MENTORING IN EDUCATION

Mentoring in Education
An International Perspective

CEDRIC CULLINGFORD
University of Huddersfield

ASHGATE

Published by
Ashgate Publishing Limited
Gower House
Croft Road
Aldershot
Hampshire GU11 3HR
England

Ashgate Publishing Company
Suite 420
101 Cherry Street
Burlington, VT 05401-4405
USA

Ashgate website: http://www.ashgate.com

British Library Cataloguing in Publication Data
Mentoring in education : an international perspective. –
    (Monitoring change in education)
    1.Mentoring in education
    I.Cullingford, Cedric
    371.1'02

ISBN-10: 0 7546 4577 0
ISBN-13: 978-0-7546-4577-1

Library of Congress Cataloging-in-Publication Data
Mentoring in education : an internatioanl perspective / edited by Cedric Cullingford.
    p.cm. -- (Monitoring change in education)
    Includes bibliographical references and index.
    ISBN-13: 978-0-7546-4577-1 (alk. paper)
    ISBN-10: 0-7546-4577-0 (alk. paper)
    1. Mentoring in education. I. Cullingford, Cedric.
    LB1731.4.M4658 2006
    371.102--dc22

                                                                2006020637

Printed and bound in Great Britain by Antony Rowe Ltd, Chippenham, Wiltshire.

Contents

List of Figures

List of Tables

Notes on Contributors

Dr Dina Al-Jamal is a lecturer at M'utah University, Jordan, and offers courses in EFL.

Chris Blamires is a lecturer in the School of Education and Professional Development, and co-designed and ran the University of Huddersfield's Management Mentor Programme.

Dr Edward Britton is a Senior Research Associate in the Mathematics and Science Programme of WestEd. in California.

Cedric Cullingford is Professor of Education at the University of Huddersfield.

Christine Farmery is Headteacher of Anston Brook Primary School, Rotherham, U.K.

Dr Tom Ganser is Director of the Office of Field Experiences at the University of Wisconsin-Whitewater, USA.

Dr Marion Jones is Principal Lecturer in Educational Research at Liverpool John Moores University.

Dr Ulla Lindgren is Associate Professor of Pedagogy at the University of Umea, Sweden.

Dr Mohammad Momany is Assistant Professor in the Faculty of Education at Yarmouk University, Jordan.

Dr Val Tarbitt is Senior Lecturer in Education at Leeds Metropolitan University and manages the Leedsmet Accredited Mentoring Awards.

Dr Gillian Trorey manages the Postgraduate Certificate in Professional Development (Higher Education Practice) at the University of Huddersfield.

Dr Sue Warren is Professional Training Research and Ethics Manager at Leeds Metropolitan University.

Preface

Mentoring has become such a global phenomenon in a number of social spheres that it needs a careful scrutiny. Educational fashions can be as powerful as they are ephemeral but the concept of mentoring has such a number of different connotations and uses that it will never simply disappear. It is an old notion constantly re-applied and used in a multitude of ways.

Whilst there are disparate uses of mentoring there are certain themes that are important and which this book analyses. Mentoring is liable to misinterpretation but it is an idea that most people find is a metaphor for an activity which is well meant and simply understood. Mentoring signifies the disinterested help given to individuals. This might mean that the help given is that of control, of helping the individual to comply with the status quo, but the association is nevertheless with support. Mentoring is also seen to be part of an almost private, unstructured, informal support mechanism. It might exist because of the unspoken and unacknowledged failures of the central system, or it might be a deliberate addition, but in either cases the relation of mentoring to more formal policies is always a matter of concern if not necessarily a matter of difficulty.

The chapters in this book are all research studies and provide empirical evidence. There are many books on how to introduce and practice mentoring but far fewer which provide a scrutiny of what actually takes place. The difference between rhetoric and reality is clear in all the studies. The authors are all keen to take a fresh look at mentoring from the point of view of what actually works and what doesn't. Between them, they also provide an overview of both the official and unofficial uses of mentoring, from national and institutional initiatives to the private endeavours to explore aspects of teaching a learning that are an alternative and more sensitive means of interaction than the mainstream.

There are certain themes that keep recurring. One of these is the issue of control and where the locus of control really lies. In Sue Warren's chapter on mentor groups and how they operate we are also presented with a useful background to the increasing use made of mentoring in teacher education. We see the tensions between the official ways forward, which reoccur in later examples of state intervention, and the private networks that sustain their own momentum or which find their enthusiasm dampened. The chapter also brings out for the first time the issue of support for all involved and the importance of the emotional issues. Mentoring depends on groups and not only on individuals.

Tom Ganser also includes the issue of teams and the ways in which people work together to use what is available. His authoritative summary of the way in which the concept of mentoring has been made official policy in the United States demonstrates how much it is assumed to be central to the delivery of teaching quality. This is especially pertinent when mentoring becomes an issue in the choice of place to work and is involved in the retention and recruitment of staff. Mentoring here is part of the classic practice of induction, imposed as part of the culture. It is the more noteworthy that we are warned against too high expectations of a system that is supposed to run itself. Teams are more subtle than that. Mentoring "can't do it all".

Induction is also the main theme for Marion Jones. Here again we see the central tensions in the communities of practice; is it inevitable that, whatever the preparation, people are drawn into the culture of the school and survive or not according to the extent with which they fit in with it? The hostility against enthusiasm is a telling insight and the incidence of failure surprisingly high. She draws attention to the problems and again suggests a more complex community approach. The subtle and detailed analysis make the many tensions clear.

The tensions between assessment and support are also central to Mohammad Momani's chapter which describes what has to be called the imposition of a mentoring system on those who are made to feel somewhat suspicious and reluctant even as they are supposed to rely on it. Official structures of mentoring can seem to be used as a shortcut measure to alleviate longer term problems. What emerges is the opposite to what is intended; difficult relationships and mistrust and the dominance of assessment over development. This demonstrates the difficulty of building a system without either the necessary recourses or the freedom of manoeuvre for individuals.

Ted Britton provides us with an exceptional opportunity to see the operations of systems in five countries. Whilst these are examples of best practice, and demonstrate the need for proper resourcing, these cases also demonstrate the need for thinking through strategies, of understanding the implications of mentoring in all its complexity. The best schemes understand the human side and give many different opportunities to learn from different people and different professional inputs, including learning from other students.

The importance of learning from different people is brought out in Dina Al-Jamal's chapter on the uses of mentoring in a specialised subject. Not only does too much depend on a single person imbued with authority but this person finds him or herself dealing with deficiencies, with making up for what is lacking rather than helping the individual student teacher to find a personal style and personal confidence. It is all too easy to revert to the dated model of personal control and example. It is like a reversion to the age old idea of patronage, and nothing should be further from the idea of mentoring than that.

In contrast, Ulla Lindgren's chapter shows the ways in which the mentoring idea can be sensitively brought out of different circumstances. She makes a strong case for the essentially personal contact between people, whatever nomenclature is used. One might have thought that in University conditions the notion of the mentor, without threat or control, would find its clearest expression, but it is apparent that, as in every other case, the shadow of control, or supervision, is always there. What is pleaded for is for mentoring to be something natural and central to the learning, rather than the teaching, process.

This point about the sensitive nature of mentoring is also brought out in Gillian Trorey and Chris Blamires' chapter on mentoring for new staff in Higher Education. The issues of power, as in having a 'protegee' as opposed to having help which is 'off-line', are clearly brought out by the contrast between the Institution's instrumental, if muddled, view of mentoring, and the staff member's appreciation of personal and informal help. The needs were those to do with the immediacies of their job rather than with fitting in. They were clearly 'bottom up'. Finding the right people, sympathetic, open-minded and with the emotional intelligence to present insights into the needs of others is an unexplored but central concept, like motivation.

Sensitivity to others and the curious complexities that can contaminate the relationship are also brought out by Val Tarbitt. The myth that online learning can replace personal interaction is unmasked again. The individual needs are more important than the systems; the starting point is the person, not the technology. This honest exploration of the uses of e-mail uncovers some surprising facts; that email is not iterative, that there is a need for personal meetings to make things work, and that there are no deep exchanges provided by the technique. The importance of students supporting each other is also brought out, together with the revelation that it is a good idea to write an e-mail in hard copy to get it 'right'. On such small interactions and etiquettes can relationships, and therefore mentoring, succeed or fail.

The strength of the collective chapters is their questioning of the term, their scrutiny of empirical evidence and their sensitive and open-minded look at the issues, whether these are large surveys or small. There are many issues that show a unity of experience and which shoulc be more than useful in both understanding and employing the idea of mentoring.

Professor Cedric Cullingford
University of Huddersfield

Chapter 1

Mentoring as Myth and Reality: Evidence and Ambiguity

Cedric Cullingford

The idea of the mentor is an attractive one. It conjures up the dream of someone showing a special interest, of someone being a personal source of information and of knowing what needs to be done. If the role of the teacher could be described in this way there would be no further interest in mentoring, but we know that teachers are overburdened with delivering the formal curriculum, organising people and materials and without the time to spend with individuals. Although mentors are always an addition to the teacher rather than a replacement, they seem in the climate of the time to be used as a panacea for all kinds of problems.

One reason for the fashion of mentoring is that the mentor appears to be a metaphor that reflects the self-imposed troubles of the time. When we trace the changes to the status and performance of teachers over the past twenty years we see a well-documented shift of emphasis to their professionalism. Certain aspects have been enhanced. These include the self-management of finances, the responsiveness to inspection, the league tables, the standard assessment tests, the targets and the instructions on how and what to teach. The assumption is that teachers 'deliver' the prescribed curriculum in ways that are carefully managed and controlled. What is played down is the view of teaching in all the pastoral aspects, the relationships with pupils, the personal nurturing and the autonomy of being able to respond to individual needs. It should be no surprise that it is in this climate that mentoring has come to the fore. Mentoring emphasises all those aspects that teachers used to cherish, and which are now taken on by ancillary workers, classroom assistants and others whilst teachers are re-branded as managers.

The idea of the mentor, therefore, brings out a long established tension. There has always been a debate about the differences between teacher centred and learner centred education. Whilst at the earlier stages of learning the teacher, as the prime source of information and instruction, is assumed to dominate, such a model cannot survive when the learners themselves become autonomous and particularly when they themselves train to be teachers. The concept of learning by precept and example, of being instructed to develop certain practices and fine tune a personal style of delivery, brings in the instructor, the coach, the advisor, and, of course, what we now term the mentor. The attention is no longer on a class full of children but on the individual. No amount of taught lessons, reading, listening and obeying, are thought to be enough in themselves, even if they were for pupils in school. Personal support and instruction take over.

There is a strong tradition on mentoring in teacher education although the nomenclature has been subtly different. Students would have carefully controlled and extended periods of teaching practice (sic) which were monitored and supported by 'supervisors'. These supervisors were the experts in pedagogy and in the subjects to be taught. They had experience and recognised expertise either of a specialist or a generic nature. Their role was clearly defined, but at the heart there was a clear tension which lies at the heart of mentoring. The supervisors were there to support, to give advice, to demonstrate, to share ideas and to encourage. At the same time their role was to make judgements. Was this student capable of teaching well? Should she pass the teaching practice? Who were the strongest and the weakest students? In the privileged role of observer and supporter, the supervisors also had to make judgements. This could be a delicate matter and demanded extremes of sensitivity and tact. At what point would it be appropriate to warn the student that she had to improve or fail? Would that undermine her confidence entirely? Or would encouragement lead to a false sense of complacency?

This ambiguity of role was accepted as a central part of the precursors of mentoring. It was also seen in the operations of local education authorities in their relationships with established teachers. The advisors were there to raise standards by enhancing good practice. At the same time their duty was to report if schools or teachers were deemed to be unsatisfactory. The advisors were also inspectors and the ambiguity of role was neatly summarised by the way in which different local authorities sometimes called them advisors and sometimes inspectors (Winkley, 1985). On the one hand the advisors were in a confidential position, sharing good practice privately and delicately with teachers who needed help. On the other, the inspectors were reporting and exposing those on whom their judgements fell.

In a time in which formal inspection has become so dominant, the role of the advisor has been removed. The role of the neutral observer is no longer carried out by an outsider but, if it is carried out, by the teachers themselves. The mentoring that takes place nowadays is nearly always a matter of induction, of easing a new entrant into a profession, into the established practices of the work place. The new teacher in school or college is assumed to need mentoring or induction. Again, the fact that it is possible to slip from one concept to another raises the question about ambiguities of the role. 'Induction' is the introduction of a new member of staff into the rules, the practices, the culture and habits of the institution. Here the 'mentors' are the gatekeepers. The new member of staff has to learn to conform, to fit in to the established practices or s/he will fail. Conformity is clearly important.

The concept of mentoring conjures up support and encouragement for the autonomous individual, of the light touch of advice rather than the heavy hand of induction. And yet mentoring is mostly used by established teachers and experienced professionals to enable someone new to fit in. This is, of course, a very subtle process. C.S.Lewis in the *Screwtape Letters* gives a good account of the way in which an individual can become caught up in the tone and attitudes of an organisation, gradually learning the assumptions, the shared values and the inner circles of private judgements, and being proud to be part of it, whatever the nature of the organisation. These are called 'Communities of Practice' (Lave and Wenger, 1991). When they are described and analysed it is clear that success lies in conformity to the shared language and attitudes. The private and arcane habits are what bind people together in the ethos of the organisation, and these are repeated without irony and without any sense that there is any danger in it.

The mentor as the agent of 'induction' has a complex role to play, but sometimes the needs of conformity dominate. The best example of this in the wider practices of official schemes is called 'engagement mentoring' (Colley, 2002). In the 'Connexions' programmes the role of the mentor became increasingly clear. Whilst cajoling and helping individuals, the practice was to control the individual to comply with the requirements of the State, or to 'reengage disaffected young people in formal labour markets...to engage their commitment to employability' (Colley, 2003). There was no question of the young people finding alternative ways forward. The duty of the connexions mentor was to create a personal trusting relationship, ostensibly helping the individual, so that he or she would learn to fit in to the requirements of the community and the demands of employability.

This side of mentoring, of controlling, ordering and making a person conform, by giving instruction and advice, has always been with us. There has always been a tension in the role of social workers, or anyone employed by the State to help the poor, the disadvantaged, and the disaffected. They possess the power of the political and constitutional organisations that employ them. And yet they often see themselves as working on behalf of the 'victim; the victim of the very same State. They try to encourage the individual to extract from the State all that he or she can. It is as if such social workers are employed to attack the very system that they represent (Hoggard, 1970). There are many examples of gamekeepers and poachers finding their ostensibly separate roles actually interdependent.

Such role conflict is less of a problem if the mentor sees the job as one of enabling conformity, of induction into new systems of organisation. Whilst the personal connection with the individual is attractive, the most instructive information is the insight given into the practices of the community. The age old notion of the mentor might have embedded within it something personal, but it has also rested on the notion of power. The mentor is the expert, the person with experience, the patron. Until recently there have always been acceptable notions of control. The mentee would have sought out only those who had greater experience, greater power and greater influence. The original root of the word 'mentor' is 'monitor': the etymological significance is of 'counsel'.

Counselling has many associations, from the all powerful legal counsel to the personal unpacker of ones private life when going for counselling. To point out the ambiguities and complexities of the terminology is not playing with words or ideas but exposing the complexities of actual practice. The difficulties of mentoring are real and they derive from the lack of clarity about the role. Stemming from the powerful 'monitor' are three different experiences, those of the teacher, those of the sage and those of the advisor. Of course roles overlap and positions change, but all these different interpretations of personal positioning are about the central issues of power and control. The sage is deemed all knowing, and the one to whom people deliberately go for help. The sage is chosen, not imposed. The teacher is there to instruct, to direct, to tell, and is inevitably someone met because they are in that role rather than sought out. The advisor is supposedly the expert, used for particular purposes, as a consultant, with a brief. The advice is professional and based on matters of fact rather than conduct.

We acknowledge at once the differences between those people deliberately sought out and those imposed, those who are there to help the individual wherever s/he wishes to go and those who are there to induct them into a community of practice. From the point of view of the mentor, the differences can lie simply in the extent to which the task and the outcomes are clear. Unlike the mentor, the coach has a specific aim, a target that is clear and which is exactly what the individual wants, using the coach clearly as a means. Whilst the coach gives goal directed advice it is the unambiguity of the target, uncomplicated by personal issues, or social pressures, that make it different. There might be all kinds of psychological pressures on the individuals involved, and they might draw on experience, but the task itself is clear and obvious. A trainer is someone who is employed to help focus on a personal target, whether this has athletic or Californian overtones. They are the means to an end. This is partly why the distinction between 'training' and 'education' is such a sensitive one to those involved in University Education Departments. The choice by the Government of the 'Teacher *Training* Agency' as the sobriquet gave a clear signal of its attitude. The teacher is a functionary who is there to learn and apply clear and measurable skills. The subtlety of personal development and individual sense of purpose, education in the broader sense, is another matter.

This brings us back to the mentor, the metaphor for making up for the deficiencies of mechanistic models, and also of making the same models function more smoothly. There have been a number of typologies of mentoring suggesting a steady progress from the apprenticeship model, copying a good or bad example, through the competency model, a systematic training, to the reflective practitioner model which emphasises the ultimate autonomy of the mentee (Schoen, 1983). Most people's experience will lead them to question whether there are clear differences and whether the original idea of reflective practice has actually made any progress. No one would question the desirability of thinking on the job, but whilst this was envisaged originally as being freed from academic institutions it is these same institutions that are most keen on promoting reflective practice as an idea (Pollard, 1987).

The mentor almost always has an official purpose and official status and this is where the difficulties lie. At one level the idea of the mentor is to give a more personal, more directed shape to induction. The mentor is the person whose advice is to be sought. The mentor is supposed to be on the side of the individual rather than the institution. No-where is this clearer than in the delicate relationship between a research student and what is still called their supervisor. The best of supervisors are akin to the concept of mentor. They help the student to direct their work and discover what they are searching for. They do not impose a prescriptive methodology. They are there to support and advise, always with comments unique to the case and always consistent in their help.

And yet, there is no question of where the ultimate power lies. The tutors, to use another term, would be of no credibility if they did not have authority, and the accumulated knowledge derived from previous experiences. As in the case of the teaching practice supervisor, the offer of support, encouragement and praise is not enough in itself (even if preferable to the opposite). Advice which is sought out is always of most use, but the advice means something because it carries weight.

In the relationship between research student and supervisor, the crucial point is the locus of control. Who essentially owns the thesis and its ideas? Is the student encouraged to develop the ideas or are ideas thrust upon him? The subtleties of support are more difficult to attain than the imposition of leadership. The crucial point is the attention paid to a student's encouragement to learn rather than the management of the supervisor's ideas. The writing of an individual thesis is clearly a learning process that needs encouragement and support. It reminds us of the essential if subtle difference between learning and being taught.

Learning does not necessarily thrive in a system which is 'top down' that is centrally directed and controlled. If the social context is not right no amount of managerialist pressures on the performance of staff will see significant improvements (Lupton, 2005). This is why the concept of mentoring has attracted both those who would seek out an antidote to the systems of imposition, and to those who realise they need an extra more subtle weapon for the system's success. Mentors are those who mitigate the worst effects of the education system and they are also the ones who make sure it works. Mentors are teachers and social workers in disguise, as well as being sucked back into the mainstream.

In the present state of the education system there is a clear difference between the policies, as measured against targets and reported in terms of outcomes, and the messy everyday reality full of complexities. Whole school measures are weighed by those involved against the individual cases of personal need, triumph and despair. There is a whole unofficial sub-culture of working practices that illustrates what is called 'underground working'. A long term funded project called Transforming Cultures in Further Education found that Further Education Tutors survive and do a good job but 'only by doing things for and with students that they are not officially supposed to be doing' (Wahlberg et al, 2005). Thus the system survives despite itself. Is this what mentoring is about?

One of the remarkable facets of the recent flurry of mentorship projects is how far they have spread. Whilst mentoring became significant in education at the time when Universities were disenfranchised and schools took over the main authority of training students and making judgments on them, the real impetus to the idea derived from Business and Community mentoring, in the 'world of work'. The initiative was based on having Industry and commerce far more involved and influential in schooling. Given the shortages of time, mentoring seemed to be an answer. As in the Excellence in Cities initiative, learning mentors were appointed and everywhere found to be beneficial, especially if those involved had their personal characteristics deliberately matched (Beddowes-Jones, 2002). Peer mentoring, or buddying, not unlike the nineteenth century Lancasterian model in schools, has been heavily promoted. But no-where was mentoring so heavily endorsed as in the Connexions service which was to transform completely all the various responsibilities of social workers and which has subsequently been abolished. It is this initiative that highlights the tensions of mentors who are acting for clients ostensibly against the State and who are responsible for meeting their official targets. The selling line of mentoring here was typically to stress the stereotype of feminine caring and concern, but the reality was of gate keeping and preserving power (Colley, 2002).

Support and Assessment make uncomfortable bed-fellows. In those roles in which people feel most comfortable there is no feeling of having to make judgements or being responsible for the outcome. There is no doubt that many mentors feel uncomfortable and unsure, a fact that is corroborated by all the empirical research, but the fact is mostly hidden. That this is suppressed is itself a telling insight into the personal feelings of accountability and the sense that to confess to difficulties is akin to accepting blame.

The role of the mentor is not just complex but emotional. Mentors take the success or failure of their mentees personally (Bullough and Draper, 2004). They want to be liked and respected. They want to be appreciated. And yet all the research into the attitudes and feelings of mentors reveal that they feel isolated and undervalued. Whilst they often enter the role with interest and enthusiasm they soon find that they are caught up in responsibilities and demands that they were not expecting. Even those who did not have mentoring thrust upon them realised that they were subtly being held accountable.

Many schools and many colleges do their best to make systems of mentoring work. There are numerable case studies which show why and how the idea was taken up and which are written up as if such schemes were the answer to innumerable problems. But when one reads between the lines and when one puts aside the insight that mentors are propping up the existing practices or limiting the damage, it is clear that the personal costs are high. This can best be summarised in one case study which came to the conclusion that the mentoring system only worked on certain conditions. These were when the mentees had the following attributes:

- They used procedures
- They appreciated the mentor
- They were good at listening
- They were willing to ask for help
- They were willing to act on advice
- They could recognise their own mistakes
- They could reflect on their experience
- They were good with interpersonal skills

If these were the prerequisites for the mentee, what more could one need? What about those who did not fulfil this condition, those who needed mentoring or some intervention programme? Here we have a description of the perfect student in any circumstances, willing to learn and able to interact with others. One imagines that mentors are necessary because such perfect students are so rare.

Fortunately from the mentoring point of view, the 'perfect student' can also be a condition. Or, to put it another way, the student can be transformed by perfect conditions. Without personal rapport it is impossible to be a guide or advisor, or any real help at all, but this can depend on the conditions in which the willingness to relate and to learn can be fostered. Let us take one example. Three groups of European students, who were brought together to learn the lingua franca of the world, were asked to spend a day discussing, designing and making a pamphlet that would give examples of differences of culture between their various nations. At the end of the day they would have produced something they had all agreed. One group was given a very explicit target. They were to produce a pamphlet that would be interesting, useful, informative and well presented. If they achieved this target, to be judged by a panel of neutral inspectors, they would be rewarded with an excursion. If they did not, they would be shamed and punished by being denied the next trip. The second group were not given the possibility of rewards and punishment, nor were they made to feel particularly competitive but they were expected to produce a worthy effort. The third group was told to spend the day enjoying discussing their cultural differences. If they felt like it, they could celebrate their findings and share them by producing a pamphlet to show the other groups. There was no pressure on them at all.

The results were obvious, emphatic and often duplicated by similar experiments. The students with the least pressure produced by far the best result. Those with clear targets and outcomes produced by far the worst (Lewis, 1991). The moral of this is clear. The conditions that are most conducive to learning are those which put emphasis on the student and on the desire to learn rather than those which are rigidly controlled. It is these conditions that mentors strive for, in constraining circumstances. Their efficacy depends on their freedom from control.

Mentors, as they are employed in most institutions, are not autonomous. They are nearly always a substitute, or an addition, to the prevailing system of organisation. They might be 'underground' workers but they are also held accountable to make judgments and to bridge the gap between the individual and the system. This means that the demands of the job are not only many but complex (Fletcher and Barrett, 2004). This is because they are contradictory. The sense of being undervalued comes about because they do not know what they are being measured against. It is not clear whether they are mediators, facilitators, or assessors, answerable to those who employ them, or therapists, protectors and supporters answerable to their mentees.

The problem for mentors is that they are often associated with the failures and difficulties of schools and colleges but they feel the pressure of making their mentees conform. This pressure is well summarised by one learning mentor.

'Some sceptics may say that mentoring is the political term for "getting kids back into the classroom and controlling them". Maybe they're not far off the mark, for mentors often feel they are only valued within schools when they have to handle disruptive children. Our role is not always understood and, as a consequence, we are not used as well as we should be. A teacher's primary objective is to educate pupils about the curriculum; a learning mentor is to educate children to become pupils (Stephenson, 2005).

The use of the word 'educate' is telling. That subtle concern to enable pupils to become perfect mentees, as in the list quoted above, is no longer the central aspect of teaching. Indeed, from the mentor's point of view, the greater the gap between him and the establishment the better.

The same learning mentor eschews becoming a teacher;

'Initially, I studied for my degree intending to become a teacher, but many staff here tell me that if I do I'll lose my special relationship with the children' (ibid).

The children do not feel they are being formally taught. The mentors are support workers and have particular attributes: they are available, they give advice on problems, they deal with parents, and are considered as friends (Vulliamy and Webb, 2003). These attributes emphasise that they are not teachers.

The concept of mentoring therefore throws an interesting light on what is happening to teachers and the education system. Given their oblique place it is not surprising to find that mentors are uncomfortable with their role whilst finding rewards despite that discomfort. The problem is that mentoring is generic (Jarvis et al, 2001). It has no specific discipline. Mentors do not feel the confidence of having a subject specialism or anything specific (Hudson, 2004). What they do or achieve cannot be measured. It is found impossible to assess the impact mentors have.

Whilst mentors have functions which are distinct from teachers, they have certain characteristics in common with them. Like teachers, they resent and fear being observed, wanting to make exclusive, hidden relationships. They are afraid of being judged, especially against those measures that are usually employed. And they feel they lack time to do all the things they would like to do.

Mentoring can be thought of as an old fashioned way of teaching at a time when the mainstream has implacably moved in a different direction. The difficulties of mentoring are as deeply felt as the individual rewards, the concern and caring that drives mentors on, whatever their circumstances. The research on mentoring has highlighted the difficulties. Mentor programmes are often a matter of chance, and are rarely well planned (Unwin and Wellington, 2001). Mentors should not work in isolation; it takes more than one to make a real impact (Vozzo et al, 2004). Students themselves do not always like the concept of a mentor (Kanan and Baker, 2002). Indeed, they resent the intrusion and the sense of being marked out as failures. Mentors in school are associated with the misfits, the unhappy, the disruptive and the 'backward'.

Books about mentoring abound, but they are nearly all about how to organise mentors and how to manage programmes (Hawkey, 1997). There is a comparatively sparse literature on what actually happens and very little on whether the students actually learn. The impact of individual relationships is very difficult to measure and yet it is clear that true learning lies in those innumerable experiences of shared personal insight and the interest of other people. The concept of mentoring is also a metaphor for concern.

Given their ambiguous place in the education system, at a variety of levels, it is no wonder that mentors often find what they are doing difficult and unrewarding. But we should also be aware of some of the sometimes unexpected and immeasurable benefits of mentoring. One is the fact that the mentors themselves are learning. As with the observation of teaching practice, it is those who observe who find themselves imbibing examples of successful and unsuccessful practice. On a full time course for in-service teachers, before such secondments were abolished, a cohort came for a special course at a University. They had the opportunity to undertake research and curriculum development useful to their school, and they could choose from a range of courses on any subject that interested them for its own sake. The were also given the opportunity to act as teaching practice supervisors. To their own surprise, it was this that gave them the most pleasure. Experienced teachers found themselves having to act as mentors. They not only observed but had to articulate their observation, give advice and act in that capacity of personal friend, sage and coach that they had not experienced before.

There are all kinds of terms for mentoring and for the different aspects of the role. There are ambiguities and complexities that give insights into the rewards and difficulties of mentoring. Those who do it are trying to enable learning in others by showing an interest in their needs. This disinterested concern for others is at the heart of education.

Concern can also be the reward, the satisfaction, which maintains the morale and sense of purpose. Of course mentors are used as part of the system, pulling recaltricant students back into the mainstream. Of course the very position of mentors reveals something of the inadequacies of the system. But mentoring can give subtle benefits. If the mentee is able to choose his or her mentor, which should not be difficult amongst colleagues, and if there is no pressure on assessing, them this form of shared learning can be not only a comfort but a benefit. Mentoring is best when it is free of pressure, and when it feels reciprocal.

Many papers concerned with mentoring begin by invoking Telemachus. This would not be so if the writers had read their Homer. The figure of Mentor in the Odyssey is quite unlike all that we think the concept stands for. Mentor is such a failure at one point that the goddess the bright eyed Athena takes over the ostensible role, and nothing could symbolise an implacable and controlling system, using people as pawns, better than her.

References

Beddowes-Jones, F. (2002), *Thinking Styles*, Consulting Tools, London.
Bullough, R. and Draper, R. (2004), 'Mentoring and the Emotions', *Journal of*

Education for Teaching, vol. 30(3), pp. 271–288.

Colley, H. (2002), 'A "Rough guide" to the History of Mentoring from a Marxist Feminist perspective', *Journal of Education for Teaching*, vol. 28(3), pp. 257–273.

Colley, H. (2003), 'Engagement Mentoring for "Disaffected" Youth: A new model of mentoring for social inclusion', *British Educational Research Journal*, vol. 29(4), pp. 521–542.

Fletcher, S. and Barrett, A. (2004), 'Developing Effective Beginning teachers through Mentor based induction', *Mentoring and Tutoring*, vol. 12(3), pp. 322–351.

Hawkey, K. (1997), 'Roles, Responsibilities and Relationships in Mentoring: a Literature Review and Agenda for Research', *Journal for Teacher Education*, vol. 48(5), pp. 325–335.

Hoggard, R. (1970), *Speaking to Each Other:About Society*, Dhatto and Windus, London.

Jarvis, T., McKern, F., Coates, D. and Vanse, J. (2001), 'Generic Mentoring: Helping trainee teachers to teach primary science', *Research in Science and Technology Education*, vol. 19(1), pp. 5–23.

Kanan, H. and Baker, A. (2005), 'Palestinian novice Teachers' Perception of a good mentor', *Journal of Education for Teaching*, vol. 28(1), pp. 35–43.

Lave, J. and Wenger, E. (1991), *Situated Learning: Legitimate Peripheral Participation*, University Press, Cambridge.

Lewis, R. (2001), *Cognitive Processes Parts 1 and 2*, Institute of Cross-Cultural Communication, Hants.

Lupton, R. (2005), 'Social Justice and School Improvement: Improving the Quality of schooling in the poorest Neighbourhoods', *British Educational Research Journal*, vol. 31(5), pp. 589–604.

Pollard, A. and Tann, S. (1987), *Reflective Teaching in the Primary School*, Cassell, London.

Schoen, D. (1983), *The Reflective Practitioner*, Temple Smith, London.

Stephenson, C. (2005), *Case Study: The Learning Mentor*, TES Friday P. 14 June 24, London.

Wahlberg, M., Diment, K., Davies, J., Colley, H. and Wheeler, E. (2005), '"Underground Working" – Understanding Hidden Labour', *Building Research Capacity*, pp. 2–4.

Winkley, D. (1985), *Diplomats and Detectives: LEA Advisors at work*, Robert Royce, London.

Unwin, L. and Wellington, J. (2001), *Young People's Perspectives on Education, Training and Employment: Realising their Potential*, Kogan Page, London.

Vozzo, L., Abusson, P., Steele, F. and Watson, K. (2003), 'Mentoring Retrained Teachers: Extending the Web', *Mentoring and Tutoring*, vol. 45(3), pp. 275–286.

Vulliamy, G. and Webb, R. (2003), 'Supporting disaffected pupils: Perspectives from the Pupils, their parents and their teachers', *Educational Research*, vol. 25(3), pp. 275–286.

Chapter 2

A Decade of Change? Mentor Groups Acting as Communities of Learners

Sue Warren

Introduction

This chapter is based on two, two-year long Case Studies investigating developments of two groups of primary teachers acting as mentors to Postgraduate Certificate in Education (PGCE) trainees. Case Study 1 (1993–95) was a collaborative action research investigation in which I researched the growth and development on nine teachers and myself working together on one of the first school-based courses. Case Study 2 (2004–06) is an on-going investigation by myself and Jude Rivers, a mentor in a Training School, in which we are researching the expectations and experiences of a group of six primary teachers working in a cluster of schools where primary PGCE trainees have been placed. Both case studies trace the life history of the groups' development as communities of learners (Lave and Wenger, 1991) in planning and executing school-based work for the trainees, how these experiences are shared and how individuals' own professional development as a mentor is affected. To date, the case study 1 group has been together for the first of two academic years of the investigation. Both groups contain experienced and new mentors and a range of teachers with senior management and/or classteacher responsibilities.

Alongside the 2004–06 investigation, I am interested in whether changes in the training of PGCE trainees over a decade may reveal similar or different issues and concerns, expectations and understandings about the mentoring role, the professional knowledge needed and the experiences the second group have. At this point in time there are several similarities between the two groups.

Context

The changing roles and responsibilities of teachers and teacher trainers can be evidenced in the structure and funding of initial teacher education/training (ITE/T) based on changes in governments' educational ideology. From 1835 (when the first government grant was given for the training of teachers) to the current day, changes have been made in: the preferred location for the training of teachers; qualification requirements; length of study; curricula content; the inspection of training; and; the role and responsibilities of qualified teachers in teacher training in a somewhat cyclical pattern (Warren, 2001).

Continual policy changes have led to differences in the balance of roles and responsibilities between Higher Education Institutions (HEI) and schools. In the latter two decades of the 20 century and the first of the 21 century, the balance between these constituencies has been more seriously challenged by political ideology than in the inaugural years of State schooling in the late 19 century. The imposition of competences (DES, 1989) and Standards (DFEE, 1998 and DFES, 2000) on the approval of teacher training courses and the awarding of Qualified Teacher Status is reflected in shifts in the language used, especially the changes in government documents from 'education' to 'training'. Changes in the power relationships amongst the government, the Council for the Accreditation of Teachers (CATE) 1989–1994, the current Teacher Training Agency (TTA, renamed the Teacher Development Agency, TDA, from September 2005), HEI tutors and teachers in schools have led to the current context of teacher training.

In 1989, the training of teachers was once again changed to become more school based and student teachers were to spend more of their time studying in schools under the tutelage of teachers, reminiscent of the 1846 pupil- teachers and stipendiary monitors. The teachers involved in the support of trainee teachers were given the title of 'mentor', and grants were made for professional development for teachers to undertake this new role. Since then, the nature of this professional development has been the scope of many reports, conferences and training routes. Tensions have been evident in both schools and HEIs ranging from, on the one hand, the insecurity of HEI tutors engaged in training serving teachers to become mentors and thus the possibility (and in some cases the actuality) of their own following redundancy, to, on the other hand, teachers' anxieties about their shifting role from teaching children to teaching adults.

Changes to Teacher Taining in the Latter Years of the 20th Century and the Beginning of the 21st Century in England and Wales

In order to place these two mentor groups in context I feel it is important to give a brief overview of important events in the recent history of the re-structuring of initial teacher education to the current initial teacher training in England and Wales.

From the election of the 1979 government, changes in the basic structure of society began to be effected in line with the political philosophy of the social market of the incoming Conservative government and the New Right. The control of education and ITT was a major issue as public services became to be seen as direct challenges to the power of the government and its focus on these market forces (Bolton, 1994; Landman & Ozga, 1995).

Following the 1983 report, *'Teaching Quality'* (DES, 1983), the Department of Education and Science established the Council for the Accreditation of Teacher Education (CATE). Initially CATE's rubric was to 'undertake an initial scrutiny of all courses of initial teacher training against the Government's criteria....' (DES Circular 24/89, para 4). CATE was given a wider remit from 1 January 1990.

Members were to 'be appointed by the Secretary of State on a personal basis and will be drawn from teacher trainers, other teachers in higher education and in schools, local authorities and the business community' (DES Circular 24/89, para 6). The control of course content, entry requirements and teaching methods to be advocated was now firmly in the remit of a personally appointed committee whose focus was to grant or rescind accreditation of HEIs. The move towards changing the nature of primary teaching away from a developmental curriculum to subjects was begun with the requirement that first degrees must contain 50% subject study of a subject of the National Curriculum. Ground rules were laid for the development of partnerships in the training of teachers in section 1 and for the length of time required for teaching practice and other school experiences in section 2, although at this point teachers were not heavily engaged in the teacher training process.

The Secretary of State for Education and Science, responding to government's belief that school-leavers did not meet the standards of literacy and numeracy of school-leavers in Britain's trading competitors in the world market place, set in motion a detailed review of the strengths and weaknesses of the education system. This led to the publication of the White Paper, *'Better Schools'* (DES, 1986) and the introduction of a new examination system which would improve the qualifications of school-leavers.

Following the publication of *'Better Schools'*, teachers came under the government's scrutiny as purveyors of 'progressive' methods of teaching as opposed to the government's preferred 'traditional' methods. Baker's 1988 Educational Reform Act laid out the required National Curriculum to which every pupil would have access. Teachers thus needed to be able to deliver this curriculum content in approved ways. Pupils' progress was to be tested and teachers' abilities judged against the national Standard Assessment Tasks (now the Standard Assessment Tests). In order for teachers to be able to deliver this curriculum using the approved (i.e. more traditional) methods they needed to be trained properly. Teacher trainers (who had trained the practising teachers) were seen as the proponents of the disapproved (i.e. progressive) methods of teaching and could not be trusted to train teachers properly, yet those very serving teachers would do the job better. Thus the requirement for training in subject knowledge and appropriate practical skills for primary teachers to be able to deliver the National Curriculum was evidence of the political move towards creating a teaching force which would meet the needs of the economy by producing a properly literate and numerate workforce using traditional teaching methods.

The speed of change can be seen in the publication of thirty reports and papers about the training of teachers over the next thirteen years as funding, qualifications, structure, curriculum and location of the training came under scrutiny yet again. The language of these reports is the language of control. In 1992, Fowler considered these documents to be 'over-worded' and that the documents showed 'intense preoccupation, pointing to "peculiarities" in the ideology of the group responsible for it.' This continues to be the state of play in the New Labour government's policy documents. It was into the *'Better Schools'* scenario that the Articled Teacher Scheme was introduced in 1989.

Government influence on the curriculum content of ITT courses continued and in 1991 the National Curriculum Council (NCC) published a consultation paper which sought to produce a National Curriculum for ITT which would provide newly qualified teachers who would be deliverers of the National Curriculum for pupils. This publication was followed by the competences of Circular 9/92 (DSE, 1992) for secondary courses and Circular 14/93 (DES, 1993) for primary courses. These Circulars further strengthened the principles of partnership and the roles and responsibilities of schools and HEIs in the tasks of the partnership. The thrust of the Circulars was the need to raise standards in schools.

Developing the Partnerships in ITT in Primary Schools

The publication of Circulars 9/92 and 14/93 caused much debate about the locus of power in partnership agreements. Whilst 'the main function of schools is to teach pupils' (CATE note of Guidance, 1993), the expectation was that schools were to become involved in ITT in new and different ways, 'Courses run by universities and colleges must be planned and delivered in partnership with schools' (Circular 14/93). Thus, the 'onus for the organisation and financing of partnerships [was to be] firmly [put] onto the schools and HEIs themselves' (Griffiths & Owen, 1995). HEIs would be penalised for turning away schools which tried to instigate partnerships and would have to justify why they had not agreed to partnerships. Schools, however, did not race to be involved over and above planning and the existing teaching practice supervision arrangements and teacher unions advised caution to HEI. The National Union of Teachers wrote to all Heads of Department and Directors of Primary PGCE and B.Ed Courses in England and Wales (July, 1993) stating that in their opinion, there were 'certain basic issues' which needed to be addressed as: HEIs

> '[Primary schools] are likely to be severely constrained in resourcing their genuine commitment to ITE ... [and]... many primary schools will regard themselves as first and foremost, educators of pupils' (Letter to Heads of Department and Directors of Primary PGCE and B.Ed Courses in HEIs in England and Wales, 15 July, 1993, p. 2)

The National Association of Headteachers also wrote to its members with similar advice the same month. Some headteachers of small primary schools who were involved with my HEI were very reluctant to be heavily involved in teaching the courses they were helping to write. Their reasons were usually rooted in the number of teachers and classes in their schools and the view that their function was to teach children not to train teachers (personal communications with teachers during the preparation of a new course, 1993).

CATE's Circular 4/93 indicated its own demise and the development of the Teacher Training Agency (TTA), which would have responsibility for the training of teachers from their ITT through to headship training. The TTA was established in May, 1994. Its remit in ITT was for the accreditation of institutions (be they HEIs or schools) which provided this level of training and the distribution of student numbers and funding. This responsibility for funding came with a requirement that the monies should be accounted for separately to the rest of University funding which caused some consternation in some Universities' accounting processes. Transitional funding was also made for the development of partnerships and the training of classteachers to act as mentors within the school-based training.

The TTA set to work immediately with a series of consultations. The first of these was a review of the preparation of the framework for developing profiles of competences (TTA, 4 November, 1994). This was followed the next month with consultation about institutional accreditation for both HE and school-based training (SCITT). Both of these consultations had to be completed by February, 1995, for implementation in September, 1995.

This focus on consultation, at first sight, seemed to indicate a political seachange in the re-distribution of some power to the HEIs; a democratic approach to initial training drawing together the opinions of schools and HEIs (Weir & Betham, 1999). However, some have argued that the reality was different. The way in which the working parties were constituted and the way in which the results of the consultations were worded on publication were criticised for lack of transparency as the evidence was used in such a way as to give the impression that there was little dissatisfaction with the TTA proposals (Hextall & Mahoney, 2000).

Circular 4/98, *'High Status, High Standards'* (DfEE, 1998) was developed as the national curriculum for ITT, and Annex I stated the 'Requirement for all courses of Initial Teacher Training'. Here the roles and responsibilities of partners were laid down. Student teachers were re-named as trainees and the 'Standards for the Award of Qualified Teacher Status' (Annex A) replaced the previous list of competences. All trainees had to be assessed and shown to meet all the Standards. Annexes B to H laid down particular subject standards and reflected the earlier National Curriculum Council's proposals (see above). This move, and the title of the circular, relate directly to another period of government concern about the standards of pupils' literacy, numeracy, and information and communication technology on joining the workforce.

In 1999, the TTA instigated the Graduate Teacher Programme (GTP) and the Registered Teacher Programme (RTP) 'to offer [you] a way to qualify as a teacher while [you] work' (http://www.teach-tta.gov.uk, 2000). These latest routes for trainees seem to draw on the experiences of the Articled (ATPS) and Licensed (LTS) teacher routes of the early 1990s. For both the GTP and the RTP, trainees had to be over 24, had found themselves employment as unqualified teachers in a school that was willing to become a recommending body (RB), or had links with a RB, and draw up an individual programme of study with an HEI. Like the ATPS and the LTS, Graduate Teachers and Registered Trainees were paid a salary (bursaries in the cases of the ATPS and LTS), schools were awarded £4,000 to cover their training costs (£2000 per trainee in the ATPS and LTS). The GTP entry qualifications were a first degree and for the RTP higher education equivalent to two years of higher education, again the same as for the ATPS and LTS. As with all trainees, English and Mathematics at GCSE grade C or above were also required. Normally these routes took one year for the GTP and two for the RTP but may be shortened according to prior experience. In both new routes, the mentor(s) in school had oversight of the trainee's progress and assessment, yet another echo of the ATPS and LTS. The most striking similarities with the ATPS and LTS routes is that the GTP and RTP had been opened as training routes at a time of acute teacher shortages, particularly in secondary schools, and that they were more generously funded than the HEI validated PGCE or shortened degree courses. Teacher training routes are advertised on the Internet, at cinemas, on television and in the press.

In the section 'Reforming initial teacher training' in the Green Paper, *Building on Success* (DfEE, 2001), statements were made that, due to the implementation of Circular 4/98, primary teacher training had 'greatly improved' and school-centred routes such as the GTP were being expanded (the RTP was not mentioned). A Flexible Route PGCE was created which gives graduates two years to qualify, generally these trainees have already some experience in working in schools and build on this whilst still being employed. The language of the paper was congratulatory and there was an implication that schools were unquestioningly involved in partnership in ITT. Much was made of OFSTED's inspections of HEI and how these reports informed TTA decision-making in allocating numbers of training places to HEI. There was no comment about inspections of school-centred ITT routes and their quality, and no indication of where the quality of the school-based trainers was to be assured. The section 'Enhancing professional development' had one comment on 'coaching and mentoring' whereby good teachers learn from each other as qualified teachers, not in the ITT context. An implication of this seemed to be that all teachers were now involved in ITT so no funding for mentor training and development was necessary.

New structures of ITT, including payment of salaries for fourth year undergraduates and postgraduates, and the possibility of Teaching Associates (undergraduate trainees working in school 'during their degree, depending on the timing of university and school terms') were made for discussion in the consultation process but, apart from bursaries for postgraduates, did not come to fruition. Much was made of the costs and funding of salaries for student teachers but no mention was made of resourcing the schools and HEIs involved with ITT. The only reference to 'mentor' was to the National Mentor Pilot and the hope that some of these mentored school students will be inspired to train as teachers themselves.

However, Kay, writing in the *Times Educational Supplement* (16 February, 2001) described a frustrating attempt she was making to train as a primary teacher in Leeds through the GTP. She wrote, 'I learned there were new in-service training schemes that would get me straight into the classroom. Schools would welcome me, the Teacher Training Agency assured me, as they would be getting a free teacher, selected and paid for by the DfEE. You try it.' Schools did not jump to take her on, 'Why should a school take on a 'tricky' case like mine – which comes with a tome of assessment papers someone has to fill in?' she asked. Yet there were some successes. One primary school known to me encouraged a Classroom Assistant they employed to gain a degree through our Individual Programme of Study Scheme in order to then register her for the GRTP.

The period of acute shortage of teachers and trainee teachers continues. The commentaries following the 'A'- level results in August, 2005, pertinently expressed the new concern of government and business leaders that the reduction of students studying Modern Foreign Languages and the affect on the training of teachers of MFL would have on the country's trade dealings.

The TTA has been active in supporting the work of its regional networks and have funded many projects. The National Partnership Project (NPP), (TTA 2001–2005) has been related particularly to the expansion of school-based teacher training and partnerships. These partnerships amongst school, LEAs and HEIs have continued to expand and the Regional Networks are strong. Some of the projects, however, have tended to be echoes or repeats of projects and work during 1990s. The Professional Development for School-based Tutors based at the University of Hull (Jackson and Cox, 2005) replicates work by, for example: McIntyre (1988), Furlong et al (1988), Warren (1989), Yeomans and Sampson (1994), Kerry and Mayes (1995), Edwards and Collinson (1996), Maynard (1997). Early Mentor Development and Training Programmes such as those at the University of Warwick, University of Cambridge, Leeds Polytechnic being but three HEIs involved in this. Many of these led to M level qualifications as part of the mentors' continuing professional development. Currently the University of Brighton and Sheffield Hallam University have recently developed M level awards in mentoring drawing from the work of the NPP.

There is now a much stronger sense of recognition of the work of mentors as the role is more a part of teachers' professional life than in the 1990s. The TTA are discussing with the Centre for the Use of Research and Evidence in Education (CUREE) how mentor training can be mapped against the National College Framework of Mentoring and Coaching to show the flow of mentoring from ITT, through Induction Stage for Newly Qualified Teachers, to headship (CUREE, 2005). This process can be seen to follow a developmental programme linked with continuing professional development in other professions. It is part of the current government's drive towards 'joined-up thinking' in the wake of changes stemming from the publication of *Every Child Matters* (DfES, 2005) and *Workforce Re-modelling*. As schools change with respect to these policies, the varieties of roles and responsibilities expand and mentoring is becoming a more embedded part of the career paths open to members of the new workforce. The next step for by the TTA and the National College of School Leadership is to work with the Learning Skills Council to develop the map of skills of mentoring.

The politically rooted tensions experienced between teacher training and the government's view of the purpose and style of the state funded education system in the late twentieth and early twenty-first centuries is not new but has existed since the beginning of the education system in the late nineteenth century and is underpinned by the politically orientated 'distribution of material resources and symbolic resources' (Ginsburg et al, 1992, p. 4), in other words, the funding of teacher training and the status then given to teachers once trained.

The Case Studies Groups' Life Histories

Case study 1 (1993–95) involved nine primary teachers and myself working together to develop knowledge and skills as mentors to post graduate trainee teachers in the Articled Teacher Pilot Scheme. This was a government pilot working towards school-based teacher training for graduates. This Postgraduate Certificate in Education (PGCE) saw graduates, the Articled Teachers, spending 80% of their training in schools and 20% in HEI for a two year period. Articled Teachers were supernumerary members of school staffs and so were to be able to undertake some facets of induction alongside their initial training. The Scheme took on board some of the practices of existing partnership models of training (e.g. the Oxford Internship Partnership). The Articled Teachers were paid a bursary and the schools were given funding for training the AT and the mentor plus a grant for resources. The resources included funding for cover for one day per week for the mentors to be released from their classroom for mentoring purposes. The Articled Teacher Pilot Scheme finished in 1995 as it had been found to be too expensive and the nature of the structure of primary schools and the teaching commitments of teachers worked against a high proportion of the training being delivered in schools. The Ofsted report on the Scheme had found that Articled Teachers were 'generally similar to those of students who have followed a one year PGCE course' (Ofsted, 1993, p. 3).

Case study 2 (2004–06) involves six primary teachers also working together as a group of mentors with a small cohort of primary postgraduate trainees in a cluster of schools led by a Training School. As for case study 1 this group of mentors contained both experienced and new mentors. The proportions of time in schools and HEI are not controlled and this PGCE award is a newly approved up-dated one year course in which the course tutors sought to link University-based work more closely with School-based work by placing all students in a small cluster of schools. This project had been discussed by the School Placement Tutor at the HEI and the Headteacher of the Training School in May 2005. The headteacher and deputy headteacher set up a cluster of schools well known to them and the HEI. Jude Rivers, the lead school's Training Manager, convened the group of mentors now called School Based Tutors (SBTs). The group was responsible for planning and executing Theory to Practice Days in which all the trainees would attend one of the schools to look into, for example, behaviour management. Only Jude has one day per week for mentoring purposes:

'To date, the group has been heavily led by myself but it is hoped that this will change over time. Indeed, other schools have indicated that they will be happy to host/chair future meetings in the forthcoming year The key reasons for me leading the work this year are that: (a) C M School put the project together so held the initial knowledge about our work to be done and (b) I have a (funded) day per week non contact time, as TS manager, to organise such things while other SBTs do not.' (Rivers, 2005)

Both groups contained experienced and new mentors and the members ranged from having senior management and/or classteacher responsibilities.

To date, both groups' life histories appear to be unfolding through the same series of inter-related and inter-connecting phases, which can be given the following titles:

- getting to know each other (and renewing old friendships)

- first flush of enthusiasm (tempered by experience)

- settling into a routine of sharing and caring (how the days' timetables began to be structured, supporting each other in professional development needs, solving problems)

- changing perspectives and relationships (frustrations and impatience, reconstituted membership)

Getting to Know Each Other

In the first phase, the members of the Case Study 1 (CS1) group who had worked together as Articled Teacher mentors renewed their old friendships made through previous mentoring work with earlier cohorts of Articled Teachers. Mentors new to the ATPGCE had met some of the experienced mentors and each other on In-Service Training courses. The mentors in Case Study 2 (CS2) also knew each other fairly well as they had all been involved with the HEI and each other's schools over a long period of time. Not all of the mentors' schools had previously been linked into the ATPGCE and these mentors welcomed the input of those mentors who had already had Articled Teachers in their schools and thus knew the processes and requirements of the Scheme.

The CS2 members brought a lot of leadership skills to the group and a firm knowledge of their individual school's educational priorities. Importantly, all the mentors had a significant level of autonomy devolved to them by their respective Headteachers, which means that they can often make decisions for their schools and know that they will be followed through. Their expectations had been based around becoming better mentors, the opportunity to train adults and give good feedback, working with, and learning from, other teachers. One, a new mentor, stated that "as this is the first time I have been a mentor I welcome the new experience of working with other schools in different ways and for supporting colleagues in school (mentor 2, 2004).

For the CS1 group, a key issue at the beginning was that the mentors themselves were not clear about the nature of the project when they first met and were not in a position to brief their own staff about what was happening. This had to be resolved before anything else could be done. 'It really made me question how far new initiatives trickle down, unless someone in a school takes responsibility to drive them though effectively. This has been resolved by everyone being more fully briefed and e-mail systems being established that cover SBTs and HTs (both groups

are routinely sent information to keep them informed)' (Rivers, 2005). This issue
had also been problematic for the CS2 group.

As both the Case Study groups came to know each other more and gained
confidence in raising and discussing concerns and doubts about the value and status
of professional knowledge held, the communities of learners (Lave & Wenger, 1991)
began to grow. The experienced members were able to share their experiences with
others in the groups who were new to this work. By talking about the mistakes they
had made and problems they had encountered when they first became mentors they
supported the new mentors in order that similar mistakes and problems might be
avoided.

First Flush of Enthusiasm

The enthusiasm of the groups has been evident in the light of devising learning
experiences, tutorial programmes and Theory to Practice Days. Some of the CS1
mentors were both wary of their own professional knowledge, whether it was up-to-
date, and keen to read the materials supplied by me in advance of those tutorials. The
first flushes of enthusiasm were tempered by the prior experience of the returning
mentors. The space and opportunity to explore how other people had responded to,
and also drawn on, prior knowledge was a great comfort and the new mentors' initial
feelings of anxiety began to diminish as the returning mentors soothed anxieties
and told stories of how they had overcome their own earlier anxieties. The support
that was given and taken began to cement the group relationships and the sharing of
experiences and care for each other's concerns consolidated the group cohesion.

In the early stages of being a mentor, most CS1 mentors had held that their most
important professional commitment, their 'centre of gravity' (Goodson, 1992), was
to the children in their class and this had caused a tension for some of the new
mentors. T commented that she had:

> 'felt that sometimes [being a mentor] impinged upon my classroom commitment but when
> I realised that this mentor role is quite different and separate from my classroom teaching,
> [it's] a professional role. When I came to terms with this I felt that a weight had been lifted
> off my shoulders.' (Warren, 2001)

For Jude the genuine situation is that 'everyone is incredibly accommodating and
flexible.... we have always come to agreement without too much difficulty. I cannot
say exactly why this should be other than we have many common traits and have a
shared desire to make the project work' (Rivers, 2005).

Settling into a Routine of Sharing and Caring

Personal support for each other in both groups has been evidenced in the caring
for group members with difficult situations. In this period of the groups' lives there
has been evidence of the building and strengthening of synergistic relationships,

when individual group members worked together to discuss problems and share ways in which they might be solved, drawing on experiences of the whole group and similar situations created effects and solutions which were better than those which the individuals working alone could develop (Lick, 1999). The co-mentoring not only aided the development of the Articled Teachers in CS1 but also how the group members' staff development needs were addressed and met with respect to professional knowledge and understanding adult learners' needs. Here the mentors generally felt at ease with each other and that they were working within a shared endeavour. They were comfortable in their relationships to be open about their problems. There was much humour and laughter in meetings, for example when it was M's turn to take the chair for the monthly progress reports of the Articled Teachers: 'Right, I'm chairing so I'll go first (M). Oh, dear, that's democracy gone! (S) South Africa's just voting for democracy! (CK)' (fieldnotes, 28/4/94).

The content of the CS2 group meetings is, as Jude states, 'incredibly open and everyone contributes ideas and opinions equally. No decision has ever been imposed because (a) if it were I would feel that we had utterly failed in our aims and (b) the group is not in a position to impose anything on a fellow school.'

As the groups came to feel more at ease with each other, the mentors became more willing and again, more comfortable, to challenge each other's practices, knowledge and beliefs; to discuss their own new learning; explain their own theories and the reasons they had for holding them. However, for both groups, sometimes the legal and Quality Assurance responsibilities of the HEI and the impossibility of changing things did lead to some frustrations.

Changing Perspectives and Relationships

As with any group of people, relationships and inter-relationships changed over time and the mood of CS1 mentors changed somewhat as new posts began to be gained and some mentors' enthusiasm waned in the preparation for exchanging Articled Teachers. At the end of the 1993–94 year, the mentors were still commenting about and sharing their surprise about 'how much it involves, you don't appreciate it until it happens.' (S, fieldnotes, 16/6/94). In sharing views about what professional learning had occurred, some mentors talked about the inappropriateness of directly transferring pedagogical skills to teaching adults, the recognition that Articled Teachers needed support in coming to terms with being learners in schools where usually adults are not learners. They spoke about their new skills: 'I've learnt a tremendous amount ... the stimulus of a challenge outside my classroom ... to practise new skills using my experience as a background...' (T) 'It does not come automatically ... I have to think ahead, to facilitate needs, to be one jump ahead' (V); 'I have had to justify both philosophy and working practice' (M) (Fieldnotes, 16/6/94).

During the similar period in the life of CS2 group (2004–05), a misunderstanding over a joint observation did lead to some unfortunate exchanges and some bad feelings in the group. However, this was addressed by the schools involved and was resolved. Judeo:'s hope is that this will in fact strengthen the group and that if another problem arises the group will be able to stand back and analyse the situation more carefully before coming to any judgements. Subsequent conversations about this incident led to the group affirming their faith in their colleagues and trust in one another. Jude feels that the members of the group 'are a fantastic group of people and I feel I know them really well now. I know that I could call them on most matters and ask for advice or a favour in future. They are really supportive and not judgmental which means one feels comfortable to speak openly and frankly about issues.'

Looking towards the 2005–06 academic year, the CS2 group has planned specific work/events such as: many more joint observations next year which will aid mentoring skills but also give the group members better insight into how the different schools work and different teaching styles. Jude is pleased that 'On top of all this, the SBT work will continue as before with people sharing new ideas and resources they have found with the group. We will still discuss difficult issues and how we handled challenging situations and get other people's feedback on how they would have handled the situation.'

Conclusion – What Was Happening Here?

The professional development of the mentors can be seen to have been underpinned by the collaboration of the groups as communities of learners. Whilst normal group dynamics have operated, in both groups the tensions and anxieties have been recognised and then subsumed as an over-arching cohesiveness and synergy came into being. Involvement in professional learning was maintained to varying degrees in both groups. There has been a shared willingness and interest in developing mentoring skills and professional knowledge as the first year of each project progressed, confidence in themselves as mentors and in their knowledge was evidenced by the way each group engaged in decision-making and problem-solving contexts where the range of mentoring skills and strategies was drawn upon reflecting this growth and development.

The two communities of learners remained strong but with reconstituted roles and levels of commitment within it. Without the continued collaborative engagement of the groups' members, I maintain that the strength of the groups would not have continued. This had also been my experience in other ITT research with teachers (Roper, Sharp and Warren, 1993).

The power of both groups came from the manner in which the contexts enabled the growth and development of the communities of learners, communities in which most of the actors were confident enough to own and share anxieties and work together to solve problems. This openness, built from within a shared endeavour, was not the usual form of engagement for in-service courses focused mainly on practical classroom pedagogical matters, but, for CS1, was more akin to award bearing further study courses in the demands it made upon the participants. The individuals within this group could easily have attended but not engaged with the

MDP, keeping their mentoring on the level of practical teaching observations and tips for the Articled Teachers' classroom survival, but all, except one, interrogated their professional knowledge in one way or another and brought concerns and anxieties about that knowledge to the group. Some of these concerns were voiced by individuals personally in group sessions, others were derived by the group from the discussions of my analyses of the data collected during the case study period. There was a ready sharing and acknowledgement that professional knowledge and educational theory were inter-linked and an important part in the education of the Articled Teachers as they became professional teachers. This is developing in the CS2 group.

The language used by both groups to report on trainee progress and the manner of that reporting has been in the form of explanations, anecdotes and stories of how similar situations had been attended to in other situations/settings. Elliott and Calderhead (1995) wrote that mentors need 'a language of practice which incorporates the complexities of training and learning.' The mentors have explained their 'knowledge-in-action' (the 'characteristic mode of ordinary practical knowledge, Schön, 1983) in metaphors: 'it's like driving a car' (C, 1994), 'watching a good teacher's like someone skating or ski-ing – it's difficult to analyse' (L, 1994). Metaphors are useful in helping reflection and in uncovering assumptions, beliefs and understandings.

By sharing these metaphors based in practice, the groups continued to develop their legitimate peripheral participation strategies alongside the routines of their meetings as the communities of learners grew (Lave and Wenger, 1991)

'Through a shift in practice to a more reciprocal and equitable sharing of experiences and solutions, we [the CS1 group] began to more actively work as a group of co-mentors in that sharing of experiences and learning, thus supporting each other's developing mentor skills and learning. How to raise confidence in background understanding and professional knowledge exercised us in our discussions' *(Warren, 2001)*

This is also evident in the CS2 group's discussions.

I believe that the issue of how to talk about practice is located more broadly within the parameters of the forms of knowledge used by teachers and the language they use to explain their knowledge-bases. Clandinin and Connelly's (1995) work on teachers' professional knowledge landscapes provides the term 'sacred story' as a metaphor of how theory tends to be given a higher status than the practical in 'out of the classroom' contexts where university teachers act as gatekeepers. The metaphor assumes that tension can arise for teachers when they move from one of the two places in that landscape to the other; from the classroom to the out of classroom communal place.

As the CS1 group recognised, mentors have to:
- Challenge the validity they give to their own educational theories and knowledge
- Recognise their ownership of that knowledge and their right to use it
- Decide what language is best to use with trainee teachers

In order to make the changes in practice from class teachers to mentors, it is necessary then to understand and be able to discuss what it is that makes our practice 'ours'. To do this we need to recall and recognise the theoretical underpinnings of our practice. The groups' members did this by investigating and sharing these understandings, working together to support new learning as co-mentors, reflecting on learning as changes to practice and developed mentoring skills occurred. In the act of describing the bases of tacit and craft knowledge, the groups began to bring to the fore all the forms of knowledge which they had internalised during their teaching lives and everyday practices.

The important influence of life histories and teaching stories on this thinking and talking about teaching and the practice of professional, or craft, knowledge (Elliott & Calderhead, 1995) cannot be overstated. Claxton (1996) writes about what it is that learners bring to situations and how they 'engage' with the activity of learning: '... the motivational issue of what creates or inhibits the learner's whole hearted commitment to the learning programme or process' (Claxton, 1996, p. 11–12). As individuals, we all brought our teaching-life histories to the group – '[our] ghosts of learning past' (Warren, 1996). The use of metaphors and stories sits alongside the developing theoretical language the mentors used as their professional knowledge bases are opened and acknowledged.

Gudmunsdottir (1992) maintained that 'to participate in a culture is to know and use a range of accumulated and shared meaning (p. 3)' and at the first meeting of CS1 we discussed our teaching stories: the experiences, learning, expertise, successes and failures of our 'teaching-selves', our ideologies, values and beliefs (Osborne & Gilbert, 1985) recognising our individual experiences within the culture of primary teaching. Through these stories and anecdotes, we explored our internalised theories of our work, how we had dealt with various situations and what we had learnt from these, recognising similarities and differences in our individual experiences and practices. Where we had been placed in the past and where we were placed now within the hierarchies of our school and what has influenced us in these roles were also items of discussion in the developing of the community of learners in CS1. Clandinin's 'sacred story' became secular and owned by the group as the use of a wider range of language genres – academic, professional, practical and metaphorical – expanded. This process is being mirrored in CS2, how it further develops for this group is the focus for the second year of this case study.

The CS1 mentors actively engaged in the interrogation of their professional development and welcomed the opportunity to extend their professional knowledge. Some were open about their anxieties about and their early lack of confidence in their theoretical knowledge. They found comfort in the group support and the assurances gained that they were not 'saying something that was out of date' (S) or 'would be later corrected by college' (M).

As a result of CS1, I was able to propose three themes from the mentors' concerns and issues over the two years:

1. theory-practice
2. pedagogy-androgogy
3. institutional support – constraint

CS2 mentors have agreed to be interviewed individually in 2005–06 and Jude and I will be exploring whether these themes apply to the second group or whether the experiences of these individuals in the intervening decade have created new themes.

The issues which underpinned the CS1 themes are shown in Table 2.1.

Table 2.1   Issues underpinning CS1 themes

Theme 1	Confidence with respect to worries that theoretical knowledge was relevant/up to date
	Commitment to read, become and keep up to date and to use this theory in tutorials
	Willingness to be challenged about theoretical knowledge as well as practical knowledge
Theme 2	Responsibility for teaching and assessing adults, rather than children
	Recognising that there are differences between teaching children (pedagogy) and adults (androgogy)
	The need to understand how adults learn and to be able to choose appropriate teaching strategies
Theme 3	Time as a resource
	Support of colleagues and institutions to enable mentors to fulfil their role and responsibilities

Theme 1

Alongside the growth of the mentors' self-confidence and recognition of their theoretical knowledge, the diffidence about whether their knowledge was appropriate, up to date and of a similar status to that held by myself and the other HEI tutors became a less daunting feature in the work of the group and a willingness to be challenged on all aspects of knowledge expanded from the sense of safety in being challenged about their practical teaching styles in the early days to a quiet confidence in being challenged about all facets of professional knowledge. Regular shared comments from reflective journal entries related to a commitment to read, learn more about how adults learn and to keep up to date with the theory.

Confidence can stem from a variety of stimuli including self-esteem, a feeling of security in one's knowledge and working practices, and excitement at passing on that knowledge to trainee teachers. Confident mentors were characterised by their willingness to openly discuss their practice, share their learning and give advice to others in order that similar problems might not be encountered by other mentors in the future. Less confident mentors were characterised by lack of participation in discussions and through the statements made in their journals which they published in the case study data sets.

It can be seen, then, that the mentors experienced and recognised growth and development in their confidence. Over time, most of the mentors moved their position between confidence in only, or mainly, the practical teaching side of their tutoring, towards a balance between their confidence in introducing and discussing theory, too. This move is reflected in their commitment to continue to update their understandings and their sense of security in discussing theory and practice using appropriate language, either metaphor or professional jargon according to the needs of their Articled Teachers.

The additional introspection involved in reviewing our own professional development may have become de-stabilising to personal, professional self-images (Argrys & Schon, 1976; Nias, 1989; Winter, 1989; Holly, 1991), creating emotional anxiety with the research (Goodson, 1992) – the tension between being an expert teacher and being insecure in the use of professional knowledge in teaching adults about teaching (Furlong & Maynard, 1995) did indeed cause anxiety and had been one of the early issues to arise. The tension between the two sites of teachers' 'professional landscapes ... the classroom working with students ... [and] the out of the classroom communal, professional place where theory is above practice and held by gatekeepers [such as] university teachers' (Clandinin, 1995, p. 28) may have been difficult to cope with. This difficulty, I believe, underpinned the issues formulated in the action cycles of the investigation. Whereas, all the group spoke about their professional knowledge and their continuing needs using a rich source of metaphors, not everyone was able to clearly articulate the complex relationship between that knowledge and educational theory (Jones et al, 1997) without the use of stories or metaphors in the early days. It was through the use of these stories that we understood each other and our group. As the MDP progressed, theoretical language became more prevalent in the discussions as we developed professional knowledge and understandings.

By working together to develop this knowledge and to overcome shared problems in an open collegiate manner everyone gained. Bruce and Easley (2000, p. 243) maintain that 'communities of enquirers who are involved in collaborative action research 'are crucial to the path of that action research.'

Although having been chosen to become the mentor had brought high esteem, the obligation to use professional knowledge in teaching contexts with the Articled Teachers which lay outside the normal work of the individuals – in discussing observations of practice, teaching new knowledge in mentor-led tutorials or marking and assessing written work – was, for some of the mentors, difficult and disconcerting. To share these concerns with the other mentors, equally expert teachers, and myself, to be open about difficulties and needs was a challenge to self-confidence and led at times to some lowering self-confidence and thereby self-esteem. Generally, the group were strong in their confidence to share and learn from each other in the learning circle we had created.

The CS2 group, as stated above, also contained teachers with varying degrees of experience and status. It does not seem to have been a difficulty to date that some are headteachers or senior members of schools and others fairly newly qualified teachers in the ways in which the discussions have unfolded. The initial discussions of the CS2 group were especially useful in building the mentors' confidence about handling trainees and one's own judgements. It removed the feeling of working in isolation. The mentors were also able to share tips and experiences they had had which were very useful to each other. They did, however, feel anxious about how far to support the trainees as they needed their trainees work to tie in with the school's work, to support the trainees fairly without giving them too much and thus not letting the trainees independently as individuals.

Theme 2

Teaching adults in a context where the adults are usually qualified or have had some input was strange and difficult for some CS1 mentors. This has become a larger part of schools' experiences in the last decade as more responsibility for school-based training has been devolved to teachers. The recognition of the learning needs of the Articled Teachers who needed teaching from scratch *about* teaching as well as *how* to teach (Furlong & Maynard, 1995) caused some consternation at times. The returning mentors had previously had the experience that the Articled Teachers' enthusiasm and/or anxieties could overwhelm them and cause them to make increasing demands on their mentor's time and knowledge. They readily shared this understanding with the new mentors giving advice to new mentors that they should set parameters and to encourage independent learning and ownership by the Articled Teachers of their learning needs to relieve possible pressure points for, even so this was a continuing cause of concern. CS2 mentors did not appear to expect to make any changes to their normal ways of working with the HEIs trainees. One commented that although she expected no changes in school, there would be a need to put aside time for planning for the Theory to Practice Days (mentor 3). A second commented that it was necessary to think more carefully about the level of the training directed at the trainees (Mentor 5).

The recognition that teaching children, teaching qualified teachers in INSET courses and teaching Articled Teachers needed different skills and strategies as well as different levels of knowledge was explored but remained an issue throughout the four action cycles. CS1 mentors discussed and reported on their wish to up date themselves and read in order to be better at teaching adults and finding out about how adults learn in addition to the reading about professional theory and subject teaching (examples from the data are to be found in chapters 6, 7 and the appendices). Some mentors became more involved in taking this part of their professional development further than the MDP by engaging in other INSET courses. This aspect of the CS2 group's development will be studied further in 2005–06.

Theme 3

Even though the CS1 schools were funded to allow for the mentors' responsibilities to take place and whole school support was given to the mentor to enact the role, the mentors did not always give themselves permission to use the mentor day per week efficiently. No matter how often we discussed the legitimacy of the day away from a class in order to fulfil all the tasks and responsibilities of the ATPS, some mentors still felt guilty at not teaching their own class everyday of the week. There was also a feeling of guilt (especially from T) that not spending the time directly in contact with the Articled Teacher was not acceptable to the rest of the busy staff. T was concerned that she was being asked why she was doing paper work, the implication being that if she was not with the Articled Teacher she should be teaching her class.

Other mentors also found it difficult to contain the mentoring tasks within the one day per week and talked about how much of their own time they used over and above the day, S was one of the mentors who was amazed at how much of his 'private time' was being taken up by his mentor responsibilities. Both Hargreaves (1997) and Day (1999) argue that teachers need time to be able to research their practice to enable them to take forward their professional development, in respect to this ATPS their comments ring true. The mentors also found time an institutional and a personal constraint upon them as they found themselves 'too busy bailing out the water to plug the leak in the boat' (Hargreaves, cited by Day, 1999, pg 226). Day gives four factors in the use of time through which teachers constrain their activities. These resonate clearly with my findings:

- the distribution of time with respect to status (micropolitical)
- the way time is constructed in schools (phenomonological)
- the claims on teachers' time by administration (socio-political)

In addition to these points, Day also added Hargreaves' (1994) comments on the ways individuals construct their priorities as a personal factor.

In CS2, there are some comments coming through about use of time, for example that taken to prepare school-based work, as a challenge to be dealt with. There is also the acknowledgement that the schools' headteachers have 'given a high level of trust/responsibility to the mentors to make this project work' (year 1 review notes, 9/6/05). There appears to be more positive feedback from their colleagues in schools such that they appear not to have as many institutional constraints upon their role as mentor. Jude has, for example, created a second group within his own school for his colleagues who are also involved in the school-based work with the trainees. This group meets weekly during assessed block teaching experience periods and hold similar discussions to the CS1 group. HE has found this to be 'incredibly successful too'.

At the end of their two years of work together, CS1 mentors listed the qualities, challenges and support the group had faced; CS1 group also listed the same aspects at the end of their first year together. The lists are very similar and are given in Table 2.2 below.

Table 2.2   Qualities, challenges and support faced by CS1 and CS2 groups

	CS1 group 1993–95	**CS2 group 2004–06**
Qualities mentors need	Responsibility, security, diplomacy, professionalism, communicator, approachability	Collaboration, professionalism, commitment, to hold similar core values
Challenges mentors face	Assessment, observations, support for trainees, to be able to challenge, inform and motivate Articled Teachers	Time, potentially money, frustration over changes, timescale, new model, some trainees, amount of work
Support for each other	Being a spring board for each other, facilitator, advisor, listener	Confidence, trust, honesty, frankness, openness, confidentiality, sharing

It will be interesting to find out whether the lists still bear such similarity when the CS2 group completes the second year together. It would seem that, when asked to list key words and phrases, the CS1 mentors considered their relationships with the Articled Teachers as well as each other whereas CS2 mentors only considered relationships within the work of the group. In the intervening ten years, mentoring trainees in schools has become the norm. In 1993–95 such work was in its infancy and the practice of the mentors was underpinned by change away from being host teachers during teaching practices where all the responsibility lay with the HEI for assessment of the training of student teachers.

Hodgkinson and Hodgkinson (2003) maintain that Lave and Wenger's approach to learning communities 'conveys a general sense of mutual agreement in an action which is defined by the negotiation of meaning both inside and outside the community' (cited by Fuller, 2005, p. 52). This is reflected in both groups' life histories. To date, similarities outweigh differences and the groups' biographies are taking the same path. As the next academic year unfolds and further work is completed by CS2 group, the meta-analysis which Jude and I will be undertaking will consider both the way in which the CS2 group's biography as a community of learners continues to unfold and also how this biography links with the on-going TTA mapping against the National Framework of Mentoring and Coaching for the career opportunities for primary teachers as we ask whether 1993–95 to 2004–04 has really been a decade of change, or is it a matter of plus ça change?

References

Argrys, C. and Schoen, D.A. (1978), *Organisational Learning*, Addison-Wesley, Reading, MA.

Bolton, E. (1994), 'Transitions in Initial Teacher Training: An overview', in M. Wilkin and D. Sankey (eds), *Collaboration and Transition in Initial Teacher Training*, Kogan Page, London.

Bruce, B.C. and Easley, J.A. (2000), 'Emerging Communities of Practice: collaboration and communication in action research', *Educational Action Research Journal*, vol. 8(2), pp. 243–259.

Clandinin, D.J. and Connelly, F.M. (1995), *Narrative and Education*.

Claxton, G. (1996), 'Professional Learning in Education: Models and Roles', in G. Claxton and E. Roper (eds), *Professional Learning in Education: models, roles & contexts*, LMU Education Papers, 1, March 1996.

Claxton, G. and Roper, E. (eds) (1996), *Professional Learning in Education: models, roles & contexts*, LMU Education Papers, 1, March 1996.

CUREE / DfES (2005), *Mentoring and Coaching CPD Capacity Building Project 2004–2005 National Framework for Mentoring and Coaching*.

Day, C. (1999), 'Researching Teaching Through Reflective Practice', in J. Loughran (ed), *Researching Teaching: Methodologies and Practices for Understanding Pedagogy*, Falmer Press, London.

DES (1983), *Teaching Quality*, HMSO, London.

DES (1986), *Better Schools*, HMSO, London.

DES (1988), *Qualified Teacher Training: A Consultation Document*, HMSO, London.

DES (1989b), *Initial Teacher Training: Approval of Courses*, (Circular 24/89) HMSO, London.

DES (1992), *Initial Teacher Training (Secondary Phase)*, (Circular 9/92) HMSO, London.

DES (1993), *The Initial Training of Primary School Teachers: New Criteria for Courses*, (Circular 14/93) HMSO, London.

DfEE (1998), *Teaching: High Status, High Standards*, (Circular 4/98) HMSO, London.

DfEE (2001), *Building on Success*, HMSO, London.

DFES (2005), *Every Child Matters*, HMSO, London.

DFES (*Workforce Re-modelling*.

DES (1983), *Teaching Quality*, HMSO, London.

Edwards, A. and Collison, J. (1996), *Mentoring and Development of Practice in Primary Schools. Supporting student teacher learning in schools*, Open University, Buckingham.

Elliott, B. and Calderhead, J. (1995), 'Mentoring for teacher development: possibilities and caveats', in T. Kerry and A.S. Mayes (eds), *Issues in Mentoring*, Routledge/Open University, London.

Furlong, V.J., Hirst, P.H., Pocklington, K. and Miles, S. (1988), *Initial Teacher Training and the Role of the School*, Open University Press, Milton Keynes.

Furlong, V.J. and Maynard, T. (1995), *Mentoring Student Teachers: The growth of professional knowledge*, Routledge, London.

Ginsburg, M.B., Kamet, S., Raghu, M. and Weaver, J. (1992), 'Educators/Politics', *Comparative Education Review*, vol. 36(4), pp. 417–45.

Goodson, I.F. (1992), 'Sponsoring the Teacher's Voice', in A. Hargreaves and M.G. Fullan (eds), *Understanding Teacher Development*, The Teachers' College Press, New York.

Griffiths, V. and Owen, P. (eds), (1995), *Schools in Partnership*, Paul Chapman Press, London.

Gudmunsdottir, S. (1992), Transforming Knowing into Telling: Narratives in pedagogical content, knowledge and teaching. Paper presented at Teachers' Stories of Life and Work: The Place of Narrative in Personal-Professional Development Conference, Liverpool, April, 1992.

Hargreaves, A. (ed), (1997), *Rethinking Educational Change with Heart and Mind*, Association for Supervision and Curriculum Development, Alexandria, V. A.

Hextall, I. and Mahony, P. (2000), 'Consultation and the Management of Consent: Standards for Qualified Teacher Status', *British Educational Research Journal*, vol. 26(3), pp. 323–342.

Hodgkinson, P. and Hodgkinson, H. (2003), 'Individuals, communities of practice and the policy context: schoolteachers' learning in their workplace', *Studies in Continuing Education*, vol. 25(1), 3–21.

Holly, M. (1989), *Writing to Grow*, Heinemann, New York.

Jackson, S. and Cox, K. (2005), Professional Development for school-based tutors in TTA (2005) *doingitt* National Partnership Project newsletter (Yorkshire and Humberside) Summer 2005, p. 5.

Jones, L., Reid, D. and Bevis, S. (1997), 'Teachers' Perceptions of Mentoring in a Collaborative Model of ITT', *Journal of the Education of Teachers*, vol. 23(3).

'KAY', article in Times Education Supplement, 16 February, 2001.

Kerry, T. and Mayes, A.S. (eds), (1995), Issues in Mentoring, Routledge/Open University, London.

Landman, M. and Ozga, J. (1995), 'Teacher Education Policy in England', in M.B. Ginsburg, and B. Lindsay (eds), The Political Dimension in Teacher Education: Comparative Perspectives on Policy, Socialisation and Society. Falmer Press, London.

Lave, J. (1988), Cognition in Practice, Cambridge University Press, Cambridge.

Lave, J. and Wenger, E. (1991), Situated learning, Legitimate peripheral participation, Cambridge University Press, Cambridge.

Lick, D.W. (1999), 'Proactive Comentoring Relations: Enhancing Effectiveness through Synergy', in C.A. Mullen and D.W. Lick (eds), New Directions in

Mentoring – Creating a Culture of Synergy, Falmer Press, London.

McIntyre, D. (1988), 'Designing a Teacher Education Curriculum from Research and Theory on Teacher Knowledge', in J. Calderhead (ed), Teachers' Professional Learning, Falmer Press, London.

National Union of Teachers (1993), Letter to Heads of Department and Directors of Primary PGCE and B. Ed Courses in HEIs in England and Wales, 15 July, 1993

OFSTED (1993a), The Articled Teacher Scheme September 1990–July 1992, HMSO, London.

Osborne, R. and Gilbert, J. (1988), 'Some Issues of Theory in Science Education', in J. Calderhead (ed), op.cit.

Rivers, J. (2005), Personal correspondence.

Roper, E., Sharp, A. and Warren, S.E. (1993), Transition to school-based ITT: researching the emerging partnerships Paper presented at BERA Annual Conference, University of Liverpool, September, 1993.

TTA (1999), Graduate and Registered Teacher Programmes, www.teach-tta.gov.uk, accessed 24/7/00

Warren, S.E. (1996), 'Ghosts of learning past: what professional knowledge do mentors bring to their role and what professional learning do they recognise?', in G. Claxton, and E.H. Roper (eds), Professional Learning in Education: Models, Roles and Contexts, LMU Education Papers, number 1, March 1996.

Warren, S.E. (2001), The Mentor's Role: an action research investigation into the professional development of primary teacher mentors, unpublished PhD thesis, Leeds Metropolitan University.

Winter, R. (1989), Learning from Experience: principles and practice in action-research, The Falmer Press, London.

Yeomans, R. and Sampson, J. (eds), (1995), Mentorship in the Primary School, Falmer, London.

Chapter 3

A Status Report on Teacher Mentoring Programmes in the United States

Tom Ganser

Mentoring programmes for new teachers are a predictable feature of public education in the United States today. Although programmes vary with respect to goals, duration, activities, and financial support, they share the central feature of providing beginning teachers with the assistance of experienced teachers. In fact, candidates for teaching positions today generally expect a mentoring programme to be available to them for at least a year, and they bear in mind the quality of the programme when considering accepting a position. Recent reports indicate that most states recommend or require induction programmes for beginning teachers (Fideler & Haselkorn, 1999; Hall, 2005). However, not all programmes call for on-site mentors and not all states provide funding for the programmes (Darling-Hammond, 2003; National Commission on Teaching and America's Future, 2003). Based on a survey of more than 5,000 teachers in 2000, a report issued by the National Center for Educational Statistics (2001) revealed that 26 percent of the respondents had served as a mentor for another teacher in a formal relationship and that 44 percent of them did so at least weekly. Twenty-three percent of the respondents indicated that they were mentored by another teacher in a formal relationship.

It is also important to bear in mind that teacher induction and mentoring programmes are not unique to the United States but are a worldwide phenomenon (Korchan & Pascarelli, 2003; McBain & George, 1995; Moskowitz & Stephens, 1997a, 1997b; Tang & Choi, 2005; Tisher, 1984; Wang, 2001; Wong, Britton & Ganser, 2005). For example, in 2005 the 12th European Mentoring and Coaching Conference (www.emccouncil.org) and in 2006 the 19th Annual International Mentoring Association Conference (www.ima.org) will occur. However, as Britton, Paine, Pimm, and Raizen (2003) are careful to point out, attempts to transplant an effective programme from one location to another – and especially from one country to another country – is unwise without first making appropriate adjustments.

The idea of formally organized and operated mentoring programmes for teachers in the United States is hardly a new idea. Some programmes were established more than 30 years ago (Darling-Hammond & Sclan, 1996). Mentoring programmes are sponsored by a variety of organizations, most typically local school districts but also consortia of school districts. As a service to local school districts, some colleges and universities sponsor mentoring programmes or support school-based programmes by providing mentor training, facilitating meetings on relevant topics, or assisting in programme evaluation (Ganser, 2002). In recent years, the two largest teacher unions in the United States, the National Education Association and the American Federation of Teachers, have become active in supporting mentoring programs for their members (American Federation of Teachers, 2000, 2001; National Education Association, 1999, 2000; NEA [National Education Association] Foundation for the Improvement of Education, 1999). Since 2000, the National Education Association/ Saturn Corporation/UAW Partnership Award (http://www.nea.org/members/ inductionaward.html) has recognized mentoring programmes throughout the United States that show a close and productive relationship between school administration and the local teachers' union. Finally, support for mentoring programmes is evident in the work of professional education groups and associations, such as the Education Commission of the States (Bonelli, 1999), the Council for Exceptional Children (White & Mason, 2001), and the National Resource Center for Paraprofessionals (Barresi & Fogarty, n.d.).

The available literature on teacher induction is extensive, and mentoring programmes as a central feature of teacher induction are typically included in this literature. Over time, the research on mentoring and mentoring programmes has evolved from descriptive studies to empirical studies, although empirical studies continue to be relatively rare. A search of the United States Department of Educational Resources Information Center (ERIC) on September 9, 2005, database using the descriptors 'Teacher AND Mentor,' 'Teacher AND Induction,' and 'Teacher AND Mentor AND Induction' resulted in 4,331, 2,532, and 732 documents, respectively. Comprehensive reviews of the literature on teacher socialization (Zeichner & Gore, 1990) and on induction are also available (e.g., Huling-Austin, 1990b; Gold, 1996; Feiman-Nemser, Schwille, Carver & Yusko, 1999).

Complementing research on teacher induction and mentoring is the extensive information available about the design and operation of mentoring programmes for beginning teachers. This information is sometimes accessible as on-line reports (e.g., Bolich, 2001; Simmons, 2000; Stansbury & Zimmerman, 2000). A host of books have been published since 2000 focusing on induction and mentor programme design (e.g., Breaux & Wong, 2003; Odell & Huling, 2000; Portner, 2001, 2005; Sweeny, 2001; Udelhofen & Larson, 2003; Villani, 2002), knowledge and skills for serving as a mentor (e.g., Boreen, Johnson, Niday & Potts, 2000; Gordon & Maxey, 2000; Jonson, 2002; Portner, 2003; Zachary, 2000) and guidelines for beginning teachers who are being mentored (Portner, 2002). Mentoring and supporting new teachers has also been the special theme for journals (e.g., *Educational Leadership*, Vol. 62, No. 8, May 2005; *Journal of Staff Development*, Vol. 23, No. 4, Autumn 2002; *Teaching Exceptional Children*, Vol. 33, No. 1, September/October 2000; *Theory into Practice*, Vol. 39, No. 1, Winter 2000).

Mentoring programmes are a prominent component of professional and staff development for beginning teachers in the United States, and likely to remain so. The fact that mentoring programmes have been developed over an entire generation of teachers suggests a history that offers a useful framework for creating new programmes and enhancing existing programmes (Ganser, 2005a). At the same time, that history also sets the snares for conceptualizing mentoring programmes based on out-dated assumptions about beginning teachers, mentor teachers, and the nature of the schools in which their professional lives intersect.

Today, the individuals responsible for the design and implementation of mentoring programmes for beginning teachers are well advised to take into account significant and shaping trends in education and in teaching as an occupation to maximize programme effectiveness. This chapter will examine five factors that require thinking about mentoring programmes in new ways to ensure their success. These factors are:

- Characteristics of beginning teachers
- Goals for mentoring
- Context of mentoring
- Selection, training, and utilization of mentors
- High-stakes dimensions of mentoring

Characteristics of Beginning Teachers

Beginning teachers are the targets for mentoring programmes, and so defining who are 'beginning' teachers and understanding their characteristics are essential. Beginning teachers today share much in common with their counterparts 25 or 30 years ago, but there have been significant changes as well. The image of beginning teachers as new graduates of teacher preparation programmes, in their early 20s, and starting a lifetime career in teaching is more appropriate for movie scripts set in the 1930s or 1940s than it is today. There is mounting evidence that variations among beginning teachers are considerable with respect to their demographic characteristics, their preparation for teaching, and their career track in teaching (Feistritzer, 2005b). Moreover, this variation is fluid over time and related to particular school settings and teaching fields.

The national Schools and Staffing Survey (SASS) conducted in 1987–88, 1990–91, and 1993–94 offers insights into newly hired teachers in public and private schools (National Center for Education Statistics, 2000). The report distinguishes among four different sources of newly hired teachers. *Newly Prepared Teachers* are first-year teachers who come directly into teaching out of college. *Delayed Entrants* are also first-year teachers who engage in other activities between graduating from college and becoming teachers. *Transfers* are teachers who move from one school to another. Finally, *Reentrants* are teachers who had taught in the past and are reentering teaching after a break in their teaching career.

Regarding gender, between 1987–88 and 1993–94 the percentage of newly hired female teachers decreased from 78.0 percent to 72.5 percent for public schools and from 79.5 percent to 76.7 percent for private schools. The age of newly hired teachers dropped only slightly, by 0.2 years for public schools and 0.8 years for private schools. However, there was a dramatic increase in the percent of minority new hires. In public schools, the increase was from 9.7 percent to 16.0 percent, and in private schools, from 6.9 percent to 11.1 percent.

In referring to a study published by the National Education Association in 1987, the National Center for Educational Statistics (NCES) (2000) report notes that 'In the 1960s ... 67 percent of newly hired teachers in public schools were new college graduates, but by the late 1980s this source supplied only 17 percent of new hires' (p. 1). This fact suggests that in the late 1980s a significant portion of new hires were either transfers or reentrants who were not at the beginning of their career. However, between 1987–88 and 1993–94 this pattern reversed, and schools hired relatively fewer reentrants and relatively more newly prepared and delayed entrants. Over this period of time, the number of first-time teachers increased from 30.6 percent to 45.8 percent for public schools, and from 25.2 percent to 42.4 percent for private schools, whereas the number of re-entering teachers dropped from 32.8 percent to 22.9 percent for public schools and from 36.7 percent to 23.3 percent for private schools.

With respect to career paths, the data upon which the NCES (2000) report are based suggest that newly prepared and delayed entrants were different from one another, whereas transfers and reentrants were quite similar across the different variables examined in the report. In general, the qualifications of delayed entrants in their primary fields of assignment were less than those of other new hires, all the more significant because of the increase in hiring delayed entrants between 1987–88 and 1993–94 from 9 to 17 percent in public schools and from 11 to 21 percent in private schools. Considering the qualification of delayed entrants, the report concludes:

> The extent to which delayed entrants lacked the standard teaching credentials suggests almost half of public and two-thirds of private delayed entrants did not plan to enter the teaching profession when they were earning their highest degrees. Over one-third of public and half of private delayed entrants transferred from other occupations, most outside the field of education. If a major or minor with certification in the primary assignment field is the standard qualification to teach a field, the data suggest that many in this group (about 45 percent of public) may be in need of alternative teacher training programs (p. 17).

Significant changes in the characteristics of beginning teachers over a span of 15 years has been reported by Feistritzer (1999). The most dramatic change she documents is a shift toward people who begin their preparation to teacher later in life and later in their academic careers. In comparing beginning teachers in 1984 and 1999, she found that in 1984 only 3 percent of teachers began their career after finishing a post-baccalaureate programme. That portion had increased dramatically to 27 percent by 1999. The average age of these post-baccalaureate programme completers was 30.2 years (compared to 22.4 years for undergraduate program completers) and more than 50 percent of them were transitioning into teaching from an occupation outside the field of education (compared to about 11 percent). Finally, over of third of them have prior teaching experience (compared to about 14 percent). All in all, they come to teaching with considerably different characteristics than their undergraduate programme counterparts. In an extension of her study to include a

2005 survey, Feistritzer (2005b) notes that 'the public teaching force in the United States continues to get more female as well as older' (p. 4).

Instructional aides are another group of individuals employed by school systems also considered as a possible target for mentoring programmes. During 2001–02 almost 3 million teachers were employed by public elementary and secondary schools in the United States. In addition to these teachers, 675,038 instructional aides directly assisted teachers in providing instruction (National Center for Education Statistics, 2003). Citing evidence from the National Center for Educational Statistics, Black (2002) notes that from 1990 to 1997, the number of paraprofessionals employed as instructional aides increased by more than 40 percent, whereas over the same period of time, the number of teachers increased by less than 15 percent.

For most of the 20th century, preparation for teaching was generally part of a four-year, baccalaureate degree programmes. In recent years, traditional preparation programmes have expanded to include five-year undergraduate programmes, or programmes combining an undergraduate program and additional graduate study, sometime leading to a master's degree. More importantly, 'alternative route' programmes preparing individuals to teach have proliferated during the past 25 years. Alternative route programmes provide a way for people with liberal arts or science degrees, people from other careers, retirees (including military), and people beginning a teaching career later in life to become teachers without returning to college to complete a traditional program of study (U.S. Department of Education, Office of Innovation and Improvement, 2004). Alternative preparation programmes are especially common for teachers in large, urban school districts where the demand to staff classrooms with traditionally prepared teachers often outstrips the supply.

In the most recent survey of states conducted by the National Center for Education Information, Feistritzer (2005a) indicates that 47 states and the District of Columbia report having a total of 122 alternative routes to teacher certification in 619 sites, compared to only eight states in 1983. She also notes that 'at least 250,000 teachers have entered teaching since the mid-1980s through some type of alternative teacher certification route' (p. 1). The reauthorization of the Elementary and Secondary Education Act, signed into law by President George Bush in January 2002 as the *No Child Left Behind Act*, allocated more than $55 million dollars in support of three programmes offering 'Innovative and Alternative Routes to Licensure': (1) Troops to Teaching, (2) Transition to Teaching, and (3) Teach for America. Individual states sponsor alternative certification programmes as well, such as the Massachusetts Signing Bonus Program that includes a $20,000 signing bonus paid over four years (Liu, Johnson & Peske, 2003).

Although many alternative route teacher certification programmes offer a level and rigour of preparation comparable to traditional programmes, others are 'poorly designed and administered and provide little appropriate training' (Laczko-Kerr & Berliner, 2003). Some programmes include intensive coursework during the summer, full-time teaching during the academic year while taking additional courses in the evening or on weekends, and coursework during the following summer. Most participants in alternative route certification programmes receive on-the-job training under the guidance of master teachers or mentors, although the role of mentor may be somewhat different in an alternative route teacher preparation programme, with an emphasis on training teachers, than the role of mentor for a graduate of a traditional programme, with an emphasis on facilitating the successful induction of teachers who have already been trained.

In the past, most beginning teachers were young adults beginning a career in education that would last a lifetime. Their career might remain that of being an elementary or secondary teacher, possibly leaving teaching for personal reasons such as raising a family and then returning. Less frequently, their career might take them into another aspect of education outside the classroom, such as school administration, guidance counselling, or school psychology, or perhaps work in post-secondary education or in a state department of education. For most teachers, however, classroom teaching would be their lifelong work.

Teacher career patterns have changed in recent years and are likely to continue changing in the future. For instance, people in the United States starting any career today are likely to make many more job changes, some of which may require additional education or training, than their counterparts in the past. A Bureau of Labor Statistics (2002) report indicates that persons born from 1957 to 1964 held an average of 7.8 different jobs between the ages of 23 and 36 years. Moreover, included among newly hired teachers are older individuals who may be changing careers in mid life to become teachers or beginning a short-term career in teaching following retirement from another line of work.

Current research conducted as part of *The Project on the Next Generation of Teachers* at the Harvard Graduate School of Education (http://www.gse.Harvard. edu/~ngt/) highlights another emerging trend among some new teachers. Susan Moore Johnson, project director, and her colleagues (Peske, Liu, Johnson, Kaufmann & Kardos, 2001; Johnson, Birkeland, Donaldson, Kardos, Kaurrman, Liu & Peske, 2004) have discovered that more of today's young adults enter teaching as a 'public service' commitment limited to a few years before moving on to another line of work. Others become teachers just to test it out as a possible career or with the view that teaching is a necessary stepping stone to become qualified for a different job in schools, such as administrator, guidance counsellor, or technology specialist. The relatively low salaries earned by school teachers in comparison with other people with a comparable level of education partially accounts for this pattern. Other reasons for a short-time commitment to teaching include the demands of the job and the relatively low status of teaching as a profession.

The increased regulation of teaching practice and the accompanying reduction of the professional autonomy of teachers in constructing their work negatively influence interest in teaching among qualified, prospective teachers. According to Grossman (2003):

> Due in large part to the confluence of increased accountability measures, including high-stakes standardized assessments and the influx of new and underqualified teachers into schools, districts around the country have begun to invest heavily in a variety of scripted

curriculum materials. Many see this move as contributing to the deskilling of teachers and the deprofessionalization of teaching. (paragraph 1).

Given a diminishment of the autonomy associated with traditional professions such as medicine or law, individuals may decide not to become teachers for that reason alone. Moreover, some new teachers may experience so much dissatisfaction in their work due to a higher degree of regulation than they anticipated that they may decide to leave teaching altogether.

Goals for Mentoring

In the first substantive review of the literature on teacher induction programmes, Huling-Austin (1990b) suggested five common goals:

1. To improve teaching performance
2. To increase the retention of promising beginning teachers during the induction years
3. To promote the personal and professional well-being of beginning teachers by improving teachers' attitudes toward themselves and the profession
4. To satisfy mandated requirements related to induction and certification
5. To transmit the culture of the system to beginning teachers

These goals are as relevant and applicable today as they were for the programmes existing in the 1980s upon which Huling-Austin (1990b) based her conclusions, and provide a useful framework for considering the goals for mentoring programmes today. Rather than calling for the elimination of any of these goals, current programme practice may suggest some differences in the relative emphasis placed on these goals.

Two of Huling-Austin's (1990b) goals are institutional in nature: satisfying mandates and increasing the retention of promising beginning teachers. Since her review, state mandates for induction programmes (generally including mentoring) have increased. Some of these mandated programmes also are funded, but many are not.

Growing numbers of states expect school districts to support the induction of beginning teachers to fulfill initial or continuing licensure requirements (Hall, 2005). For example, Wisconsin school districts are obliged to provide all beginning teachers (as well as beginning school administrators and student support personnel) who are issued a non-renewable 'Initial Educator' license with the services of a qualified mentor for at least one year (Wisconsin Department of Public Instruction, 2000). The districts are also required to provide on-going, collaboratively-designed orientation to new teachers and support seminars related to ten Wisconsin Teacher Standards. In Wisconsin's new licensing system, mentors are called upon (at least informally) to assist initial educators in developing a 'Professional Development Plan' required for the second license stage, 'Professional Educator.' However, the mentors are not part of a three-person team, including another teacher, a school administrator, and a representative of higher education, that must approve the design of the Professional Development Plan and verify its implementation. Other states, such as Ohio, link continuing licensing for beginning teachers to successful performance on assessment instruments such as the Educational Testing Service's Praxis III instrument.

The goal of increasing and retaining promising beginning teachers is of continuing importance, especially in areas such as mathematics, science, bilingual education, and special education where the pool of prospective teachers is relatively shallow. Failure to keep good beginning teachers is costly in many respects, including the financial investment in hiring new teachers as well as the investment in providing them with staff development services (Alliance for Excellence Education, 2005). Thomas G. Carroll (2005), president of the National Commission on Teaching and America's Future, recently noted:

> ... the real school staffing issue is teacher retention, not recruitment. America produces enough teachers each year to fill the schools, but it loses them like water draining through a leaky bucket. They leave for many reasons, but lack of support is at the top of the list. (p. 199)

In an era when the economic support of education has eroded, the wasted money invested in hiring and supporting new teachers who leave within a few years is a cause of great concern (Johnson, Berg & Donaldson, 2005). At the same time, implicit in the goal of retaining *promising* beginning teachers is encouraging the departure of beginning teachers who are *not* promising.

A new goal for mentoring programmes as related to the retention of promising teachers has emerged recently (Strong, 2005): viewing a mentoring programme as a recruitment device. Applicants for teaching positions take into account a school district's induction programme, including mentoring, in deciding whether or not to accept a position if it is offered. A certain portion of teacher education graduates are willing to take a position in a school district that offers a good mentoring programme even at a reduced salary compared to other districts not offering a quality mentoring programme (Ganser, 2005b). Several years ago, the district supervisor of full time mentors in a large, urban school district investing approximately one million dollars in the mentoring programme commented that the most important value of the programme was convincing prospective new hires that the school district supported new teachers, but with little regard as to whether or not newly hired teachers were more effective because of the mentoring programme and the money spent to support it (Ganser, 1997, personal communication).

For many experienced teachers, what draws them to service as a mentor is the opportunity 'to promote the personal and professional well-being of teachers.' Providing emotional guidance and support to beginning teachers as they start to construct a professional identity is at the heart of this goal (Gold, 1996). Wang and Odell (2002) describe this as the 'humanistic perspective' on teacher mentoring, aimed at helping new teachers to come to terms with the 'reality shock' of teaching and to remain as teachers in spite of it. This goal remains very important today, even more for a portion of beginning teachers who are 'undercertified' (Lackzko-Kerr & Berliner, 2000) for teaching, or who are given 'out-of-field' teaching assignments for which they have not been adequately prepared (Ingersoll, 1999; Jerald, 2002).

The goals to 'promote ... the professional well-being of beginning teachers' and to 'transmit the culture of the system to beginning teachers' imply a focus on the organizational context of teaching. Although the notion of transmitting the culture of the system to beginning teachers suggests a continuation of the status quo, it is also possible that the culture of the school promotes innovation. The emphasis in these goals lies in the practical dimensions of teaching, and here the mentor may function as a 'local guide' and 'educational companion' as the new teacher comes to understand the curriculum, available resources, and the culture of teaching in the school (Feiman-Nemser & Parker, 1992). These goals are compatible with Wang and Odell's (2002) description of the 'situated apprenticeship perspective' on teacher mentoring, and range from addressing the common problems of beginning teachers, such as classroom management and student motivation (Veenman, 1984), to becoming familiar with local policies and procedures.

As is the case in providing personal and emotional support to new teachers, veteran teachers serving as mentors generally are comfortable in serving as local guides. Stated differently, interacting with beginning teachers in learning about how their school and school district operate comes naturally to many teachers. Since these goals for mentoring are more-or-less intuitive to mentors, providing them with training that focuses on meeting these goals may be viewed as unnecessary. In the case of mentoring programmes with meager resources for mentor training, the goals for the programmes may intentionally be limited to this kind of support and orientation to the local school culture.

Huling-Austin's (1990b) first goal, 'To improve teaching performance,' seems to be the most important of all five goals, and yet it is the most challenging. Focusing on teaching performance – and by implication, student learning – presents far different expectations for mentoring than providing emotional support, help with policies and procedures, and understanding local school culture. It moves the rationale for mentoring from ensuring that new teachers will stay in teaching to influencing what kind of teachers they will become (Feiman-Nemser, 2000). Feiman-Nemser, Schwille, Carver, and Yusko (1999) observe that policy-makers tend to view 'induction' as a programme rather than a process and they point out that 'induction' also refers to 'a unique phase (or stage) in teacher development and 'a time of transition when teachers are moving from preparation to practice' (p. 4). From this perspective, newly hired teachers are not finished products whom mentors assist in fitting into particular teaching assignments. Instead, mentors are charged to work with beginning teachers during a period of significant professional development. Wang and Odell's (2002) description of the 'critical constructivist perspective' on mentoring provides a good example, since it 'clearly aligns with the goal of transforming teaching' (p. 499).

The goal of improving teacher performance as part of induction influences the structure of a mentoring programme, including mentor selection; mentor training and support; and accessibility of beginning teachers and mentors to one another for conversations and to each other's classroom for the purpose of observing teaching. This goal also suggests the role of mentor as expert teacher or, at the very least, as an expert facilitator of teaching improvement. In an occupation that historically has been relatively flat and with few distinctions among teachers based on expertise, identifying the mentor as 'expert' challenges the existing structure. However, changes like this have become increasingly evident in how teaching as a line of work is organized. On the one hand, more leadership roles are now available for teachers, such as team leader for a group of four or five seventh grade teachers in a middle school. On the other hand, new licensing systems recognize differences in level of expertise as reflected in the nomenclature of licensing, such as 'Initial Educator,' 'Professional Educator,' and 'Master Educator' in Wisconsin.

Mentoring programmes are also being considerably influenced by the standards-based reform movement that is based on performance. Accreditation, state approval of teacher preparation programmes, and licensing systems are routinely linked to state standards (e.g., Wisconsin Teacher Standards [Wisconsin Department of Public Instruction, 2000]), national standards (e.g., Interstate New Teacher Assessment and Support Consortium, 1992), or standards of professional organizations (e.g., Council for Exceptional Children, 2003). Moreover, the work of teachers is also linked to learning standards for children (e.g., Wisconsin Model Academic Standards [Wisconsin Department of Public Instruction, 1998]). With respect to mentoring programmes, external standards serve to provide an external foundation to mentoring (Odell & Huling, 2000). This is a considerably different approach than 'mentoring by intuition.' For example, the Center for Strengthening the Teaching Profession (2005) outlines 'Standards for Beginning Teacher Induction,' offering them as 'principles of practice and not "must-dos" in a prescriptive model' (p. 3, emphasis in original). However, Wang and Odell (2002) also caution that the current emphasis of many mentoring programmes on emotional support and technical assistance makes mentored learning to teach in ways consistent with standards and reforms difficult to achieve.

The Context of Mentoring

Mentoring occurs within the context of school, and so how schools are staffed is especially important. Changing staffing patterns influences how best to design mentoring programmes so as to avoid falling into a 'one size fits all' trap. Fortunately, recent research on the staffing of schools and on the nature of the teaching workforce has provided more sophisticated and valuable information. One of the important insights gained is that what appears to be a 'shortage' of qualified teachers is far less of a problem of an inadequate supply of teachers and much more the result of failing to retain teachers after they are hired (National Commission on Teaching and America's Future, 2002, 2003). From this vantage point, mentoring emerges as one variable out of many that can promote the retention of teachers, but without being a panacea or 'silver bullet.' For example, in a study of seven mid-western states, Hare and Heap (2001) include new teacher support programmes and mentoring as an important recruitment and retention strategy, but they also recommend several other strategies, such as (1) including teachers in decision-making, (2) making scheduling and structural changes necessary to increase collaboration between teachers, (3) creating smaller learning environments through smaller schools or 'schools within schools,' (4) supporting 'grow your own' programmes, and (5) increasing the flexibility of pay schedule to be more market-driven. Johnson and Birkeland (2003) describe as 'voluntary movers' teachers who have not given up on teaching entirely but who decide to move to schools that make good teaching possible in ways that cannot be addressed by mentoring alone.

In recent years, the case for mentoring programmes has been based on the projections that the United States will need about 2 million additional teachers over a span of ten years due to a convergence of several trends: (1) increasing enrollments due to birth rates, (2) a retirement wave of teachers hired in the 1960s and 1970s, (3) increased immigration, and (4) policies that result in smaller class size (e.g., expansion of full-day kindergarten or reduction of class size in California in early primary grades to 20 pupils). The picture was one of large numbers of experienced teachers leaving teaching and being replaced by even larger numbers of beginning teachers. However, Richard Ingersoll, using a large, national dataset, offers a different analysis of the situation (Ingersoll, 1999, 2001, 2002; Ingersoll & Smith, 2003; Smith & Ingersoll, 2004).

Ingersoll's body of research differentiates between teachers who leave the professional altogether because of retirement or entering a different line of work, and teachers who migrate from one school to another due to dissatisfaction (salary, level of administrative support, characteristics of students served, etc.). Ingersoll finds that there is more than an adequate supply of newly prepared teachers to replace veteran teachers who are leaving due to retirement. The problem is that the number of new teachers being produced cannot match the total of the number of teachers who retire, combined with the number of teachers who exit the profession due to dissatisfaction. Ingersoll's findings paint a picture of a sizeable number of experienced teachers moving from one school to another. From the standpoint of those schools to which the teachers move – and their mentoring programmes – these teachers are indeed new to the school although they are not new to the profession. Historically, district-based mentoring programmes with scant resources have targeted their services on beginning teachers at the start of their career, not experienced teachers new to the district.

State-of-the-art teacher mentoring programmes take into account the changing balance between new teachers and veteran teachers in a school. Hargreaves and Fullan (2000) suggest that this changing balance requires rethinking about how mentoring is recognized in schools. With a notable bifurcation in some schools between older teachers and younger teachers, the challenge for mentors may not be so much to 'counsel individuals' as to 'bring together the cultures of youth and experience' (p. 54).

The Project on the Next Generation of Teachers at the Harvard Graduate School of Education presents a somewhat different picture. Liu and Kardos (2002) find evidence of three types of professional cultures in schools. In the *Veteran-Oriented Culture* the concerns and habits of veteran teachers determine professional interactions with minimal focused or organized support for novices. There is also minimal focused or organized support for novices in the *Novice-Oriented Culture*, where new teachers either work together at a fever pitch or in isolation, but without the help of the experience or expertise of veteran teachers. Novice-Oriented Cultures are frequently found in charter schools or in struggling schools that have been re-constituted or re-organized and in which entire staffs are replaced at once. Finally, in the *Integrated Professional Culture*, there is a faculty wide, shared belief – regardless of experience level – in the importance of teacher interaction around issues of curriculum and teaching. The result is frequent open and reciprocal exchange among all teachers. In an investigation of new teachers' experiences in California, Florida, Massachusetts, and Michigan, Kardos (2003) finds that Integrated Professional Cultures are rare. Clearly, the function of mentors varies according to the type of culture into which beginning teachers are inducted. Indeed, formal mentoring programmes are far less important in an Integrated Professional Culture where the principles of mentoring are already part of the culture.

Selection, Training, and Utilization of Mentors

In the early days of mentoring programs, mentor selection, training, and utilization was fairly simple and straightforward. The primary selection criterion was willingness to serve as a mentor with no reduction in teaching responsibilities and with few, if any, extrinsic incentives. The existing body of literature suggested that mentors have between 7 and 15 years of teaching experience and that their teaching assignment should be identical or at least very similar to that of their mentee. If any training was provided to mentors, it was generally limited, offered at the beginning of the assignment, and focused on general principles of beginning teaching rather than grade-level or subject specific training. Often no training was offered, based on the belief that being an effective mentor involved the same knowledge, skills, and dispositions associated with being an effective teacher. Mentoring was viewed as a one-on-one, face-to-face relationship between mentor and mentee. This approach to selecting, training, and using mentors was and continues to be justifiable to some extent when the goals for mentoring are limited to emotional support, a low level of technical assistance, and an orientation to the local culture. However, increasing the expectations for mentoring to include an emphasis on teaching and curriculum influences the selection and training of mentors, all the more so if the mentor role is constructed as a new role for teachers, not just an 'add on' role to their unaltered work as teachers, that may include financial incentives.

Today, the selection process for mentors is often more complex and includes criteria that extend well beyond a willingness to serve. Selection may be the responsibility of a group rather than an individual such as a principal. This group might include current or former mentors, teachers who received services as beginning teachers, school administrators, and teacher union officials. Prospective mentors may be required to provide evidence that they are qualified to serve as a mentor through interviews, narrative statements, letters of support, verification of successful experiences related to mentoring (e.g., serving as a cooperating teacher for a student teacher or as team leader for a group of teachers), and evidence of effective teaching (e.g., videotapes of teaching or professional portfolios). Naturally, as the complexity of the application procedure increases, so too does the need for integrity in the process and a reasonable and ethical basis for deciding which a candidate is or is not qualified to serve as a mentor.

The selection process might be less stringent than expected due to the pool of prospective mentors. The retirement of large numbers of teachers over time means that the availability of experienced teachers to serve as mentors diminishes. In addition, the shrinking group of veteran teachers are also under pressure to serve in other leadership roles in the school or district, or for the profession in general (e.g., serving as a cooperating teacher for student teachers or on the 'Professional Development Team' for a beginning teacher in Wisconsin). This situation has led to using teachers with relatively few years of teaching experience or retired teachers as mentors, a phenomenon that should be addressed in mentor training since mentees may question the suitability of mentors with relatively few years of teaching experience or presuppose that retired teachers may not be able to empathize fully with their experiences as beginning teachers.

Changes in goals and expectations for mentoring in recent years call for changes in the level of mentor training and on-going support. For example, as observation of teaching as part of mentoring grows in prominence, so too does the need to provide mentors with training in systematic observation of teaching, a constellation of skills that is generally not addressed in undergraduate or alternative route teacher preparation programmes. In addition, the sequence of mentor training has been influenced by training techniques in business and industry. For example, rather than using an exclusively 'up front' model of delivery, mentor training also includes a 'just in time' approach to training based on the premise that the best time to provide training is shortly before it is needed, when the motivation to learn the skills is high and the application of the training is immediate. Finally, the increasing importance of mentoring also means that mentors require on-going support over time. Accordingly, there is a good reason to include in the structure of a mentoring programme a way to provide mentors with opportunities to engage in facilitated discussions regarding their experiences as mentors and to seek the advice of fellow mentors when necessary.

Perhaps the most significant change in mentoring programmes in recent years is how mentors are utilized. As suggested above – and reflecting naturally occurring mentoring – teacher mentoring programmes have been based on a model of one mentor serving one mentee in a relationship that is primarily face-to-face. The shrinking pool of prospective mentors and the increasing focus of mentoring that is grade-level or subject specific call for alternative approaches to mentoring. For example, a new teacher may work with two mentors. The primary mentor may be a teacher in the mentee's school but whose teaching assignment or experience may be considerably different than the mentee's. The secondary mentor's grade level or subject area may be identical to the mentee's, and this mentor may be in the same school as the mentee or possibly in a different school. Another approach is for a mentor to work with more than one mentee in a 'group' mentoring situation.

Technology has introduced electronic alternatives to 'one-on-one' and 'face-to-face' (Babione, Givens, Hoeppner & Shea, 2002; Guy, 2002; Korchan & Pascarelli, 2005; Single & Single, 2005). For example, a National Science Foundation award in 2002 supported the development of the *e-Mentoring for Student Success* (eMSS) project. This national project includes online networks for beginning and experienced science teachers and scientists to promote professional development through dialogue and online mentoring for beginning science teachers by trained mentors who teach the same discipline (Teacher Induction: e-Mentoring for Student Success, n.d.). Futurist Michael Zey (2005) predicts an increased use of 'telementoring' and 'cybermentoring' strategies, including use of e-mail, electronic bulletin boards and chat rooms, and, as the technology improves and the costs come down, eventually 'virtual mentoring.' As an example that combines multiple mentors and technology, a teacher with expertise in assessment might host an electronic chat room for a week or two for beginning teachers focusing on issues related to authentic student assessment. Over the course of the year, other teachers who are not 'official' mentors might interact with new teachers in this way on a variety of topics, for a limited period of time and at a relevant point in the school year.

High Stakes Dimensions of Mentoring

Requiring induction programmes and mentoring programmes, and tying them to requirements for licensure increases the stakes involved in mentoring. Under these circumstances, mentoring programmes are transformed from a nicety, made available at the generosity of a school district, to an essential part of the profession. Newly licensed teachers whose career may depend in some respects on the quality of the mentoring they receive add a 'high stakes' dimension to mentoring that is new.

As the importance of mentoring increases, especially as related to a teacher's license stages and career, so too does the need to select mentors carefully, provide them with adequate training and on-going support, and support them in delivering the two central features of effective mentoring: meeting with mentees regularly and observing mentees in their classrooms. Moreover, the support provided by mentors is almost universally conceptualized as 'formative' in nature, with 'summative,' or job performance assessment, being reserved to the school administrator. Not surprisingly, new teachers whose continuing certification or employment is terminated may contend that the mentoring they received was inadequate, causing veteran teachers to hesitate becoming mentors.

   The growing importance of mentoring has resulted in a need for more and better research on mentoring and mentoring programme is developing. Until recently, research on mentoring has been based largely on the self-report of mentees, although some research has explored relationship between mentoring and retention (e.g., Serpell & Bozeman, 1999), the perspectives of the multiple stakeholders in mentoring programs (e.g., Trenta, Newman, Newman, Salzman, Lenigan & Newman, 2002), specific elements of the mentor/mentee relationship (Ringler, 2000; Strong & Baron, 2004), and the impact of mentoring on mentors professional development (Riggs & Sandlin, 2002). A report by the NEA Foundation for the Improvement of Education (2002) outlines ways in which programme data can be used systematically for program improvement. In the most comprehensive review of empirical research on the effects of mentoring programmes, Ingersoll and Kralik (2004) cite only eight empirical studies. In one of these studies using a national dataset, Smith and Ingersoll (2004) conclude that having a helpful mentor in the new teacher's field is only one of five components that are part of a 'package' associated with reducing a new teacher's risk of leaving teaching by 72 percent. The other components are: (1) common planning time with other teachers in their subject area, (2) regularly scheduled collaboration with other teachers on issues of instruction, (3) participation in a network of teachers, and (4) regular or supportive communication with their principal, other administrators, or department chair.

Final Thoughts

More than 15 years ago, Huling-Austin (1990b) made the elegantly simply observation that the success of beginning teachers is based on three components: (1) the knowledge and skills beginning teachers possess before they start teaching, (2) the workplace conditions (e.g., teaching assignment and responsibilities, the culture of the school, etc.) they encounter, and (3) the induction support, including but broader than mentoring, offered to them. Her analysis suggested that mentoring is one of many factors associated with successful beginning teaching, and perhaps not the most significant one. As Fulton, Yoon & Lee (2005) note, "Mentoring, when done well, can provide an important component of induction, but it is only one piece of what should be a system of induction (p. 4, emphasis in original). Accordingly, it is important to ask what can reasonably be expected as outcomes of even the most carefully designed, delivered, and supported mentoring programme in the absence of an acceptable, beginning level of teacher knowledge and skills (Carver & Katz, 2004) or in a setting characterized by negative or dysfunctional workplace conditions. Wong's (2001) answer to question is to the point: 'Mentoring can't do it all.'
   The personal challenge faced by all beginning teachers is learning to teach and to formulate their professional identity in a very public and incredibly complex forum. As Feiman-Nemser (2003) stresses, it is a mistake to consider new teachers as 'finished products' whose emergent needs are signs of deficiency and whose primary task is to refine an existing and nearly complete set of skills. In teaching, as in many

occupations, a certain amount of learning on the job is natural and inescapable, and it should be the primary role of the mentor to facilitate that learning. The potential for learning in a quality mentoring relationship extends to mentors as well. With adequate training and support, serving as a mentor can reinvigorate veteran teachers and prepare them for leadership roles in schools (Moir & Bloom, 2003). Over time, the learning experiences of both mentor and mentee are woven into the fabric of a school, transforming it into a professional learning community.

In the justifiable effort to make mentoring more than just a means of 'coping' with the challenges of beginning teaching through psychological support and assistance with technical problems, it is critical to preserve the human, person-to-person dimension of mentoring and the very powerful connection between teachers that mentoring can engender (Norman & Ganser, 2004). 'Good teaching is not just a matter of being efficient, developing competence, mastering technique, and possessing the right kind of knowledge,' observes Hargreaves (1997). 'Good teaching also involves emotional work. It infused with pleasure, passion, creativity, challenge, and joy. It is ... a passionate vocation' (p. 12). That passion for teaching must continue to be the heart of mentoring and mentoring programmes as well if they are to reach their full potential.

References

Alliance for Excellence Education. (2005, August), Teacher attrition: A costly loss to the nation and to the states. IssueBrief. Washington, DC: Author. Retrieved on September 9, 2005, from www.all4ed.org/publications/TeacherAttrition.pdf

American Federation of Teachers. (2000), Building a profession: Strengthening teacher preparation and induction. Report of the K-16 Teacher Education Task Force. Item No. 36-00697 4/00. Washington, D.C.: Author. Retrieved July 11, 2005, from www.aft.org/pubs-reports/downloads/teachers/k16report.pdf

American Federation of Teachers. (2001), Beginning teacher induction: The essential bridge. *AFT Educational Issues Policy Brief*. Number 13. Washington, D.C.: AFT Educational Issues Department. Retrieved July 11, 2005, from www.aft.org/pubs-reports/downloads/teachers/policy13.pdf

Babione, C., Givens, N., Hoeppner, C. and Shea, C. (2002), Electronic mentoring for special needs teachers. Paper presented at the annual meeting of the Association of Teacher Educators, Denver, CO.

Barresi, A. and Fogarty, J. (n.d.). A Paraeducator training program and mentoring system. National Resource Center for Paraprofessionals. Retrieved July 11, 2005, from www.nrcpara.org/resources/careerladder/clarticle1.php

Black, S. (2002), 'Not just helping hands', *American School Board Journal*, vol. 189(5), 42–44. Retrieved July 11, 2005, from www.asbj.com/2002/05/0502research.html

Bolich, A.M. (2001), Reduce your losses: Help new teachers become veteran teachers. Atlanta, GA: Southern Regional Education Board. Retrieved July 11, 2005, from www.sreb.org/main/HigherEd/ReduceLosses.asp

Bonelli, J. (1999), Beginning teacher mentoring programs. Education Commission of the States (ECS) State Notes. Retrieved July 11, 2005, from www.ecs.org/clearinghouse/13/15/1315.htm

Boreen, J., Johnson, M.K., Niday, D. and Potts, J. (2000), *Mentoring beginning teachers: Guiding, reflecting, coaching*, Stenhouse, York, Maine.

Breaux, A.L. and Wong, H.K. (2003), *New teacher induction: How to train, support, and retain new teachers*, Harry K. Wong Publications, Mountain, View, CA.

Britton, E., Paine, L., Pimm, D. and Raizen, S. (2003), *Comprehensive teacher induction in five countries: Launching early career learning*, Kulwer Academic Publishers, Dordrecht, Netherlands.

Bureau of Labor Statistics. (2002), Number of jobs held, labor market activity, and earnings growth among younger baby boomers: results from more than two decades of a longitudinal survey. (USDL 02-497). Washington, DC: U. S. Department of Labor. Retrieved July 12, 2005, from www.bls.gov/nls/nlsy79r19.pdf

Carroll, T.G. (2005), 'Induction of teachers into 21st century learning communities: Creating the next generation of educational practice', *The New Educator*, vol. 1(X), pp. 199–204.

Carver, C.L. and Katz, D.S. (2004), 'Teaching at the boundary of acceptable practice: What is a new teacher mentor to do'? *Journal of Teacher Education*, vol. 55(5), pp. 449–462.

Center for Strengthening the Teaching Profession. (2005, May), *Effective support for new teachers in Washington State: Standards for beginning teacher induction*. Silverdale, WA: Author. Retrieved on August 19, 2005, from www.cstp-wa.org/Navigational/Policies_practices/Teacher_induction/Complete_Guideline.pdf

Council for Exceptional Children. (2003), CEC Code of Ethics for Persons with Exceptionalities. Retrieved July 12, 2005, from www.cec.sped.org/ps/ps-ethic.html

Darling-Hammond, L. (2003), 'Keeping good teachers: Why it matters, what leaders can do', *Educational Leadership*, vol. 60(8), pp. 6–13.

Darling-Hammond, L. and Sclan, E.M. (1996), 'Who teaches and why: Dilemmas of building a profession for the twenty-first century', in J. Sikula, T.J. Buttery and E. Guyton (eds), *Handbook of research on teacher education* (2nd ed.) (pp. 67–101), Macmillan, New York.

Feiman-Nemser, S. (2000), From preparation to practice: Designing a continuum to strengthen and sustain teaching. Occasional Paper Series, No. 5 (April 2000). New York: Bank Street College of Education.

Feiman-Nemser, S. (2003), 'What new teachers need to learn', *Educational Leadership*, vol. 60(8), pp. 25–29.

Feiman-Nemser, S. and Parker, M.B. (1992), Los Angeles mentors: Local guides or educational companions? (Research Report 92-10). East Lansing, MI: National Center for Research on Teacher Learning, Michigan State University.

Feiman-Nemser, S., Schwille, S., Carver, C. and Yusko, B. (1999), A conceptual review of literature on new teacher induction programs. Washington, DC: National

Partnership for Excellence and Accountability in Teaching. Retrieved July 12, 2005, from www.edpolicy.org/publications/NPEAT/induction2.pdf

Feistritzer, C.E. (1999), The making of a teacher: A report on teacher preparation in the U.S. Washington, DC: Center for Education Information. Retrieved July 12, 2005, from www.ncei.com/MakingTeacher-rpt.htm

Feistritzer, E. (2005a), Alternative teacher certification: A state-by-state analysis 2005. Washington, DC: National Center for Education Information. 'Introduction' and 'Overview' retrieved on July 12, 2005, from www.teach-now.org/booktoc2005. html

Feistritzer, E. (2005b), *Profile of Teachers in the U.S. 2005*, National Center for Education Information, Washington, DC.

Fideler, E.R. and Haselkorn, D. (1999), *Learning the ropes: Urban teacher induction programs and practices in the United States*, Recruiting New Teachers, Belmont, MA.

Fulton, K., Yoon, I. and Lee, C. (2005, August), Induction into learning communities. Washington, DC: National Commission on Teaching and America's Future. Retrieved on August 19, 2005, from www.nctaf.org/documents/nctaf/NCTAF_ Induction_Paper_2005.pdf

Ganser, T. (2002), 'Building the capacity of school districts to design, implement, and evaluate Effective new teacher mentor programs: Action points for colleges and universities', *Mentoring & Tutoring*, vol. 10(1), pp. 47–55.

Ganser, T. (2005a), 'Learning from the past – Building for the future', in H. Portner (ed), *Teacher induction and mentoring: The state of the art and beyond* (pp. 3– 19). Corwin, Thousand Oaks, CA.

Ganser, T. (2005b), The willingness of prospective beginning teachers to accept less salary for the benefit of a good mentoring program. Unpublished study.

Gold, Y. (1996), 'Beginning teacher support: Attrition, mentoring, and induction', in J. Sikula, T.J., Buttery and E. Guyton (eds), *Handbook of research on teacher education* (2nd ed.), pp. 548–594. Macmillan, New York.

Gordon, S.P. and Maxey, S. (2000), *How to help beginning teachers succeed.* (2nd ed.). Association for Supervision and Curriculum Development, Alexandria, VA.

Grossman, P. (2003, January/February), 'Teaching: From *A Nation at Risk* to a profession at risk', *Harvard Education Letter, Research Online*, Retrieved July 12, 2005, from www.edletter.org/past/issues/2003-jf/nation.shtml

Guy, T. (2002), 'Telementoring: Shaping mentoring relationships in the 21st century', in C.A. Hansman (ed), *Critical perspectives on mentoring: Trends and issues* (pp. 27–37). Columbus, OH: Ohio State University. ERIC Reproduction Service No. 465045.

Hall, J. (2005), 'Promoting quality programs through state-school relationships', in H. Portner (ed), *Teacher mentoring and induction: The state of the art and beyond*, pp. 213–223. Corwin Press, Thousand Oaks, CA.

Hare, D. and Heap, J.L. (2001, May), Effective teacher recruitment and retention strategies in the Midwest: Who is making use of them. Elmhurst, IL: North Central Regional Educational Laboratory. Retrieved July 12, 2005, from www. ncrel.org/policy/pubs/html/strategy/index.html

Hargreaves, A. and Fullan, M. (2000), 'Mentoring in the next millennium', *Theory into Practice*, vol. 39(1), pp. 50–56.

Huling-Austin, L. (1990a), 'Mentoring is squishy business', in T.M. Bey and C.T. Holmes (eds), *Mentoring: Developing successful new teachers* (pp. 39–50), Association of Teacher Educators, Reston, VA.

Huling-Austin, L. (1990b), 'Teacher induction programs and internships', in W.R. Houston (ed), *Handbook of research on teacher education* (pp. 535–548), Macmillan, New York.

Humphrey, D.C. and Wechsler, M.E. (2005, September 2), 'Insights into alternative certification: Initial findings from a national study', *Teachers College Press*, Retrieved on September 9, 2005, from http://www.tcrecord.org/PrintContent. asp?ContentID=12145

Ingersoll, R.M. (1999), 'The problem of underqualified teachers in American secondary schools', *Educational Researcher*, vol. 28(2), pp. 26–37.

Ingersoll, R.M. (2001), 'Teacher turnover and teacher shortages: An organizational analysis', *American Educational Research Journal*, vol. 38(3), pp. 499–534.

Ingersoll, R.M. (2002), 'The teacher shortage: A case of wrong diagnosis and wrong prescription', *National Association of Secondary School Principals Bulletin*, vol. 86(631), pp. 16–31.

Ingersoll, R. and Kralik, J.M. (2004), The impact of mentoring on teacher retention: What the research says. *ECS Research Review*, Denver, CO: Educational Commission of the States. Retrieved on August 30, 2005, from www.ecs.org/ clearinghouse/50/30/5036.htm

Ingersoll, R. and Smith, T.M. (2003), 'The wrong solution to the teacher shortage', *Educational Leadership*, vol. 60(8), pp. 30–33.

Interstate New Teacher Assessment and Support Consortium. (1992), Model standards for beginning teacher licensing and development: A resource for state dialogue. Report No. 202/336-7048. Washington, DC: Council of chief State School Officers.

Jerald, C.D. (2002, August), All talk, no action: Putting an end to out-of-field teaching. Washington, DC: The Education Trust. Retrieved July 12, 2005, from www2. edtrust.org/NR/rdonlyres/8DE64524-592E-4C83-A13A-6B1DF1CF8D3E/0/ AllTalk.pdf

Johnson, S.M., Berg, J.H. and Donaldson, M.L. (2005), *Who stays in teaching and why: A review of the literature on teacher retention*. The Project on the Next Generation of Teachers, Harvard Graduate School of Education. Retrieved on September 9, 2005, from http://assets.aarp.org/www.aarp.org_/articles/NRTA/ Harvard_report.pdf

Johnson, S.M., Birkeland, S.E., Donaldson, M.L., Kardos, S.M., Kauffman, D.K., Liu, E. and Peske, H.G. (2004), *Finders and keepers: Helping new teachers survive and thrive in our schools*, Jossey-Bass, San Francisco, CA.

Johnson, S.M. and Birkeland, S.E. (2002), Pursuing 'a sense of success': New teachers explain their career decisions. Paper presented at the annual meeting of the American Educational Research Association, New Orleans, LA. Retrieved on July 12, 2005, from http://gseweb.harvard.edu/~ngt/Johnson_Birkeland_Oct_ 2002.pdf

Johnson, S.M. and Birkeland, S.E. (2003), 'The schools that teachers choose', *Educational Leadership*, vol. 60(8), pp. 20–24.

Jonson, K.F. (2002), *Being an effective mentor: How to help beginning teachers succeed*. Corwin, Thousand Oaks, CA.

Kardos, S.M. (2003), Integrated professional culture: Exploring new teachers' experiences in four states. Paper presented at the annual meeting of the American Educational Research Association, Chicago, IL. Retrieved on July 12, 2005, from www.gse.harvard.edu/~ngt/Kardos%20AERA%202003%20Final.pdf

Korchan, F.K. and Pascarelli, J.T. (eds). (2003), *Global perspectives on mentoring: Transforming contexts, communities, and cultures*, Information Age, Greenwich, CT.

Korchan, F.K. and Pascarelli, J.T. (eds). (2005), *Creating successful telementoring programs*, Information Age, Greenwich, CT.

Lackzko-Kerr, I. and Berliner, D.C. (2003), 'In harm's way: How undercertified teachers hurt their students', *Educational Leadership*, vol. 60(8), pp. 34–39.

Liu, E. and Kardos, S.M. (2002), Hiring and professional culture in New Jersey schools. Retrieved on July 12, 2005, from www.gse.harvard.edu/~ngt/Hiring%20 and%20Prof%20Culture%20in%20NJ%20Schools.pdf.

Liu, E., Johnson, S.M. and Peske, H.G. (2003), New teachers and the Massachusetts signing bonus: The limitations of inducements. Retrieved on July 12, 2005, from www.gse.harvard.edu/~ngt/Liu,%20Johnson%20&%20Peske%20-%20MA%20Signing%20Bonus.pdf.

McBain, R. and George, M. (1995), *Proceedings of the Third European Mentoring Conference*, European Mentoring Centre, London.

Moir, E. and Bloom, G. (2003), 'Fostering leadership through mentoring', *Educational Leadership*, vol. 60(8), pp. 58–60.

Moskowitz, J. and Stephens, M. (1997a), *From student of teacher to teacher of students: Teacher induction around the Pacific rim. Asia-Pacific Economic Cooperation*, U. S. Department of Education, Washington, DC.

Moskowitz, J. and Stephens, M. (1997b), *From student of teacher to teacher of students: Teacher induction around the Pacific rim. Asia-Pacific Economic Cooperation. Selected findings of the study*. Washington, DC: U. S. Department of Education. Retrieved July 12, 2005, from www.ed.gov/pubs/APEC/findings.html

National Center for Education Statistics. (2000), Teacher supply in the United States: Sources of newly hired teachers in public and private schools, 1987–88 to 1993–94. NCES 2000-309. Washington, DC: U. S. Department of Education. Retrieved on July 12, 2005, from http://nces.ed.gov/pubs2000/2000309.pdf

National Center for Education Statistics. (2001), Teacher preparation and professional development: 2000. NCES 2001-088. Washington, DC: U. S. Department of Education. Retrieved on July 12, 2005, from http://nces.ed.gov/pubs2001/2001088.pdf

National Center for Education Statistics. (2003), Public school student, staff, and graduate counts, by state: School year 2001-02. NCES 2003-358. Retrieved on July 12, 2005, from http://nces.ed.gov/pubs2003/2003358.pdf

National Commission on Teaching and America's Future. (2002), Unraveling the 'teacher shortage' problem: Teacher retention is the key. Washington, DC: Author.

National Commission on Teaching and America's Future. (2003), No dream denied: A pledge to America's children. Retrieved on July 12, 2005, from www.nctaf. org/article/index.php?c=4&

National Education Association. (1999), Beginning now: Resources for organizers of beginning teachers. Author, Washington, D.C.

National Education Association. (2000), A better beginning: Helping new teachers survive and thrive (A guide for NEA local affiliates interested in creating new teacher support systems). Retrieved on July 12, 2005, from www.nea.org/ teachershortage/betterbeginnings.html#preface

NEA Foundation for the Improvement of Education. (1999), Creating a teacher mentoring program. Retrieved July 12, 2005, from www.nfie.org/publications/ mentoring.htm

NEA Foundation for the Improvement of Education (2002), Using data to improve teacher induction programs. Retrieved on July 12, 2005, from www.nfie.org/ publications/inductionib.pdf

Norman, D.M. and Ganser, T. (2004), 'A humanistic approach to new teacher mentoring: A counseling perspective', *Journal of Humanistic Counseling, Education, and Development*, vol. 43(2), pp. 129–140.

Odell, S.J. and Huling, L. (eds) (2000), *Quality mentoring for novice teachers*, Kappa Delta Pi, Indianapolis, IN.

Peske, H.G., Liu, E., Johnson, S.M., Kauffman, D. and Kardos, S.M. (2001), 'The next generation of teachers: changing conceptions of a career in teaching', *Phi Delta Kappan*, vol. 83(4), pp. 304–311.

Portner, H. (2001), *Training mentors is not enough: Everything else schools and districts need to do*, Corwin Press, Thousand Oaks, CA.

Portner, H. (2002), *Being mentored: A guide for protégés*, Corwin, Thousand Oaks, CA.

Portner, H. (2003), *Mentoring new teachers* (updated edition), Corwin Press, Thousand Oaks, CA.

Portner, H. (ed) (2005), *Teacher induction and mentoring: The state of the art and beyond*, Corwin Press, Thousand Oaks, CA.

Riggs, I.M. and Sandlin, R.A. (2002), Professional development of mentors during a beginning teacher induction program: How does the garden (mentors) grow? Paper presented at the annual meeting of the American Educational Research Association, New Orleans, LA. ERIC Reproduction Service No. ED465752.

Rigler, S.E. (2000), Gender differences in beginning teachers' metaphors for mentoring. ERIC Reproduction Service No. ED447070.

Simmons, A. (2000), A guide to developing teacher induction programs. Recruiting New Teachers, Belmont, MA.

Single, P.B. and Single, R.M. (2005), 'E-mentoring for social equity: Review of research to inform program development', *Mentoring & Tutoring*, vol. 13(3), pp. 301–320.

Smith, T.M. and Ingersoll, R. (2004), 'What the effects of induction and mentoring on beginning teacher turnover'? *American Educational Research Journal*, vol. 41(3), pp. 681–714.

Stansbury, K. and Zimmerman, J. (2000), Lifelines to the classroom: Designing support for beginning teachers. San Francisco: WestEd. Retrieved July 12, 2005, from http://web.WestEd.org/online_pubs/tchrbrief.pdf.

Strong, M. (2005), 'Teacher induction, mentoring, and retention: A summary of the research', *The New Educator*, vol. 1(X), pp. 181–198.

Strong, M. and Baron, W. (2004), 'An analysis of mentoring conversations with beginning teachers: Suggestions and responses', *Teaching and Teacher Education*, vol. 20(1), pp. 47–57.

Sweeny, B.W. (2001), *Leading the teacher induction and mentoring program*, Skylight Professional Development, Arlington Heights, IL.

Tang, S.Y.F. and Choi, P.L. (2005), 'Connecting theory and practice in mentor preparation: Mentoring for improvement of teaching and learning', *Mentoring & Tutoring*, vol. 13(3), pp. 383–401.

Teacher Induction: E-Mentoring for Student Success (eMSS). (n.d.). Retrieved on September 2, 2005, from http://newteachercenter.org/eMSS/index/php

Tisher, R.P. (1984), Teacher induction: An international perspective on provisions and research, in L.G. Katz and J.D. Raths (eds), Advances in teacher education (Vol. 1), 113–123. Ablex, Norwood, NJ.

Trenta, L., Newman, I., Newman, C., Salzman, J., Lenigan, D. and Newman, D. (2002), Evaluation of a teacher mentoring program using a mixed methods approach. Paper presented at the annual meeting of the Eastern Educational Research Association, Sarasota, FL. ERIC Reproduction Service No. ED463295.

Udelhofen, S. and Larson, K. (2003), *The mentoring year: A step-by-step guide to professional development*, Corwin, Thousand Oaks, CA.

U. S. Department of Education, Office of Innovation and Improvement. (2004, November), *Innovations in education: Alternative routes to teacher certification*. Washington, DC: Author. Retrieved on August 23, 2005, from www.ed.gov/admins/tchrqual/recruit/altroutes/index.html

Veenman, S. (1984), 'Perceived problems of beginning teachers', *Review of Educational Research*, vol. 54(2), pp. 143–178.

Villani, S. (2002), *Mentoring programs for new teachers: Models of induction and support*, Corwin, Thousand Oaks, CA.

Wang, J. (2001), 'Contexts of mentoring and opportunities for learning to teach: A comparative study of mentoring practice', *Teaching and Teacher Education*, vol. 17, pp. 51–73.

Wang, J. and Odell, S.J. (2002), 'Mentored learning to teach according to standards-based reform: A critical review', *Review of Educational Research*, vol. 72(3), pp. 481–546.

White, M. and Mason, C. (2001), Mentoring induction principles and guidelines. Draft. Council for Exceptional Children. Retrieved July 12, 2005, from www.cec. sped.org/spotlight/udl/mip_g_manual_11pt.pdf

Wisconsin Department of Public Instruction. (2000), Chapter PI 34, Teacher Education Program Approval and Licenses. Madison, WI: author. Retrieved on July 12, 2005, from www.dpi.state.wi.us/dpi/dlsis/tel/newrules.html

Wisconsin Department of Public Instruction. (1998), Wisconsin Model Academic Standards. Madison, WI: Author. Retrieved on August 27, 2005, from http://www. dpi.state.wi.us/dpi/standards/

Wong, H.K. (2001), 'Mentoring can't do it all', *Education Week*, vol. 22(43), pp. 46, 50.

Wong, H.T., Britton, T. and Ganser, T. (2005), 'What the world can teach us about new teacher induction', *Phi Delta Kappan*, vol. 86(5), pp. 379–384.

Zachary, L.J. (2000), *The mentor's guide: Facilitating effective learning relationships*. Jossey-Bass, San Francisco.

Zey, M. (2005), Cybermentoring and beyond: Using technology to overcome physical distance in formal mentor programs. Presentation at the annual meeting of the International Mentoring Association, Oakland, CA.

Zeichner, K.M. and Gore, J.M. (1990), 'Teacher socialization', in W.R. Houston (ed), *Handbook of research on teacher education* (pp. 329–348), Macmillan, New York.

Chapter 4

The Balancing Act of Mentoring: Mediating between Newcomers and Communities of Practice

Marion Jones

Introduction

Following the relocation of teacher education from an academic into a vocational domain in 1992 (DfE), mentoring was introduced as a key component in teachers' professional training and continuing development. Since its introduction the role of the school-based mentor has evolved in accordance with the statutory requirements set out in the original and revised standards frameworks for initial teacher training (ITT) (DfEE, 1998; DfES, 2002) and induction (DfEE, 1999; DfES, 2003). The considerable shift that has taken place from theory-laden university-based teacher education to practice-related school-based training is reflected in the literature generated in relation to the support of trainees and newly qualified teachers (Wildman, 1992; Feiman-Nemser et al, 1993; Maynard & Furlong, 1993; McIntyre et al, 1993; Dormer, 1994; McLaughlin, 1994; Abell et al, 1995; Ballantyne et al, 1995; Yau, 1995; Veenman et al, 1998)

Against the backdrop of this shift away from the theoretical 'standard paradigm' (Beckett & Hager, 2002) towards a conceptualisation of learning that is practice-based and embedded in social activity (Lave, 1988; Brown et al, 1989), there is now a need to examine the contribution of mentoring in assisting newly qualified teachers to manage the transition from initial training to professional practice and in their socialisation into the profession. While emphasis has predominantly been placed on supporting newly qualified teachers in maintaining the *Qualifying to Teach* (DfES, 2002) and achieving the *Induction* Standards (DfES, 2003), scant attention has been paid to the structural, social and cultural factors inherent in the various settings within which induction takes place and the tensions they can generate within the mentoring process.

In spite of the comprehensive guidance materials available from the TTA and compulsory training provided for Induction Tutors within each LEA, mentoring practice remains highly diverse. While it is recognised that it plays a significant role in the induction process of newly qualified teachers, there is evidence which suggests that quality provision is inconsistent, raising issues of entitlement and equity on behalf of the mentees (Tickle, 2000; Bubb, 2000; 2002; Jones, 2002; Totterdell et al, 2002; Roden, 2003; Kyriacou & O'Connor, 2003).

By drawing on empirical evidence from a research project concerned with the evaluation of the experiences of ten newly qualified teachers during their first year in teaching (Jones, 2001), this paper intends to concentrate on aspects of induction support which are not explicitly addressed in the induction framework (DfES, 1999; DfEE, 2003), but which are central to successful socialisation into the profession. Reference will also be made to Lave and Wenger's (1991) conceptualisation of learning, which centres on the notion of 'participation in social practice' and 'belonging to a community' and as such is of relevance to the discussion of issues related to the mentoring of newly qualified teachers. According to Lave and Wenger, the experiences of newcomers to a profession, their relationships with colleagues and their involvement in professional and social activities determine to a large extent the quality of their learning. This is where induction tutors/mentors play a crucial and pivotal role as 'mediators' between the newcomer and the profession and 'facilitators' in providing access to opportunities for learning through co-participation. However, all too often, the structural, social and cultural factors inherent in the various settings influence the quality and extent of learning that takes place. By using extracts from the accounts of the ten newly qualified teachers participating in Jones's (2001) research, it is the intention of this paper to illustrate the crises, conflicts and dilemmas experienced by them and to identify the challenges and tensions inherent in the mentoring process.

The chapter is organised in five Sections. Following the Introduction, conceptualisations of mentoring employed as a key strategy in initial teacher training and induction programmes are examined by explaining the process by which new entrants to a profession are assisted in acquiring the skills, knowledge and understanding necessary to manage the transition from training to professional practice. In this context three aspects of the mentoring role are selected as particularly relevant to the Induction Tutor's remit, namely that of 'mediator', 'facilitator' and 'assessor'. While the first two are akin to more traditional conceptualisations of mentoring and can be related to Lave and Wenger's (1991) approach to 'situated learning', according to which learning is perceived as 'an integral part of generative social practice in the lived-in world' (1991:35) and allows 'newcomers [to] become part of a community of practice' (Ibid:29), the latter presents itself as more problematic in terms of the influence it may have on the balance of power and control within the induction process. The third section provides an overview of a research project, which evaluated the induction experience of ten newly qualified teachers (Jones, 2001) in terms of the support and guidance they received during their first year of teaching. Next, the empirical evidence generated by each case will be examined in order to illustrate the crises, conflicts and dilemmas experienced by newcomers to the profession and the tensions arising. The discussion will focus on phenomena frequently cited in the research on induction, such as the 'reality shock', the reconciliation of 'teacherhood' and 'personhood', the balance of 'autonomy' and 'conformity' and 'developing a sense of belonging'. Induction tutors in their role of mentors play a pivotal, catalytic role in welcoming newly qualified teachers into the profession by facilitating opportunities for learning embedded within an open, co-operative and supportive culture.

Conceptualisations of Mentoring

Since 1992 mentoring constitutes a formal element in initial teacher training in England and since 1999 it is implicit in the induction process of newly qualified teachers. In spite of the comprehensive guidance and training provided for mentors of trainee teachers and newly qualified teachers, practice remains variable.

Defining mentoring is problematic as different schemes will prompt different purposes and the different structural, social and cultural parameters inherent in the various settings will result in diversity of practice, which may change over time. Stammers (1992) argues that there is no 'single animal called a mentor, rather a group of tasks associated with the role'. Zey (1984) defines mentoring as a relationship whereby the mentor oversees the career and development of another person, usually a junior. He posits a mutual benefit model whereby the whole organisation gains. Mentoring can thus be perceived as a helping process (Caruso, 1990), a teaching-learning process (Ardery, 1990), as an intentional, structural, nurturing, insightful process either developing along stages or rhythms, but not in series of events (Roberts, 2000). Bennetts (1996) adds a pedagogical, democratic dimension by stating that mentoring is learner-centred and progresses at the rate determined by the mentor and mentee. In relation to the modern, professional world, the spirit of mentoring is aptly captured by Roberts (2000) when he describes it as:

> 'a formalised process whereby a more knowledgeable and experienced person actuates a supportive role of overseeing and encouraging reflection and learning within a less experienced and knowledgeable person, so as to facilitate that person's career and personal development.' (Robert, 2000:162).

However, mentoring today may not always aspire to such levels of altruism, which are synonymous with 'trusted friend' and 'protector', as during the past twenty years there has been a trend towards the professionalisation of the role, reflected in systematic training, increased regulation and accreditation.

In industry, business and commerce, mentoring has been viewed as a key component in management development and has been employed as an effective strategy on training and induction programmes. In education and health care, mentoring schemes have been used to assist trainees as well as qualified staff in their early and continuing professional development. In education the concept of mentoring became popular in the 1980s, concomitant with a growing desire to improve the quality of teaching and learning. Educationalists became aware of the need to provide on-the-job support and advice to teachers early in their professional career (Little, 1990), the idea being that experienced teachers would act as mentors and models for their junior colleagues, assisting them in 'learning the ropes'. It was hoped that practice related learning through school-based models of training would facilitate smooth transition from student to qualified teacher, from novice to competent professional. This approach to learning is akin to Lave and Wenger's (1991) conceptualisation of 'situated learning'. This presents a contrasting perspective to the conventional 'standard paradigm' of learning (Beckett & Hager, 2002), which ignores the social dimension present in work based learning environments, such as school-based models of initial teacher training and induction.

Mentoring and 'Communities of Practice'

Studies concerned with teachers' professional development indicate that where the personal dimension to be measured in the relationship between newly qualified teachers and their induction tutors/mentors and other colleagues had been neglected, the emotional and physical welfare of newcomers to the profession was affected, and consequently their effectiveness in the classroom (Tickle, 2000). For example, Turner (1994) and Tauer (1998) confirmed that where the pastoral support was strong, newly qualified teachers flourished in terms of professional and personal growth. Where it was lacking, confidence and performance were suffering. These findings suggest that the mentor-mentee relationship is at the heart of the learning process and therefore needs to be nurtured, but equally, support provided by other colleagues is important in generating a sense of belonging and identity as well as providing opportunities for learning through sharing and collaboration of knowledge, skills and expertise. This is where Lave and Wenger's (1991) notion of 'community of practice' and 'legitimate peripheral participation' are of relevance. They believe that 'learning is not merely situated in practice – as if it were some independently reifiable process that just happened to be located somewhere; learning is an integral part of generative social practice in the lived-in world' (Lave & Wenger, 1991:35). The 'community of practice' within which these processes are embedded is defined as 'groups of people who share a concern, a set of problems, or a passion about a topic, and who deepen their knowledge and expertise in this area by interacting on an ongoing basis' (Wenger et al, 2002).

From a mentoring perspective, Lave and Wenger's (1991) theoretical approach can be transferred to the context of the induction process of newly qualified teachers in an attempt to explain the learning experiences of newcomers to the profession. Accordingly, becoming a member of a community of practice is concomitant with participating in social practice, which in turn facilitates learning. However, the extent and quality of the learning experience will depend to a large extent on the structural, social and cultural factors determining social and professional practice within the setting. For example, the quality of relationships established between the newly qualified teacher and the Induction Tutor /mentor(s) as well as other colleagues, the values and beliefs promoted by the school as a whole and the tacitly agreed norms of teacher behaviour can act as a catalyst or present barriers to gaining access to learning opportunities via 'peripheral participation'. Issues of power and control are unavoidable and need therefore be addressed in order to illuminate the overt and covert mechanisms taking place within the mentoring process. To allow mentors and mentees to engage in honest, open, dialogue it is helpful if a democratic, co-operative spirit can be generated within the school. However, for this to be achieved, it is a prerequisite to develop and maintain a climate of trust and mutuality between all members of the community of practice. For example, the mentor's status within the school may have an intimidating effect on an inexperienced novice and/or other colleagues. Similarly, gender, age, race and ethnicity can determine the extent of access to learning opportunities, as they are often perceived as demarcation lines determining a newcomer's membership status in relation to certain communities of practice.

The Role of the Induction Tutor of Newly Qualified Teachers

In spite of a general acceptance of mentoring hailed as 'the new panacea' (Stephenson, 1997) in professional training and development, studies have revealed that its effectiveness is highly dependent on the quality of the mentoring relationship and, in turn, the nature of the setting within which it is located. In initial teacher training and induction emphasis is placed to a large extent on modelling good practice, providing guidance and support, monitoring progress and assessing competence against predetermined criteria (Jones, 2004). It is therefore paramount to provide clarity on, and agree, the purposes of mentoring as well as the practicalities to be confronted by those who are at the heart of the process. Although TTA guidance provides a clear description of induction tutors' roles and responsibilities, the main aspect to be considered is that of monitoring and assessment of newly qualified teachers' progress measured against the standards (DfEE, 2003). Inevitably, the requirement to assess introduces elements of power and control into the mentoring process, which can seriously interfere with newcomers to the profession developing a sense of security, belonging and identity. During induction, Qualified Teacher Status is conditional and is only confirmed once the required standards are achieved. Whether the newcomer will become a member of the profession will largely depend on the judgements of Induction Tutors, who act as gatekeepers.

The role of 'assessor', however, is at odds with more traditional notions of mentoring, which are related to nurturing and caring, portraying the mentor in the role of confident and guardian rather than judge. Moreover, a programme which is structured and driven by processes of monitoring and assessment leaves little room for accommodating a democratic, pedagogical dimension (Caruso, 1990; Roberts, 2000), which is learner-centred and progresses at the rate determined by the mentor and the mentee, allowing the latter to assert his/her own values and targets in an open brief (Bennetts, 1996; Butters, 1997). As a result of mentors' individual perceptions of their role, the statutory requirements of induction and the structural, social and cultural parameters defining each setting, mentoring support for newly qualified teachers remains inconsistent and idiosyncratic, raising issues of equity and entitlement. The complexity of the mentoring role and the tensions inherent, are often reflected in the conflicting demands made upon them. On the one they are expected to establish a trusting, friendly relationship with their mentees, on the other they act as assessors, whose professional judgement must not be compromised by their relationship with the mentee. The frequently cited notion of 'critical friend' seems to appropriately define this inherent tension, by adopting a critical stance in the role of 'assessor', but simultaneously acting as a 'friend' in the role of mediator and facilitator.

As a result of mentors' and mentees' individual perceptions, the multiple purposes it serves and the various settings within which it occurs, the mentoring process harbours a multitude of tensions, which can lead to personal and professional conflicts and dilemmas. In the context of accountability and professional standards, the ancient ideal of the 'older, trusted and loyal friend, who is responsible for the growth and development of the protégé and whose characteristics were integrity, wisdom and personal involvement, is no longer seen as appropriate.

The following five cases reported here formed part of a research project which evaluated the induction experience of ten newly qualified teachers, when the statutory induction framework (DfEE, 1999) was introduced in schools in England. The findings provide an opportunity to explore contexts of practice related learning and professional development, where mentoring was intended to assist newly qualified teachers to become members of the profession as well as the school community within which induction took place. While in initial teacher training mentoring is frequently employed to assist trainee teachers in developing technical and to some extent clinical competences in the classroom, the accounts of the five newly qualified teachers serve to highlight the importance of supporting the socialisation process and in assisting them in reconciling their personal values and beliefs with those of the school community within which they are located and those of the profession as a whole.

While in some schools the duties associated with induction support remained the sole responsibility of either the subject head or the designated induction tutor, usually a member of the senior management team, in others they were equally shared between the two. Both individual and shared arrangements had their particular advantages and disadvantages. Where the head of department performed the role of mentor/induction tutor there was concern that under the constant pressure of monitoring and assessment, newly qualified teachers would feel obliged to conform to the expectations of their line managers and refrain from exploring alternative, potentially risky strategies in their teaching. With reference to the tensions arising from conflicting roles and issues related to quality provision, Tickle (2000) questions whether it is appropriate for heads of department to be allocated this role.

The empirical data generated by the five case studies suggest that 'communities of practice' can be highly effective by embedding learning in practice contexts and by involving both novice and experienced practitioner in collaborative activities. However, in view of the variable quality of mentoring during induction reported by the ten newly qualified teachers and the effect this experience had on their future career development as teachers, emphasis needs to be placed on the need to explore individual settings in greater detail. On successful completion of their induction period two of the ten newly qualified teachers resigned from their posts. Both had suffered the negative consequences of isolation and lack of integration within their respective schools. It is undeniable that their negative experiences during their year of induction played a part in their decisions to resign from their posts. One needed to reconsider her options altogether, as she was unsure whether teaching was the right profession for her. The other was confident that teaching was the right profession for her, but not within the paradigm prevailing in England. Consequently she applied to teach in a school abroad. In both cases their mentors had failed to help them become members of the 'community of practice' within which they were placed.

Five Cases

The research evaluating newly qualified teachers' induction experiences makes explicit the link between membership of a community of practice and the desire to continue teaching within it. It also highlights the mentor's role in liaising between the newcomer and experienced practitioners, mediating between the novices' ideal and the reality of the classroom and providing the newly qualified teachers with learning opportunities by means of collaborative activities in the form of 'legitimate peripheral participation'. While the mentor's role of assessor was generally regarded as potentially problematic, it appeared that where a trusting relationship had been established between mentor and mentee, tensions were kept to a minimum. Newly qualified teachers highly valued the advice and constructive feedback of their more experienced colleagues. Rather than the ubiquitous threat of assessment, it was the culture prevailing in individual departments or the school as a whole that created potential barriers to newly qualified teachers' successful integration and membership. While some induction tutors played a central role in mediating between newcomers and communities of practice and facilitating access to learning opportunities, this was not the case in all settings.

The following cases are concerned with aspects of the socialisation process of five newly qualified teachers. By providing an account of their anxieties, feelings and opinions the vignettes are intended to provide an insight into the overt and covert mechanisms involved in their following the rites of passage.

Desperately seeking membership – Hilary's story

Prior to embarking on teacher training, Hilary (27) had worked abroad teaching English as a foreign language. As a trainee she was described as highly enthusiastic, committed, hard working and setting herself high standards. She had obtained excellent reports from both her practice school and was looking forward to commencing her induction year at a highly academic, oversubscribed 11–19 secondary school. Having familiarised herself with the new statutory framework for newly qualified teachers (DfEE, 1999), she was looking forward to working alongside more experienced colleagues, who would be prepared to share their expertise and experience with the newcomer.

> I suppose, in the beginning, I thought, 'Oh, right, I am going to be a teacher.' And I had really high expectations. High, high, high! And then I realised that that's completely selfish and that is doesn't get you very far with all children, of course. (Hilary)

However, instead of engaging in open dialogue and collaboration, they tended to display a rather defensive, almost hostile attitude towards her, which she found difficult to understand.

> The greatest challenges, let's think! Establishing a relationship with the new department. I found that was quite tricky in fact. I underestimated it, because you start very enthusiastically, and I underestimated people's opinions of NQTs. And I think that some people felt a bit threatened, that they were having somebody straight off the, you know, production line as it were and were worried about just the level of enthusiasm, ... that you show when you are starting a new job. I didn't notice it. It was pointed out to me in, well, a very complicated way of going into it. But you know, it was brought to my attention.

Hilary's experience is recognised by Roden, who believes that by displaying high levels of enthusiasm and idealism, a characteristic of the early stage in teacher development (Furlong & Maynard, 1995), newly qualified teachers can make enemies amongst older, highly experienced colleagues, who view the newcomer with suspicion, which can be equated with 'committing professional suicide' (2003: 201).

Staff turnover at Hilary's school was very low as the school's academic achievements were reflected in a high GCSE/GCE league table position and was heavily oversubscribed. Consequently, the majority of staff were reluctant to leave and had been teaching there for a considerable time and were entrenched in their daily routines and habits which they had established over the years and were not prepared to engage in critical review and evaluation of their practice, neither as individuals not as a department. Perhaps, to some extent, they feared competition from a newly trained teacher, who would possess up-to-date knowledge and skills superior to theirs and, through her innovative practice, might introduce the elements of change and development they had resisted within the secure environment of their closed culture.

A second factor of concern was the competitive climate prevalent in all aspects of school life, which allowed little scope for sharing of practice, collaboration and critical dialogue. At first, Hilary was confident that she would win over her colleagues' co-operation with regard to the joint planning of lessons and the production of resources, and frequently took the initiative by sharing her ideas and materials. However, contrary to her expectations, her colleagues within the department became increasingly protective of their territories:

> I have tried with a few people to say I wouldn't mind, you know, just coming to see things that they are doing. But instantly, ... people think that you just want to go and see how

badly they're doing or something. And it is not that! And people have been very defensive and I have found that not only once, since I have started work, but also on teaching practice as well. (Hilary)

To her great disappointment, her curriculum mentor/induction tutor, who was also Head of the Modern Languages Department, appeared to have difficulty responding appropriately to her needs as a result of a loyalty conflict between his colleagues and the newcomer. This is how Hilary describes the situation:

I think Ofsted interfered with the induction process, definitely, in as much as the staff weren't able to give us as much of their time, because they were obsessed with their own performance and a had a lot of work before the inspectors were coming.

Even though it had been a highly successful inspection, it had taken its toll in terms of staff's lack of willingness to engage in any further scrutiny, observations and critical reflection of their practice. To Hilary's disappointment her mentor failed to address and resolve the issue of lack of collaboration and support within her department and instead left her to her own devices.

A third factor for Hilary's negative experience was that fact that the induction support she received was not tailored to her day-to-day needs, but consisted of informal conversations with the Professional Mentor/Induction Tutor concerned with issues related to school policy. Through her own efforts she tried to establish relationships with colleagues across the school and get involved in cross-curricular activities with the intention of developing a sense of belonging, which helped her survive the year. Within her own department she remained an outsider and intruder. It seemed as if the values and beliefs about teaching modern languages and about education were at odds with those of her colleagues, most of whom had become victims of attrition and cynicism. Isolated and excluded Hilary decided that teaching was for her, but not in this school and not in this country.

'I feel relieved that I have finished. I really do, because the last six months have been, ... well ... I have done nothing the past six months apart from the job and think about leaving. And it crossed my mind that I did want to go abroad, where I feel that certain systems abroad take more of a pedagogical interest in the kids as opposed to this, the pastoral bureaucratic side.'

After successful completion of the induction period, Hilary accepted a post in an English school abroad.

Who is my mentor? – Francis's story

Similarly to Hilary, Francis (34) had already gained experience in the world of work as a public sector employee before embarking on teacher training, possessing good communication and interpersonal skills, which she used effectively in her class management. During her training she had impressed mentors and tutors through her unstinting commitment and diligence. A mother of two, she had family commitments, but never allowed this to interfere with her work as a teacher. Her preparation and planning of lessons was immaculate reflecting the highest standards. Everything was set for a promising start! However, almost immediately into starting her induction year at a popular, highly performing secondary school, she realised that an Induction Programme did not exist and that the mentoring support to which she was entitled was not forthcoming. There was also ambiguity about the identity of the induction tutor acting as her mentor. The deputy head who introduced himself to her as the designated Induction Tutor had delegated his duties to Francis's Head of Department, who felt that she could not do the role justice, as she had neither the training nor the resources, i.e. time, required to perform the role adequately and, after all, officially it was not her job.

> I don't really know who my induction tutor is, because the induction tutor has not been formally identified to me. [...] The Deputy Head was the induction tutor, but seems to be under the impression that he has delegated down to the heads of department. But the heads of department are not really aware of it. So, it's really a bit mixed up.

Positioned between a deputy head who had transferred his mentoring responsibilities to a head of department who was clearly overworked, Francis found it difficult to approach either of them, eventually resigning to the fact that she had to manage on her own as best as she could.

> We haven't really received any [support]. It is a bit sort of trial and error at the moment. Try out what you think and see how it works. But we haven't had any discussions about how we are going to approach it as a department. We have been left to our own devices.

After four months into induction, Francis had neither been observed, nor received feedback on her practice. Her feelings of isolation and abandonment were compounded further by the fact that the morale within the school as a whole was at its lowest point. In contrast to Hilary who tried to establish relationships with colleagues outside her department, Francis deliberately refrained from joining the staff room at lunchtimes to avoid the negative atmosphere that was being generated through bickering and cynicism about the school, pupils and education as a whole.

> Well, there are a lot of people who have been there for a very long time and there is a lot of moaning and whinging and complaining going on all the time. It's just not a very nice atmosphere to sit in there, day in day out, when people are just talking school, school, school all the time and it's nothing but complaints. So, I tend to stay away from the arguing and petty falling out that goes on. I have been part of a working party for literacy during the school year. I tend to really not go into the staff room at lunchtime, because ..., I don't really like the atmosphere in there. So in that respect I haven't sort of integrated myself, really, because I have tended to keep away and keep to my own sort of room. I think I have been accepted by [my colleagues]. I think they sort of view me as a bit strange, maybe, that I don't go in the staff room at lunchtime and sit in the group ... probably. (Francis)

However, in her endeavour to develop her competence as a teacher and meet the prescribed standards she joined several working parties. While she shared her concerns about her lack of mentoring support with one other NQT, she felt that she had no opportunity to openly discuss these issues with her mentor or other more experienced colleagues. Her involvement with them remained entirely 'professional', relating the operational aspects of day-to-day teaching, class management and assessment. In her distress she contacted her union representative and sought advice from the LEA adviser, neither of whom were able to help her. She, too, had been abandoned by her mentors and as a result had only gained marginal access to the community of practice of her school. The process of learning and professional development that had taken place in isolation, and as such lacked moderation and input from other perspectives representing the wider range of perspectives of the school community.

> 'I am glad to be finishing the school completely, because I handed my notice in, and I'll be leaving by the end of this term. It's a combination of reasons, really. But ... partly, it has to do with the fact that the induction year has been virtually non-existent. I haven't really had any support at all from the so-called induction tutor.'

On successful completion of her induction period, Francis decided that, in view of her negative experience, she needed to reconsider her career options and decided to resign from the post that was offered to her at the school.

The mentor as moderator between ideal and reality – Sam's story

Similarly to Hilary and Francis, Sam (33) also had gained extensive experience in the world of work and possessed good interpersonal and organisational skills. She was also a mother of two and was highly enthusiastic about teaching and had successfully completed her initial training. In contrast to Hilary and Francis, however, both of whom worked in high achieving schools, she had obtained a post in a secondary school where academic performance was below the national average and where challenging pupil behaviour and negative parent attitudes posed considerable challenges to new as well as experienced teachers. In spite of this difficult environment, Sam remained optimistic throughout the entire induction period, highlighting the excellent mentoring support she had been given by her curriculum and professional induction tutor in the form of a structured induction programme and regular meetings with her mentors as well as other colleagues. She praised the positive approach prevalent across the whole school and the open, collaborative culture apparent in colleagues' behaviour and attitude towards newcomers to the profession and the school:

> I speak to people in the department [and] see how they handle situations. They handle situations and you handle situations, but not in the same way. I think that different things work for different teachers and the whole part of this is just finding what works for you.

This does not mean that Sam's induction experience was trouble free. On the contrary, due to retaining the high standards she had set herself and pupils during her initial training, she had repeatedly experienced serious self-doubt and lack of confidence in her ability as a teacher and had found her own values and beliefs about teaching and education incompatible with the reality encountered in everyday practice. Following her first parents evening, her self-image as a teacher had been seriously dented, as she felt that teachers were not given the respect they deserved.

> When I started, I thought teachers were more profile that they are, ... in that, ... status may be. But now I am actually a teacher ... things with parents, not agreeing with you, not supporting you. The attitudes, ... and the attitudes of pupils and sometimes the attitudes of other teachers, in that they don't feel high profile .... Because of the comments.

In the classroom she realised that she had to either lower her standards in relation to pupil behaviour or risk constant confrontation.

> I started off with very high standards and I have high expectations for behaviour and work. And, I think, because I have had to fit into the school, I think, I have gone down, which is disappointing for me. I know it's the school. The only way I have survived is by lowering them. I don't think, if I hadn't lowered them, I would have survived. They are still in the back of my head. Since then, I haven't got over the fact, thinking, 'Well, this is the way it's done here' ... I am just going to be flexible and get along and get on with it. Then, I feel as if I have become a better teacher. I have been getting along better with the pupils and I feel happier in myself. (Sam)

This is where her mentor played a crucial role in mediating between ideal and reality, between personal and professional values and beliefs, and by providing the emotional, pastoral support required to help newcomers to the profession to develop a sense of belonging. In spite of the absence of a reference to the pastoral dimension in the statutory induction framework, there has been widespread belief amongst the research community that the provision of personal and emotional support is crucial in a newly qualified teacher's overall development (Olson & Osborne, 1991; Turner, 1994; Tauer, 1998). Hardy (1999:114) goes as far as to maintain that the opportunity of having 'someone to turn to' is 'the single most helpful aspect' of the induction programme. Such an arrangement allowed newcomers to the profession to share their problems freely with their 'buddy mentor' who they regarded as someone ' who is willing to listen and to hear what you are saying, someone who empathises and remembers what it is like to be a new person or on probation', as one NQT expressed it.

Although Sam felt that her competence as a teacher was constantly challenged, she never considered the option of giving up. On successful completion of the induction year she was offered a post which she happily accepted.

Two mentors and a buddy! – Pat's story

Pat presents a special case in that he had completed his final block practice at the same school as his induction period. This meant that to some extent he was already affiliated with the school and had established himself at least a peripheral member of the school community of practice. He was familiar with the tacitly agreed routines and behaviours established within the school community and had become a member of the school staff soccer team, which placed him in a strategically favourable position in terms of establishing informal relationships with staff, who could act as his informal mentors in relation to specific aspects of teaching, including information transmitted via the grapevine.

In addition to the social contacts which Pat had been able to establish, he valued the multi-mentoring system that had been implemented. It was highly sophisticated in terms of its structure, allocating each newly qualified teacher a professional mentor, curriculum mentor and 'Friend Tutor', all of whom had specific responsibilities attached to their role. In terms of status, age, experience and seniority the 'friend Tutor' was not too dissimilar to the mentee and was always located outside the faculty to avoid conflict of interests, bearing resemblance to the concept of 'buddy' mentoring, which is explored by Ballantyne et al (1995) in their research of a sample of beginning primary teachers. The division of roles drew a distinct line between providing emotional support as well as professional assistance with regard to developing effective classroom skills and teaching behaviour, and as such avoided the dilemma of accommodating conflicting demands within one role. While the professional mentor (deputy head) organised forums for all NQTs to discuss whole school issues, the curriculum mentor was available on a daily basis, providing guidance and advice on subject specific and departmental matters. Both acted as assessors. Conversely, the function of the 'buddy' was to be understood as a peer mentoring role, and, as such, it was detached from the ubiquitous threat of monitoring and assessment and free from conflict of interests and loyalties. By distinguishing between these three dimensions of mentoring, the school had embraced induction in a comprehensive way and acknowledged that the socialisation of teachers must be perceived as a holistic process, which takes into account the needs of the whole person. In addition, there was a fourth dimension present within the school, which was less tangible than the other three and more difficult to define. It manifested itself in an open, collaborative culture, suffused by a strong commitment of all staff to having an input in the induction process of newly qualified teachers by welcoming them into their community, professionally as well as socially.

> I had a full day where I could choose what I wanted to observe. You could see what other people do and how they do it. So, that was good. You pick bits up.

Consequently, Pat felt safe, supported, welcome and needed, as he was allowed and encouraged to engage in collaborative activities with colleagues in his own and other departments.

Professional values and practice – Who is in control? – Joe's story

Similarly to Hilary, Joe (26) had gained teaching experience as a Foreign Language Assistant prior to entering initial training. However, she was born and educated in France, which still shaped the values and beliefs she held about education in general and teaching in particular. Like Sam and Pat, she described the mentoring support provided by her school as 'excellent' and was happy to continue teaching at the same school after successfully completing her induction period. However, one incident involving disciplinary action and communication with parents over a pupil's unacceptable behaviour in the classroom plunged her in a profound crisis, provoking her to reconsider her personal and professional beliefs about principles and values underpinning teachers' practice. This is her account:

> 'I confiscated this fingerboard from Year 9 and I kept it for four weeks. After that time I received a letter from the parents, asking me to clarify why I had kept this fingerboard, because they felt it was time for me to give it back. I answered the letter. I told them, well, I clarified why I confiscated the fingerboard; because the pupil was playing with it just in front of me, smiling and looking at me, finding it really amusing. So I said to the parents that I was concerned about the pupil's progress in school rather than his entertainment. But this was too direct and the letter was changed. I showed the letter to the co-ordinator and she said it would be fine. But someone a bit higher decided that it was too bad and then there were other words. ... It ended up ... the letter was saying that the pupil had made wonderful progress and that ... It's not really what I wanted to say. It made me make the decision that next time, I will ... next time, I will send my own letters, without asking anyone else to read them and express what I want, and say what I want, without lying to the parents. It would definitely make me feel a lot better!'

In cases of pupils' misdemeanour, she felt that parents had a right to an honest account of events that had taken place, and, equally, in their communication with parents, teachers were entitled to express their opinion openly. Joe was taken by surprise and reacted angrily when she learnt that the tenour of her letter had been changed. By doing so, she felt that Senior Management had undermined her authority as a teacher and had not acted honestly. She also felt extremely disappointed that her mentor had not supported her in defending her point of view, and instead had tried to mediate between her point of view and the interests of the school as a whole. In recognition of her position as a newly qualified teacher, Joe was fully aware of the imbalance of power apparent in this scenario, which is why she reluctantly agreed to the procedure, however, with grave misgivings and doubts about the integrity of the profession as a whole.

Discussion

The five case studies indicate different levels of socialisation and integration into the school community and illustrate the challenges involved in mentoring newly qualified teachers. They also suggest a link between the degree of socialisation and new entrants' desire to continue or resign from teaching. Given that the national issue of retention has now replaced that of recruitment, it is important to take note of such findings. In an attempt to explore and explain some of the tensions arising for mentors and mentees during induction, the discussion will focus on the following three areas:

- The socialisation of new entrants to the profession
- The balance of power and control apparent within the induction setting
- The reconciliation of teacherhood and personhood

The process of socialisation

Gaining access Hilary's isolated position within her subject department can be seen in parallel to Francis's deliberate choice to distance herself from the staff room. In both cases the mentors failed to assist the newly qualified teachers to become members of the community of practice. One explanation for the reluctance displayed in welcoming Hilary unconditionally into the department could perhaps be rooted in colleagues' lack of mutual trust and fear of loss of self-esteem, which prevented them from engaging in collaborative practice and sharing of experiences. Such preference for privacy at the expense of interdependent collegiality was interpreted with reference to observations made by Hargreaves and Fullan (1992, p. 62) who maintain: 'When teachers ... act as 'gatekeepers' to their isolated 'kingdoms' rather than as professional colleagues, the prospects for positive educational change [and the professional development of newly qualified teachers] are reduced'. In a similar vein Sam deplores the inequality of opportunities as it manifested itself in a group of colleagues who behaved as if they possessed certain pre-established rights that were denied to other teachers:

> It's difficult to explain. I think, things within the school are quite sort of, ... certain teachers do certain things and certain teachers don't even get asked if they want to do things. Those teachers do it all the time and if you are new to the school, you don't even get asked. 'It's an established right. They have this right, and I think it is hard to feel part of a community when you don't get involved in things. (Sam)

Such settings make the limitation of the dyadic mentoring model explicit. Although Hilary and Francis joined working parties which provided them with opportunities to develop knowledge and skills in a specific area of the curriculum, it could not create the informal environment conducive to casual conversation. The importance of 'ongoing conversation about teaching, views of self-as-teacher and the context of teaching' is highlighted by Bullough and Baughman (1993, p. 94). Often, ad hoc chats during a morning or lunch break bears the potential of leading to unexpected, alternative solutions to problems. Unlike the two above cases, the majority of the ten newly qualified teachers benefited from a staffroom culture that can encourage the generation of informal networks and caring and empathic relationships which helped the newcomers to the profession in overcoming initial difficulties (Turner, 1994).

Making friends Apart from a general reticence displayed by staff, the choice of 'friends' or 'allies' can be influenced by internal politics reflected in the social and professional segregation of staff. Hargeaves (1992) refers to these negative effects of 'balkanisation' in terms of poor communication, indifference and groups going their separate ways. The option to subscribe to a subgroup and be assured of their solidarity was particularly tempting for Francis when feelings of vulnerability or isolation had been generated:

> Well, to be honest, there were two camps in the school as it stands at the moment in as much as there are five NQTs and four of them are leaving completely at the end of this term. [...] There are also about five or six new members of staff who started when we did and they have been very unhappy as well. So, it's tended to be the NQTs and these new people that have tended to stick together, really, and talked about their problems and the problems, you know, that are in the school as we see them.

The importance of having someone to talk to is highlighted by Francis, who opted out of her school's staff room community, but occasionally felt the need to confide in someone:

> Errr, you know, [...] I wouldn't feel comfortable approaching someone personally. ... Well, I wouldn't really talk to anyone at the school other than ... I do have, errm, an NQT colleague and I will sort of talk, if things have not gone too well, or if I feel too unhappy about something. (Francis)

Such situations raise issues for mentors. If their mentees select their strategies to obtain collegial support and collaboration in allegiance to the colleagues with whom they identified most, rather than in relation to their professional needs, the depth and breadth of their induction programme could not be guaranteed. According to Wu, (1998) values and attitudes are powerful forces in determining the quality of new teachers' relationships with other staff. Consequently, opportunities for interacting with as wide a cross-section of experienced teachers as possible and engaging in 'legitimate peripheral participation' would be missed, resulting in an unbalanced, narrow experience.

The balance of power and control

Meeting whose needs – the mentee's or the school's? Membership was not the issue in Joe's case. On the contrary, she described her relationship with her mentors as excellent and was fully integrated in the school community. Far from being isolated and excluded, Joe was well supported, perhaps too well. This example epitomises the conflict experienced by a new teacher, whose personal and moral values were in contradiction with school policy. It also highlights the status differential that existed between the newly qualified teacher and senior management, as it manifested itself in the autocratic manner in which the matter was dealt with. In this respect, MacDonald's (1995) conclusion about the close link between lack of status, limited decision making and teacher dissatisfaction was of particular relevance here, in that the newly qualified teacher was excluded from the process of resolving the issue. Such procedure is difficult to reconcile with the notion of reflective practice and a collaborative culture within which newcomers to the profession could 'articulate their voice, as a way of constructing and reconstructing the purposes and priorities in their work, both individually and collectively' (Hargeaves & Fullan, 1992, p. 5). Joe's judgement was ignored, causing resentment and possibly encouraging retreat to a position of individualism or 'strategic compliance' (Lacey, 1977). Accordingly, she complied with the authority figure's definitions or constraints of the situation, but retained private reservations about them. The issues to be raised here are related to the conflict arising from professional values and practice as defined by individual schools and newly qualified teachers' personal beliefs, resulting in coerced collaboration. Where was the mentor who would act as mediator between her personal stance and that of the senior management? By including Joe in the decision making process, and thus facilitating 'legitimate peripheral participation', she could have developed a sensitivity towards whole school issues and at the same time maintained her personal dignity and professional pride. However, in the light of the ubiquitous pressure of monitoring and assessment, she compromised her values and beliefs, although reluctantly.

In the cases of Hilary and Francis, the potential tension between professional practice and personal values and beliefs became increasingly accentuated, eventually leading to a critical state of polarisation. It remains open to speculation whether Francis's resignation and Hilary's opting out of the English education system could have been prevented through a more proactive mentoring approach, which would have explained the tacitly agreed norms of teacher behaviour within the context of the respective schools.

The double-edge sword of mentoring and assessment The current induction framework (DfES, 2003) allocates mentors an array of important duties and responsibilities with an emphasis on training rather than education. Given that one of their roles is that of assessor, who measures the quality of new teachers against national standards prior to entering the profession, the notion of the mentor as gatekeeper lies at the heart of the tension inherent within the mentoring role and generates conflict and dilemma for mentor and mentee. Particularly in the case of weak or awkward novices it could be used to ensure that they are 'either supported or eased out of the profession' (Taylor, 1997, Appendix 25, p. 65), thus providing a 'bridge or a barrier into teaching' (ATL, 1999). In this sense, the metaphor of the double-edged sword is by no means an exaggerated visualisation of the constant threat of failure experienced by newly qualified teachers, as Sam illustrates:

> We've already passed our PGCE. Why should we be tested again? Why should there be a failure point at the end? It puts you under too much pressure.

If assessment is at the forefront of mentors' and mentees' thinking, it is likely that it affects the balance of power within the mentoring relationship in a potentially detrimental way (Dormer, 1994:130) and restricts new teachers in their development of their own style. While in some relationships the differential in status and power is somewhat tempered by the nurturing, collaborative, supportive environment within which mentoring occurs, in other situations it may prevent the mentee from becoming an active participant in and having some ownership of the learning process, and, ultimately, from emancipating themselves.

Acting as assessor and judge over who will be deemed competent enough to join the profession and who will be failed (Smith, 2001) inevitably bestows power on the mentor, which can potentially impair the quality of the relationship established with the mentee and the learning process. The potential tensions arising from such an imbalance of power are inextricably linked to notions of honesty and trust, all of which are prerequisites for establishing and maintaining positive mentoring relationships. If the pressure of assessment is ubiquitous, it is highly questionable to what extent mentors and mentees are prepared to engage in honest, critical dialogue, admitting weakness on the one hand and providing feedback on the other.

If we intend newly qualified teachers to engage in honest, critical reflection of their practice, we must ensure that they can do so freely without fearing the pressure of repercussions affecting the outcome of the induction period or their future career. Ironically, Hilary valued the aspect of regular assessment by the induction tutor, in so much as it provided her with feedback and moral support during a time of loneliness and exclusion:

> I wasn't worried, because I was quite glad, because I wanted a little bit of attention in a perverse way and some feedback, because I did feel quite isolated, really, in the department. There wasn't a great sense of team work, team spirit, so it was quite a pleasure, really, to have visitors come into the class, because you got some feedback from them.

The desire to be observed, to receive feedback and to be acknowledged seemed to constitute fundamental needs articulated by each of the ten newly qualified teachers, which can be aligned to Lave and Wenger's (1991) notion of learning through participating in social practice. Only where observations and feedback formed an integral element of the induction/mentoring programme, were newcomers provided with opportunities for 'legitimate peripheral participation', which took place in the form of constructive dialogue with their more experienced colleagues. It also helped them to obtain reassurance with regard to areas of uncertainty and to feel integrated within the school community.

In contrast, Francis was deprived of such co-participation and as a result never developed a sense of belonging within her school or as a member of the profession as a whole.

> I had two observations in total during the year, one from the deputy head himself and one from the head of department. I have not had any discussions with him at all. In fact, when he observed me, I had to sort of demand that he told me what he had written about me and I have never been given a copy of that. I feel that I am not being assessed properly and I have doubts in my mind all the time. 'Am I doing this right? Am I doing this wrong?' And as I say, you still feel on the one hand that you're still the student.

As described by Barrington (2000:2), assessment meetings constitute 'important milestones' for new teachers on their journey of development, in that it serves as acknowledgement of the progress they have made towards their destination, the completion of induction and the confirmation of Qualified Teacher Status. And yet, mentors need to be cognisant of the potential dangers inherent in a learning model that is driven primarily by the need to monitor and assess newly qualified teachers against prescribed standards. The balance of power and control can easily be weighted in favour of the assessor, thereby removing the democratic, mutual aspect of 'legitimate peripheral participation', which according to Lave and Wenger (1991) is crucial for situated learning to take place.

Professional autonomy versus conformity The tension between freedom and restriction, autonomy and conformity was also experienced by the other newly qualified teachers, but not to the same extent. Although the legal framework as well as school policies and procedures provided guidelines for professional behaviour, they could not always assist newly qualified teachers in negotiating ethical, moral or personal dilemmas and conflicts confidently. And even where rules and professional expectations were clearly defined, the prescribed course of action might be often in conflict with the teachers' personal beliefs and values, as the following example demonstrates:

> I need to know what other people think, but then I would see if what they do is what I think is right. If it is, I will follow them, but otherwise, if I still think that I have not said what I wanted, if I decide it's not what I want to do, then I am not going to ... unless there is high pressure. (Joe)

> School issues ... dealing with the hierarchy in the school ... it's related to classical teaching, to functions, policies and generally the school's code of conduct. You realise that you have to follow the school rules. (Hilary)

The strong opinions expressed by the two new teachers with regard to conforming to externally defined standards and norms proved corroborating evidence to support the argument that indicated that an unequal distribution of power can encourage uncritical behaviour at the expense of a reflective-reflexive approach, particularly at a time when the 'cloak of rationality shrouds the training' and the induction experience of new entrants to the profession (Wright & Bottery, 1997:1). Furthermore, it highlights the potential power exerted by training curricula that are driven by a need for compliance and accountability. A similar control mechanism can be set in motion as a result of tacitly agreed values and beliefs that are indicative of the idiosyncratic culture of a particular community of practice, which aims to reproduce itself rather than engage in critical dialogue about their established practices and existing patterns of teacher professionalism. This raises an interesting issue with regard to the reference points that are used by mentors/induction tutor in the assessment of competence.

Mediating between ideal and reality

Mentors arc cxpcctcd to play a pivotal role in facilitating the successful transition from training to professional practice, and thus assist beginning teachers to manage the often cited 'reality shock, which manifests itself in the discrepancy of expectations and actual situations experienced (Veenman, 1984; Huberman, 1992; Koetsier & Wubbels, 1995). This is compounded further when the newly qualified teachers' self-image of a professional is at odds with the reality encountered. For example, workload and remuneration, low staff morale and the general lack of respect for teachers provoked a re-examination of their personal and professional values and beliefs about education and teaching.

Workload The idealised picture of teaching portrayed in marketing materials may evoke unrealistic expectations in newly qualified teachers, many of whom feel overwhelmed by the unexpected amount of work they are expected to do:

> I think that people generally don't realise how many hours, extra hours, teachers really do, until they are doing it themselves. (Sam)

> Everything is new at once. The greatest challenge has been the planning, organising myself to be ready each day and be enthusiastic each day with different classes. I found that quite hard; the workload and the fact that every single week, there always seems to be something happening. You either have to get some grades ready or prepare yourself for a parents evening. (Francis)

Low staff morale The comments provided by a newly qualified teacher strengthened the view that an understanding of the structural, social, cultural and personal and factors involved in teachers' career histories, has to be facilitated for newcomers to the profession to adopt a differentiated approach in an attempt to make sense of some of their disturbing experiences. 'Constant moaning about the profession, constant complaining ... and bickering between staff and bickering about other members, groups of members of staff', as witnessed by Francis, is certainly not helpful in promoting a positive image of the profession and may seriously dampen the high levels of enthusiasm, commitment and self-esteem expressed prior to induction. MacLure (1993) related the issue of disaffection and cynicism amongst longer serving colleagues to the dramatic changes in the social perception of teachers, resulting in denial of identity, esteem, trust, authority and expertise and highlight the relevance of these undesirable behaviours to newly qualified teachers' development of self-esteem, confidence and professional pride and the formation of negative attitudes (Smyth, 1995; Hardy, 1999). And yet, Sam's enthusiasm for teaching was not dampened. Her mentor, whom she described as 'friendly', 'easy to talk to', 'a good listener' and 'caring', played a crucial role in moderating her idealistic expectations and the high standards she had initially set herself on the one hand and her pupils' disaffection and underachievement on the other. In addition, he provided her not only with professional, but also emotional support during periods of self-doubt, disillusionment and confidence. In this sense, mentoring contained a pastoral dimension and constituted 'an individualised form of training which was tailored to the needs of the individual (Brooks & Sikes, 1997: 35). The importance of recognising the 'personal' element in mentoring is highlighted by Goodson when he contends that 'in understanding something so intensely personal as teaching, it is critical we know about the person the teacher is' (1981: 69).

High standards, high status? The image of teaching portrayed by the Department for Education and Employment as a profession reflecting 'high standards' and 'high status' (1998) did not quite live up to Sam's expectations prior to induction. In an attempt to adjust her personal and professional standards to those of the school, Sam had to make painful compromises, which resonates with Bleach's observations (1998, p. 59) that newcomers to the profession display a tendency 'to accept things as they are', unless they are encouraged to adopt new perspectives. In Sam's case, however, the decision to lower standards was not reached lightly and was based on the assumption that by doing so a better rapport could be established amongst pupils and teachers, which would lead to an improved quality of teaching and learning overall. The newly qualified teacher's confession, '[the standards] are still in the back of my head' (Sam), implied a strategy of 'pragmatic compliance', which is not unlike Lacey's (1977) concept of 'strategic compliance'. Accordingly, original values are retained, but are not in synchrony with the actions performed within the constraints of the situation. The potential danger inherent in this situation is that of a possible reaction from compliance to disaffection, as a result of circumstances denying newly qualified teachers the opportunity to incorporate their personal values in their professional conduct (Butt et al, 1990).

Mediating between teacherhood and personhood

Sam's self-image of a professional, whose contribution to society is described as 'invaluable' (TTA, 2000), was at odds with her experiences at school. In contrast to Joe, who adopted a course of action of 'strategic compliance', Sam deliberately breached school policy when she intervened to stop two boys fighting. As a result of her action she received a blow to the face.

> But although I was told I shouldn't have got between them, I think I'd get between them again. I felt I didn't want them to hit each other. [...] Although I was told I did wrong, it's a reaction, and it's something you just do, isn't it. I'd still do it again. I think it's because I'd react like that automatically. I think being a [parent] influences you as well. I couldn't have stood by and watched them fight. [Sam]

Sam's course reaction reflects how powerful personal factors can be in influencing teachers' decision making and highlights the fact that in performing their daily duties as professional, teachers also act as individuals with reference to their own biography. Accordingly, Sam's values and beliefs embedded in her identity as a parent collided with those prescribed by the profession's code of conduct.

Sam's and Joe's experiences present themselves for comparison in that they relate to similar issues, namely the reconciliation of a personal and professional identity, and yet they differ in the way in which they responded to this predicament. While Sam's reaction was spontaneous and was provoked by a deep-felt, motherly concern for the children's safety, Joe's moral dilemma arose out of a clash between her definitions of honesty and fairness and how these values should be interpreted in her professional practice and the official line adopted by the school's senior management. To what extent these values were also intertwined with her identity as an individual who had been born and educated in France remains open to speculation. What these examples illustrate is that professional practice, such as teaching, is personal, including a strong investment of self (Clandinin, 1986; Nias, 1989; Huberman, 1993). Hargreaves and Fullan (1992, p. 16) lend further support to this stance:

> 'Understanding teacher development involves understanding not only knowledge and skills that teachers should acquire, but also understanding what sort of person the teacher is and the context in which most teachers work'. (Hargreaves and Fullan, 1992:6)

They also draw attention to the negative implications of coerced collaboration for the profession as a whole when they maintain that 'where purposes are imposed and consensus is contrived, there is no place for practical judgements and wisdom of teachers'. Similar concern is expressed by Wright and Bottery (1997: 1) who believe that the absence of an education developing a wider sense of professionalism can encourage uncritical behaviour at the expense of a reflective-reflexive approach, particularly at a time when the 'cloak of technical rationality shrouds the training' and consequently the induction experience of new entrants to the profession. Bearing this caveat in mind, mentoring must not exclusively be perceived as a training device in relation to measurable outcomes, but needs to encompass a host of other dimensions, one of which is of a pastoral nature, and as such, emphasises the humanistic, person-centred aspects of mentoring (Turner, 1994; Tauer, 1998; Jones, 2000; Tickle, 2000).

Conclusions

Competence beyond the standards

Within the current paradigm of competence-based learning, it is questionable whether the focus on the technical aspects of teaching and classroom management is sufficient in equipping new teachers adequately to become members of, and contribute to, a community of practice that engages in critical reflection that extends beyond the boundaries of the statutory standards framework. This, of course, would require mentors to perceive learning as a process that is embedded in social activity and as such transcends the boundaries of the conventional, dyadic mentoring relationship and thereby act in the role of mediator and facilitators within a 'multi-support system' (Fabian & Simpson, 2002). Accordingly, mentoring would comprise a team of 'critical friends' at various levels of seniority and representing a wide range of professional experience and expertise. Such a multi-support model of mentoring would have the capacity to assist new teachers in the development of the four levels of competence identified by Zimpher and Howey (1987):

1. Technical competence, which refers to the effective use of teaching skills in the classroom.

2. Clinical competence, which relates to the ability to assess problematic situations and respond to them appropriately.

3. Personal competence, which is reflected in the capacity of clarifying and developing one's own values and beliefs.

4. Critical competence, which manifests itself in teachers who engage in the critique of social institutions and structure and their consequences for individuals.

By addressing all four levels, mentors could assist new teachers in extending their mastery of technical competence into the realm of reflection and reflexivity, which involves ethical and moral judgement and ultimately the teacher as a person.

The pastoral dimension and socialisation

In light of the frustration and anxiety reported by some of the ten newly qualified teachers there appears to be a need for incorporating a pastoral dimension into mentoring, in spite of the imperative to operate in a strictly professional manner. Given the high attrition rate amongst new teachers (Teachernet, 2005), Induction tutors as mentors need to be seen as occupying a key position in providing opportunities for socialisation and integration into the school community and the profession as a whole. For, according to Turner (1994), socialisation is one of the key factors in individual adjustment to the role of a professional in an organization, a view which resonates with Olson and Osborne's (1991) emphasis of new teachers' needs for affiliation and security. In this sense 'fitting in' generates feelings of security and belonging and as such constitutes a pre-requisite for expressing self-doubt and engaging in critical reflection and collaboration. The insecurity characterising the socialisation process of newly qualified teachers and the tentative behaviour displayed by them towards their colleagues is aptly encapsulated by Pat:

> Yes, I do feel part of the staff. I don't think I am quite at the stage when you air your opinions openly, because you are still sort of sifting through who speaks to whom.

Further evidence which suggests that 'people are profoundly affected by the social setting in which they are involved' has been produced by Wu's (1998, p. 214) investigation into ways in which the work environment influences the professional development of teachers. Accordingly, interpersonal relationships are regarded as a crucial component of the school environment. It could be argued that there was a connection between the new teachers' development of professional competence and the degree to which their values and attitudes were congruent with those promoted by the school culture, a view strongly supported by Handy and Aitken (1986).

The five case studies indicate that, at least to some extent, socialization can be attributed to the staff culture prevalent within a particular school, in the way in which the structural and social parameters determine the pattern of interactions. As 'culture itself is not visible' (Van Maanen, 1988: 3), mentors can act as guides and mediators in making explicit the beliefs, values and norms that have been tacitly agreed within a school and ensure that newcomers are welcomed into the community of practice and gain access to teachers' isolated 'kingdoms' (Hargreaves and Fullan, 1992: 62). In her endeavour to 'fit in', one of the ten newly qualified teachers participating in Jones's study (2001) provides the following advice:

> You have to stick to the policy as much as possible. If you are not seen to be sticking to procedure, then you are frowned upon, really, by the whole school.

However, Sparkes (1994) expresses concern over restrictive, intimidating cultures, as unconditional surrender to the structural, procedural and cultural demands imposed in a setting could result in the depersonalisation of teaching, self-blame and a removal of the sense of individualism. In situations where new teachers experience ethical conflict and moral dilemmas arising out of conflicting values, it is vital for the community of practice to function as a learning environment in which mentors act as their advocates, who may negotiate on their behalf, and thereby reduce the potential of negative stress and burnout (Russel et al, 1987; Hardy, 1999). This function is aptly encapsulated in the way in which one of the ten Induction Tutors was described (Jones, 2001):

> She is a very good spokesperson for the group [of NQTS], will take our queries and complaints to Senior Management for us and support us in anything we feel is badly dealt with or unfairly treated.

Facilitating a collaborative model of learning

The findings of this study point towards a collaborative model of induction as one that is favoured by newcomers to the profession, but is not yet embraced by the wider community of practice. For example, Francis's school invested generously in newly qualified teachers' professional learning and development, but, contrary to Lave and Wenger's (1991) concept of 'legitimate peripheral participation', it was delivered externally in discrete units:

When we first started at the school, there was this sort of feeling that ... you know, ... they were quite proud of the fact that they were going to send us on a lot of courses, and that they were spending a lot of money on us. My argument would be that, yes, it's very nice to go on courses and it's very nice to have a day out of school, but you really need to settle into the job, you know, and get to grips with things a bit better. (Francis)

This strategy has several disadvantages. External training was detached from the actual context within which it was intended to be applied, absence due to course attendance resulted in disruption of planning and teaching patterns and opportunities for collaborative activities with colleagues were minimised.

There is a strong desire apparent in newly qualified teachers to interact and communicate with other teachers, both experienced colleagues ands peers alike, and not exclusively in a professional capacity.

Just sharing experiences, really, because you feel a bit on your own sometimes. You just want to talk. 'Is this happening to other people as well?' And just to get together and do that, was really good; and to meet people within my school, who were NQTs; and I had not had the opportunity to chat with them and go and see them. (Jones, 2001: Alex).

In search of reassurance concomitant with the desire to integrate into the profession, teaching issues, as well as personal problems, were shared and discussed. The social dimension reflected in the need to meet with other teachers indicated that the newly qualified teachers' selves could not be detached from their professional lives, a fact which is not taken account of in the statutory induction framework, not in the provision of mentoring support, which is predominantly defined in terms of monitoring and assessing progress.

The data of Jones's study (2001) confirm Hardy's (1999) belief that induction takes place on a general and a personal level, following an official and a private agenda and that effective mentoring is contingent on a multitude of factors, not least of all the social contexts and nature of the relationship between individuals within (Rippon & Martin, 2003; Lucas, 2001).

Indeed, Hargreaves and Fullan (1992:90) emphasise the interrelationship between personal, educational and social reference points which they consider an 'important catalyst for teacher development' and the multiple demands made upon mentors in performing their demanding and often conflicting role. For example, the preponderance with technical aspects of competence often prevents mentors from adopting a more holistic approach, which incorporates a humanistic, pastoral dimension, and allows space for individuals' identities as teachers and persons. Acting as mediators between newcomer and 'community of practice', facilitators of 'legitimate peripheral participation' (Lave & Wenger, 1991) and gatekeepers to the profession can prove highly problematic. Similarly, conflicting loyalties and tensions can be generated in an attempt to balance their own needs as teachers with those of their mentees, their colleagues' expectations and the school's goals.

In conclusion, it is argued that in order to provide new teachers with the adequate professional and personal support as well as collaborative models of learning the conventional dyadic model of mentoring is deemed inappropriate. Instead it is proposed that, a multi-dimensional, multi-disciplinary, holistic approach needs to be adopted, one which transcends departmental boundaries and pervades the entire 'community of practice' within and without a school's boundaries. By perceiving 'mentorship as a community' every teacher will act in a mentoring capacity, thus, alleviating the pressure incumbent on mentors in conventional models of mentoring. Within such a collective approach, it is hoped that the potential for tensions arising from the multiple, often conflictual demands inherent in the mentoring role can be minimised and that the burden of responsibility and accountability can be shared. Accordingly all teachers within a school would play an active role in assisting newly qualified teachers in becoming a member of their community of practice by allowing them to participate in the accumulation and generation of knowledge, practices and approaches the value of which is not merely instrumental for their work, but also accrues a personal satisfaction of knowing colleagues who understand each other's perspectives (Wenger et al, 2002). It is hoped that through social interaction and dialogue, relationships between newcomer and experienced colleagues can be developed, generating a sense of belonging and professional identity. Further in-depth studies investigating the perspectives of newly qualified teachers and induction tutors in a wider range of contexts would be helpful in gaining a deeper understanding of the conflicts and tensions inherent in mentoring newcomers to the profession.

References

Abell, S.K., Dillon, D.R. and Hopkins, C.J. (1995), '"Somebody to Count on": Mentor/Intern Relationships in a Beginning Teacher Internship Program', *Teaching and Teacher Education*, vol. 11(2), pp. 173–188.

Ardery, G. (1990), 'Mentors and Protégés: from Ideology to Knowledge', in J. McCloskey and H. Grace (eds), *Current Issues in Nursing*, Mosby, St Louise.

Ballantyne, R., Packer, J. and Hansford, B. (1995), 'Mentoring Beginning Teachers: a Qualitative Analysis of Process and Outcomes', *Educational Review*, vol. 47(3), pp. 297–307.

Barrington, R. (2000), 'An Investigation into the Induction Period which Considers the Perspectives of NQTs and their Induction Tutors', paper presented at the *British Educational Research Association Conference* (BERA) Cardiff University, September 7–10.

Beckett, D. and Hager, P. (2002), *Life, Work and Learning: Practice in Postmodernity*, Routledge, London.

Bennetts, C. (1996), 'Interpersonal Aspects of Informal Mentor/Learner Relationships: a Research Perspective', *Proceedings of the Fifth National Mentoring Conference*, Manchester, April 30th, 1996.

Bleach, K. (1998), 'Off to a Flying Start? Induction Procedures for Newly Qualified Teachers in Secondary Schools in the Republic of Ireland', *Mentoring and*

Tutoring, vol. 6, pp. 55–65.

Brooks, V. and Sikes, P. (1997), *The Good Mentor Guide*, Open University Press, Buckingham.

Brown, J.S., Collins, A. and Duguid, P. (1989), 'Situated Cognition and the Culture of Learning', *Educational Researcher*, vol. 18(1), pp. 32–42.

Bubb, S. (2000), 'Statutory Induction – a Fair Deal for All?' *Viewpoint* no 12. University of London Institute of Education, London.

Bullough, R.V. and Baughman, K. (1993), 'Continuity and Change in Teacher Development: first Year Teacher after Five Years', *Journal of Teacher Education*, vol. 44(2), pp. 86–95.

Butt, R., Townsend, D. and Raymond, D. (1990), 'Bringing Reform to Life: Teachers' Stories and Professional Development', *Cambridge Journal of Education*, vol. 20, pp. 255–268.

Butters, S. (1997), 'Authority and Power in Mentoring: some Comparisons between Teaching, Engineering, Design and Social Work', in J. Stephenson (ed), *Mentoring – the New Panacea*, Peter Francis, Norfolk.

Caruso, J.E. (1990), *An Examination of Organised Mentoring: the Case of Motorola*, British Thesis Service, DX 147810.

Clandinin, D.J. (1986), *Classroom Practice: Teacher Images in Action*, Falmer Press, London.

Department for Education (DfE) (1992), *The Initial training of Teachers (Secondary Phase) Standards for the Award of Qualified Teacher Status*, Circular 9/92, DfE, London.

Department for Education and Employment (DfEE) (1998), 'Standards for the Award of Qualified Teacher Status', *Teaching: High Status, High Standards*, Circular 4/98, Teacher Training Agency (TTA), London.

Department for Education and Employment (DfEE) (1999), *The Induction Period for Newly Qualified Teachers*, Circular 5/99, DfEE, London.

Department for Education and Skills (DfES) (2002), *Qualifying to Teach*, Teacher Training Agency, London.

Department for Education and Skills (DfES) (2003), *Into Induction*, Teacher Training Agency, London.

Dormer, J. (1994), 'The Role of the Mentor in Secondary Schools', in M. Wilkin and D. Sankey (eds), *Collaboration and Transition in Initial Teacher Training*, Kogan Page, London.

Fabian, H. and Simpson, A. (2002), 'Mentoring the Experienced Teacher', *Mentoring and Tutoring*, vol. 10(2), pp. 117–125.

Feiman-Nemser, S., Parker, M.B. and Zeichner, K. (1993), *Are Mentor Teachers Teacher Educators*? in D. McIntyre, H. Hagger and M. Wilkin (eds), *Mentoring: Perspectives on School-based Teacher Education*, Kogan Page, London.

Fullan, M.G. and Hargreaves, A. (1992), *Understanding Teacher Development*, Teachers College Press, New York.

Furlong, J. and Maynard, T. (1995), *Mentoring Student Teachers*, Routledge,

London.

Goodson, I.F. (1981), 'Life History and the Study of Schooling', *Interchange*, vol. 11(4), pp. 62–76.

Handy, C. and Aitken, R. (1986), *Understanding Schools as Organisations*, Penguin, Harmondsworth.

Hardy C.A. (1999), 'Perceptions of Physical Education Beginning Teachers', First Year of Teaching: Are We Doing Enough to Prevent Early Attrition?, vol. 3(1), pp. 109–127.

Hargreaves, A. and Fullan, M.G. (eds) (1992), *Understanding Teacher Development*, Teachers College Press, New York.

Huberman, M. (1992), 'Teacher Development and Instructional Mastery', in A. Hargreaves and M. Fullan (eds), *Understanding Teacher Development*, Teachers College Press, New York.

Huberman, M. (1993), *The Lives of Teachers*, Cassell, London.

Jones, M. (2000), 'Trainee Teachers' Perceptions of School-based Training in England and Germany with Regard to their Preparation for Teaching, Mentor Support and Assessment', *Mentoring and Tutoring*, vol. 8(1), pp. 63–80.

Jones, M. (2001), 'Mentors' Perceptions of their Roles in School-based Teacher Training in England Germany', *Journal of Education for Teaching*, vol. 27(1), pp. 75–94.

Jones, M. (2002), 'Qualified to become Good teachers: a Case Study of Ten Newly Qualified Teachers during their Year if Induction', *Journal of In-service Education*, vol. 28(3), pp. 509–526.

Jones, M., Foster, R., Groves, J., Parker, G., Rutter, T. and Straker, K. (2004), 'How Do Mentors Know What they Know? An Investigation of Mentors' Professional Knowledge Base', *British Educational Research Association Conference*, Manchester, September 2004.

Koetsier, C.P. and Wubbels, J.T. (1995), 'Bridging the Gap Between Initial Teacher Training and Teacher Induction', *Journal of Education for Teaching*, vol. 21(3), pp. 333–345.

Kyriacou, C. and O'Connor, A. (2003), 'Primary newly qualified teachers' experience of the induction year in its first year of implementation in England', *Journal of In-service Education*, vol. 29(2), pp. 185–200.

McLaughlin, T.H. (1994), 'Mentoring and the Demands of Reflection', in D. McIntyre, H. Hagger and M. Wilkin (eds), *Mentoring: Perspectives on School-based Teacher Education*, Kogan Page, London.

Lacey, C. (1977), *The Socialisation of Teachers*, Methuen, London.

Lave, J. and Wenger, E. (1991), *Situated Learning*, Cambridge University Press, Cambridge.

Lave, J. (1988), *Cognition in Practice: Mind, Mathematics and Culture in Everyday Life*, Cambridge University Press, Cambridge.

Little, J.W. (1990), 'The Mentor Phenomenon and the Social Organisation of Teaching', *Review of Research in Education*, vol. 16, pp. 297–351.

Lucas, K.F. (2001), 'The Social Construction of Mentoring Roles', *Mentoring and*

Tutoring, vol. 9(1), pp. 23–47.

MacDonald, D. (1995), 'The Role of Proletarisation in Physical Education Teacher Attrition', *Research Quarterly for Exercise and Sport*, vol. 66, pp. 129–141.

MacLure, M. (1993), 'Arguing for Your Self: Identity as an Organising Principle in Teachers' Jobs and Lives', *British Educational Research Journal*, vol. 19, pp. 311–321.

Maynard, T. and Furlong, J. (1993), 'Learning to Teach and Models of Mentoring', in D. McIntyre, H. Hagger and M. Wilkin (eds), *Mentoring: Perspectives on School-based Teacher Education*, Kogan Page, London.

McIntyre, D., Hagger, H. and Wilkin, M. (eds) (1993), *Mentoring: Perspectives on School-based Teacher Education*, Kogan Page, London.

Nias, J. (1989), *Primary Teachers Talking*, Routledge, London.

Olson, M.R. and Osborne, J.W. (1991), 'Learning to Teach: the First Year', *Teaching and Teacher Education*, vol. 78(4), pp. 331–343.

Rippon, J. and Martin, M. (2003), 'Supporting Induction: Relationships Count', *Mentoring and Tutoring*, vol. 11(2), pp. 212–226.

Roberts, A. (2000), 'Mentoring Revisited: a Phenomenological Reading of the Literature', *Mentoring and Tutoring*, vol. 8, pp. 145–170.

Roden, J. (2003), 'Bridging the Gap: the Role of the Science Co-ordinator in Improving the Induction and Professional Growth of Newly Qualified Teachers', *Journal of In service Education*, vol. 29(2), pp. 201–219.

Russel, T., Munby, H., Spafford, C. and Johnston, P. (1987), 'Learning the Professional Knowledge of Teaching: Metaphors, Puzzles and the Theory-Practice Relationship', in P.P. Gimmett and G.L. Erickson (eds), *Reflection in Teacher Education*, Teachers College Press, New York.

Smith, P. (2001), 'Mentors as Gatekeepers: an Exploration of Professional Formation', *Educational Review*, vol. 57, pp. 313–324.

Smyth, D.M. (1995), 'First-year Physical Education Teachers' Perceptions of their Workplace', *Journal of Teaching in Physical Education*, vol. 14(2), pp. 198–214.

Sparkes, A.C. (1994), 'Self, Silence and Invisibility as a Beginning Teacher: a Life History of Lesbian Experience', *British Journal of Sociology of Education*, vol. 15, pp. 93–118.

Stammers, P. (1992), 'The Greeks had a word for it (five millennia of mentoring)', *The British Journal of In-service Education*, vol. 18(2), pp. 76–80.

Stephenson, J. (ed) (1997), *Mentoring – the New Panacea*, Peter Francis, Norfolk.

Tauer, S.M. (1998), 'The Mentor-protégé Relationship and its Impact on the Experienced Teacher', *Teacher and Teacher Education*, vol. 14, pp. 201–218.

Taylor, C. (1997), Memorandum submitted to *Education and Employment Committee Sixth Report: The Professional Status, Recruitment and Training of Teachers*, Appendix 25, HMSO, London.

Teachernet (2005), *The Secrets of Teacher Wellbeing, TeacherNet*, www.teachernet.

gov.uk/teachingand learning/library/retention/. Accessed on 17 April 2005.

Tickle, L. (2000), *Teacher Induction: the Way Ahead*, Open University Press, Buckingham.

Totterdell, M., Heilbronn, R., Bubb, S. Jones, C. and Bailey, M. (2002), *Evaluation of the Effectiveness of the Statutory Induction Period: Final Report*, DFES, London.

Teacher Training Agency (TTA) (2000), *Teaching – a Guide to Becoming a Teacher*, Teacher Training Agency, London.

Turner, M. (1994), 'The Management of the Induction of Newly Qualified Teachers in Primary Schools', *Journal of Education for Teaching*, vol. 20, pp. 325–341.

Van Maanen, (1988)

Veenman, S., De Laat, H. and Staring, C. (1998), 'Evaluation of a Coaching Programme for Mentors of Beginning Teachers', *Journal of In-service Education*, vol. 24(3), pp. 411–427.

Veenman, S. (1984), 'Perceived Problems of Beginning Teachers', *Review of Educational Research*, vol. 54, pp. 143–178.

Wenger, E., McDermott, R. and Snyder, W. (2002), *Cultivating Communities of Practice*, Havard Business School Publishing, Havard, MA.

Wildman, T.M. (1992), 'Teacher Mentoring: an Analysis of Roles, Activities and Conditions', *Journal of Teacher Education*, vol. 43(3), pp. 205–231.

Wright, N. and Bottery, M. (1997), 'Perceptions of Professionalism by the Mentors of Student Teachers', *Journal of Education for Teaching*, vol. 23, pp. 235–253.

Wu, J. (1998), 'School Work Environment and its Impact on the Professional Competence of Newly Qualified Teachers', *Journal of In-service Education*, vol. 24(2), pp. 213–225.

Yau, C.K. (1995), 'From a Student Standpoint: My Views on Mentoring', *Mentoring and Tutoring*, vol. 3(2), pp. 45–49.

Zey, M.G. (1984), *The Mentor Connection*, Dow Jones-Irwin, Illinois.

Zimpher, N.L. and Howey, K. (1987), 'Adapting Supervisory Practices to Different Orientations of Teaching Competence', *Journal of Curriculum and Supervision*, vol. 2, pp. 101–127.

Chapter 5

Introducing Mentoring Systems in a Centrally Controlled State: A Case Study

Mohammad Momany with Cedric Cullingford

Introduction

The Jordanian government has taken education very seriously, arguing that in a country with few natural resources there was no other option than to invest in human resources, especially in its strategic position. This has meant that Jordan has been in a hurry to introduce reforms and, to use a term invoked in other countries, to 'drive up' standards. Mentoring has become part of this drive.

The Educational Reform Plan of 1987 had a major impact on initial teacher training in Jordan, and marked the introduction of several initiatives designed to improve both initial and inservice education and training. It meant an expansion in the number of supervisors. Mentoring itself was introduced for the first time in 1996 when the pre-service teacher training courses in the State Universities were established.

The fact that mentors are envisaged as central to the development of the existing system can be understood. For all the complexities of the role, the emphasis is supposed to be clear and simple; the raising of standards, particularly in student teachers. Mentoring represents the concept of a personal interaction between an experienced person in teaching with someone ignorant but willing to learn. The connection is supposed to contribute to the improvement of their skills and personality in general. Hagger et al (1995) defined the mentor in initial teacher training as:

'The person in the school with responsibility for managing and co-ordinating the student's learning as it relates to subject teaching' (p. 14)

This definition of 'mentors' is concerned with the mentor's role inside the classroom and his or her responsibility in organising and managing the trainees' development in the teaching of their subjects. Shaw (1995) defined a mentor as a qualified and experienced teacher:

'Experienced but not very senior ... someone committed to good teaching and professional development' (p. 261)

Shaw (1995) and Hagger et al (1995) emphasise the mentors' experience in teaching and their professional role. They do not reflect on the personal and social role of mentors.

Campbell and Kane (1996) reiterated that being a mentor is not easy. The role needs an understanding of professional issues related to teaching and demands personal and social skills, as well as the ability to deal with professional and personal problems that arise during the mentoring process. Certain conditions are necessary for good mentoring: inter-personal skills, a collaborative ethos with the trainees and the training team in general, whole school awareness, and constructive management by the headteachers. Dagmar's (1992) research revealed that student teachers can simply model and copy their mentors' behaviours and strategies in teaching rather than using what they learn from the theoretical and general principals that they studied at the university or training institution. This limits their ability to vary their teaching strategies. The mentors' role in initial teacher training programmes is more influential than the tutors, because of their closeness to trainees. Jones (1993) proposed no less that eleven different roles of the mentor, from supporter and catalyst to reporter and manager.

The roles suggested by Jones cover all those anticipated but there is no indication of when and how these roles should be used in a practical situation. Balch and Balch (1987) suggested that the mentors' roles change over time. They introduced their proposed roles of mentors as stages of the mentoring process, and the significance and amount of time spent on each role was supposed to vary depending on the personality, strengths, and weaknesses of each student teacher. The role of the mentors was seen as a crucial element in ITT and the researchers emphasised the importance of training the mentors for supervising the student teachers. Some studies' outcomes (Duquette, 1994; Duquette, 1998) showed that the mentoring process was seen as an opportunity for the professional development of mentors themselves. Many of studies revealed that the mentoring process and the relationship between mentors and student teachers influenced the professional development of the experienced teachers and enhanced their teaching competencies.

The findings of the previous studies showed that there was a lack of mentors' qualifications and the insufficient role for mentors in the training process. Moreover, the mentors did not vary their use of different training methods and tended to use traditional methods of training their student teachers. (Fagan and Waiter, 1982; Gusky, 1986; Duquette, 1994; Stanulis, 1994; Tauer, 1998; Ismail, 2001). Despite the complexities of the role, the assumption has been made that the very comprehensive nature of mentoring can be a kind of short cut to the improvement of student and teacher performance.

The Mentoring System in Jordan

Co-operative teachers in the partner schools have the role of mentor in supervising student teachers. Their responsibilities include managing the student teachers' learning about teaching in collaboration with the teacher education institutes and helping student teachers to become familiar with the textbooks, curriculum and teaching manuals. The mentors provide personal support for the student teachers who will often experience both insecurity and failure, perhaps on a greater scale and in a more personal sense than ever before. They also participate in assessing the student teachers' performance during their training in partner schools (Al-Sagrat, 1999).

The principals of the partner schools choose the co-operating teacher (mentor). They receive a letter from the University informing them of the numbers of student teachers who are going to train in their schools. The headteachers then make the arrangements for attaching each student teacher to a mentor according to his field regardless of the mentors' experience and qualifications. Because there is little choice of mentor within schools, any of the teachers available may become mentors. The University does not require any conditions or attributes for the mentors and there are no criteria set for their selection (Owais, 1999). The functions of the mentors in the school-based work include the role of instructor, evaluator and counsellor. Both tutors and mentors' duties are the same for all, regardless of their subject specialism. There is no particular mentoring approach that is developed, promoted or recommended by the universities. The way in which the mentoring process is carried out is similar to the apprenticeship approach because it is easier for mentors, and they have no idea about other mentoring approaches.

University Supervision

The University Tutor is mainly responsible for guiding and supervising the student teachers during their placement at partner schools. He/she is the only person from the universities to visit the trainees at schools. The tutors' duties in the pre-service teacher training course are very similar to the mentors' duties, in working directly with student teachers and guiding them. In addition, they act as co-ordinators between the universities and schools. If we analyse the tutors' responsibilities we will find the following functions for the University supervisors. These are shown diagrammatically in Figure 5.1.

In Figure 5.1 we can see that the tutors have six functions in pre-service teacher training course. They are:

1. *Instructors (trainers)*. They are responsible for training student teachers and following their progress in the school-based work of ITT.

2. *Counsellors*. They help student teachers with any academic and social problems during their placement at partner schools.

3. *Co-ordinators*. The University tutors are considered the main link between the University, partner schools, and student teachers. They provide the pre-service teacher training administration with reports about the mentors and student teachers' performance as well as the training process in general. They are also responsible for explaining the training instructions and curriculum plan as well as the responsibilities of the mentors and headteachers.

4. *Lecturers*. They teach some of the theoretical modules in teaching methodology.

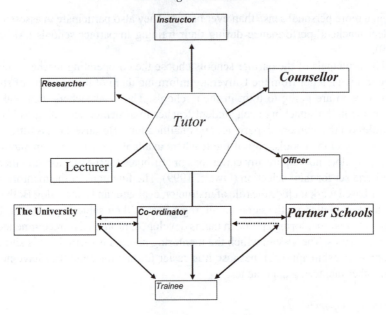

Figure 5.1   The tutors' functions in Pre-Service Teacher Training Course in Jordan

5. *Researchers and research assistants*. They conduct research studies and help other University Researchers to conduct theirs.

6. *Officers*. They do any work required by the administration, for example: organising the examinations and participating in organising conferences.

The headteachers of partner schools also participate in supervising the student teachers. They participate in the evaluation of student teachers' performance. The duties of the headteachers of the partner schools in pre-service teacher training course are to:

1. Act as a co-ordinator between the University and partner schools in selecting mentors and placing student teachers.

2. Support student teachers and mentors.

3. Motivate student teachers in their administrative performance like attending on time and obeying the schools rules.

4. Provide student teachers with the facilities they need.

Mentoring and monitoring the mentors work and performance with student teachers is the responsibility of the headteacher of the partner school and the university tutor. They are also responsible for co-ordination between the universities and partner schools. Training and guiding the student teachers inside the classroom is shared between mentors and tutors. The assessment of student teachers is shared between the mentors, tutors, and headteachers.

The Research Methodology

The subjects in the research were drawn from the student teacher population at the Jordanian State Universities, all the Primary Education Tutors at all the Universities, mentors in partner schools who agreed to take part in the study, and a random sample from the headteachers of partner schools. 178 questionnaires were distributed to all of the student teachers, and 146 were returned, a response rate of 80%, (12% Male and 88% Female). A random sample of headteachers of co-operating primary schools consisting of fourteen subjects who collaborated with the Jordanian Universities, twenty-four primary co-operating teachers (mentors) and eleven tutors were also involved. Both qualitative (interviews) and quantitative (questionnaire) methods were used.

The Findings

This chapter presents the findings related to the supervisory visits and tutors' roles in the school-based work of ITT and also reveals the findings related to the mentors' role in school-based work. The findings from the questionnaires and interviews addressed the following specific research question:

> To what extent are trainees satisfied with the roles of their mentors and tutors during their school-based work of ITT?

Supervision

The university tutors' role is to help the prospective teachers to benefit from the school-based work of ITT at partner schools and to develop their teaching competencies, by visiting them in the schools, observing their performance and evaluating them. In addition to the academic duties, the tutors have some social duties in helping prospective teachers to sort out their problems at schools and to build good relationship with school staff and their mentors (Yarmouk, 1996; Owais, 1999). The findings related to the tutor's role in the training course are divided into two main areas: the supervisory visits by tutors to student teachers in the partner schools and their role in training the student teachers.

Supervisory visits

In Jordan the student teacher is supposed to be visited and observed by tutors. Each of the student teachers officially receives 3 to 5 guidance and evaluation visits and a weekly workshop. Some supervisors also meet their student teachers in regularly scheduled group meetings. Tutors are required to follow the student teachers' teaching practice during their training at co-operating schools through the regular visit to student teachers (Mu'tah, 1996; Yarmouk, 1996; Jordanian University, 1996; Al-Sagrat, 1999). Table 5.1 shows the student teachers' satisfaction on the quality and quantity of supervisory visits during their placement at partner schools.

The findings of the questionnaire in Table 5.1 show that the number of supervision visits to student teachers at the partner schools was not felt to be sufficient by half (53%) the student teachers. 'Lack of supervision visits' was reported by student teachers as one of the major problems they faced in the partner schools. They claimed in the open-ended questions that there was no organisation or timetable for the tutors' visits, and they did not have any information about the supervisory visits. They used many comments to express their dissatisfaction for the supervision visits when they reported their problems and weaknesses of their field experience at partner schools such as: 'unexpected visits, late visits, lack of visits, lack of following-up from mentors and tutors'. These results indicate the need for on-going support from the university tutors in order to ensure that the quality of teaching and learning is consistently maintained, particularly as the tutors have expertise in their subjects, and have the main responsibility in the assessment and the decision about whether trainees have reached the expected or acceptable level of teaching competencies.

The mentors and headteachers of partner schools in the interviews expressed similar views about the lack of supervision visits and indicated that they considered the number of supervisory visits inadequate. One of the mentors said that:

'The tutor of my trainee visited him twice during the training term, and it is insufficient to give the trainee the guidance needed'

The tutors claimed that they visited their trainees between three to four visits per training term. One of the tutors said:

'We made our best to offer at least three supervision visits for each student teachers, and the majority of them received four visits'

The gap between the intention and the reality is clear. Tutors are required to visit their trainees between three to four visits each training term. In the way the tutors defended themselves and explained the lack of supervision visits, they revealed the

Table 5.1   Supervisory vists

Item	Agree		Disagree	
	F	%	F	%
The number of tutors visits is adequate	69	47%	77	53%
The variety of supervision visits is adequate	59	40%	87	60%

F: Frequencies of the sample. %: The percentages of the frequencies.

truth of the findings. The failure to fulfil their obligations was minimised by them. They consider it is due to the large load of trainees for each one of them. The ratio of trainee to tutor is approximately 20:1. They indicated that they do have not sufficient time to take care of their student teachers and to visit them more than two or three times at the partner schools. One of the tutors' recommendations was 'to reduce the number of student teachers for each tutor' to enable them to increase the supervisory visits to the student teachers. A tutor said that:

'We have a lot of student teachers, and they are distributed in many schools. Sometimes we cannot visit more than one or two student teachers per day'

A large number of partner schools are situated at such a distance from the university that it is impossible for tutors to visit more than one or two trainees per day. Some tutors claimed that they have a timetable for their visits to student teachers but they cannot announce it to the student teachers because they cannot guarantee their visits because of the unpredictable nature of their university commitments. The tutors also indicated that the student teachers did not inform them if they are going to be absent from schools. Four tutors justified unannounced visits because they want to observe their student teachers in a 'normal' situation. One of the tutors said that:

'The student teachers as a teacher trainee should be prepared at any time. We want to observe them in the normal situation'

Not only were the number of supervision visits held to be insufficient for the student teachers, but the variety of supervision visits were seen to be inadequate for the majority (60%) of student teachers, as shown in Table 5.1. There are two kinds of supervisory visits. The first one is the guidance visit that aims to support student teachers on how to teach and manage the teaching-learning process inside the classroom. The second kind is the evaluation visit that aims to assess the student teachers' performance in school-based work. The student teachers claimed that their tutors ignore the guidance visit and that all of the supervisory visits were used for assessment. The tutors mostly visit their student teachers as 'examiners' rather than trainers. Thirty-seven of the student teachers reported that 'all of the supervisory visits are for evaluation' and there is 'lack of guidance supervision visits', and they indicated that this type of visits makes them anxious. From the point of view of the student teachers all visits were like an examination, a threat. This affected the kind of the feedback the trainees receive from their tutors. There was no neutral support. The student teachers suggested that:

- The number of supervision visits should be increased.
- The supervision visits to placement should be at the beginning of the training term.
- The first two visits should be for guiding trainees not for evaluation.
- Trainees should be given warnings of visits.

• The number of supervision visits should be increased.

Tutors' guidance and feedback

Pajak (2001) emphasised that classroom observation and feedback have been the mainstays in the supervision of both pre-service and in-service teaching for many years and are likely to continue to play an important part in the ongoing quest to further the professional growth of beginning and experienced teachers. Table 5.2 shows the student teachers' responses about the tutors' guidance and the feedback they received at the end of the supervisory visits.

The tutors' guidance was seen to be sufficient by more than two thirds (79%) of the student teachers when it was recieved. Table 5.2 shows that 84% of the student teachers are satisfied with their tutors' feedback about their performance at the end of every supervision visit. When they did visit what was said was seen to be useful. This highlights the significance of the lack of formative visits. The tutors were capable of being helpful when there, but the ambiguity of the nature of the visits undermined their effectiveness.

In addition to the academic work, the tutors are required to support their student teachers at partner schools and to help them with any problems or obstacles with their mentors or with the partner school staff. The tutors are in the main responsible for student teachers during the school-based work. Table 5.2 shows that the majority of student teachers (64%) indicated that their tutors were helpful in sorting out their problems at partner schools when they did visit. A quarter (26%) were not happy with their tutors' role as supporters and in helping them with their problems at partner schools. This result may be related to the lack of supervisory visits to the student teachers or in not discussing the student teachers' problems in a neutral atmosphere. The American Association of Colleges for Teacher Education (AACTE, 1999) points out that tutors must consider not only the academic needs of student teachers but also their human needs and varied social circumstances.

In general the student teachers' responses in Table 5.2 related to the tutors' role in the school-based work indicated that they were happy with the nature of the tutors' guidance. But they were dissatisfied with the number of the supervisory visits and the purpose of these visits, since the majority of the supervisory visits are simply for assessment.

Table 5.2   Tutors' guidance and feedback

Item	Agree		Disagree	
	F	%	F	%
I feel the tutor guidance was not very helpful	31	21%	115	79%
The feedback which my tutor gave me at the end of every visit was not helpful	24	16%	122	84%
My tutor helped me with my problems at school	108	64%	38	26%

F: Frequencies of the sample. %: The percentages of the frequencies.

Table 5.3   Mentors and Training instructions

Item	Agree		Disagree	
	F	%	F	%
My mentor fulfilled the training programme instructions	55	38%	91	62%

F: Frequencies of the sample. %: The percentages of the frequencies.

School-based Mentoring

The mentoring process in Jordan is a new arrangement for pre-service teacher training courses and it is new for the schoolteachers. The mentors, during the school-based work, are expected to:

- Observe the student teachers performance and stay with them in the class in the beginning and try to leave them alone at the end of the training course.
- Attend the trainees lessons and leave them alone step by step.
- Give the student teachers chances to use a variety of teaching methods which are appropriate to the schools needs and the needs of pupils (Yarmouk, 1996; Owais, 1999).

The duties of mentors are very similar to the tutors' duties, working directly with student teachers and giving them feedback about their performance, as well as helping them with any difficulties they may face during their training. The duties of tutors and mentors are the same regardless of their subject specialisation. Adey (1997) indicated that student teachers during their school-experience preferred mentors who would give them direct professional guidance about teaching and provide them with organised and structured opportunities for learning. Table 5.3 presents the trainees' opinions about the extent to which their mentors confirmed this intention.

Table 5.3 shows that the majority of student teachers' responses (62%) indicate that the mentors did not abide by the training programme instructions. 15 student teachers reported that their mentors left them alone inside the classroom from the beginning and did not observe them. Nor did the trainees observe the mentors. Tutors also indicated that the mentors did not follow the training plan. It appeared that instead of a judicious blend of instruction and trust, knowing when to intervene and when to leave them alone, the mentors followed either one extreme or the other. They either abandoned the student to their own devices or were anxious is seeing everything they did, presumably correcting them as they did so. Sometimes they set tasks beyond the capabilities of the student teachers. like controlling the classes and drawing up timetables. Tutors (eight of eleven) felt that mentors were not familiar with their role, and that the University did not explain the responsibilities of mentors clearly. One of tutors said that:

'The mentors did not have a clear idea about their real role in the training course, and they did not co-operate with tutors in applying the training plan'

Another tutor said that:

'The mentors did not know the stages of training course. Some of them sent students to teach in the classroom alone from the beginning of the training semester before the observation period, and the student teachers cannot manage the classes by themselves'

The universities stated that the mentors should give the student teachers opportunities to use a variety of teaching methods appropriate to the school's needs and the needs of pupils (Yarmouk, 1996). Twenty-three student teachers, however, reported that their mentors did not give them the chance to practise their own approaches and experiment with different teaching methods. A trainee reported that:

'The mentors did not give us the opportunity to use and develop our own teaching strategies during the teaching practice phase'

This finding was supported by the interviews in which tutors expressed the same view. They indicated that some mentors did not discus the link between theory and practice in teaching, and did not encourage the students to find their own best teaching style. Instead, they appeared to want the student teachers to copy them. One of the tutors commented:

'The mentors should realise that they should not force student teachers or persuade them to copy their strategies of teaching, but they should understand that their role is to help trainees to try and develop their own ways in teaching'

Three of the tutors and 15 student teachers emphasised that the mentors rejected the student teachers' opinions and did not accept any comments on their teaching from student teachers, because they believed they are more experienced and knowledgeable. One of the tutors pointed out that:

'Some mentors did not accept criticism from student teachers, and they consider themselves as knowing every thing related to teaching, and they do not make any mistakes'

Owais (1999) indicated that student teachers demanded that their co-operating teachers should be willing to accept criticism and improve their own knowledge and experience as well as being experienced, knowledgeable and helpful.

Mentors' guidance and feedback

The main responsibilities of mentors in school-based work are to discuss academic issues related to student teachers' performance in the classroom and provide them with constructive feedback (Owais, 1998). Kostner et al (1998) described the feedback as:

'Offering a specific description of observed and demonstrable behaviour of the other person, one's own experiencing of that behaviour, and the effects it has on oneself, in such a way that the recipient is able to recognise and accept the information' (p. 82) (Kostner, Korthagen and Wubbels, 1998)

This description of feedback sees it as a two-way interaction between mentors and mentees where the student teacher also has a role to play. Positive and constructive feedback should be given to student teachers in helping them to become aware of their strengths and weaknesses, and to reveal the teaching-learning process (Ismail, 2001). Table 5.4 shows the student teachers' responses about the mentors' guidance and feedback:

Table 5.4 shows that more than half of the student teachers indicated that their mentors' guidance about their teaching practice, as well as the feedback they received from them, was insufficient and unhelpful in the development of their teaching skills. This indicated the weaknesses of the mentors in their professional role. The mentors were negative and critical rather than constructive. They focussed on the negative skills of trainees in order to show them that they are more experienced and capable.

The mentors should be positive in providing trainees with feedback, and they should appreciate their performance and encourage them to develop their skills. Adey (1997) asserted that the skilful mentor should make student teachers feel one of the school staff, be welcoming in the classroom, encouraging pupils to behave with student teachers as they behave with their own teachers.

The mentors were seen to be unqualified for the training task by half (55%) the student teachers. This result agreed with Dunne and Bennett's (1997) results in the UK that indicated that although mentoring is a very influential role it is often poorly conceived. Her Majesty Inspectors (1993) reported that many mentors are unclear how to help their trainees, and unfamiliar with the content of the trainees in the training institution (Dunne and Bennett, 1997).

The mentors' role is very influential in the pre-service teacher training courses, not as it should be, but as a negative and depressing effect. One can see from the above findings that the mentoring process in Jordan is very weak, and many mentors do not show any commitment to their role or are not serious in their task. Why were they seen to be unqualified by their mentees and tutors? Why did mentors not follow the training instruction or plan? Why were they having a negative rather than a constructive influence?

The mentors claimed that they did not have a clear idea about the training plan, and the universities did not provide this in advance or at the start of the training term. They complained about the lack of meetings between the programme staff in schools and the universities to explain their duties and the training procedures. One of the mentors commented that:

Table 5.4   Mentors' guidance and feedback

Item	Agree		Disagree	
	F	**%**	**F**	**%**
I feel the mentor guidance was not helpful	85	58%	61	42%
The feedback which my mentor gave me at the end of every lesson was not helpful	82	56%	64	44%
I consider my mentor qualified for the task of training	66	45%	80	55%

F: Frequencies of the sample. %: The percentages of the frequencies.

'We did not receive any formal documents from the university about the training plan or our responsibilities'

Five mentors indicated that the university sent a small booklet about the training instructions, but the interactions were insufficient and it was ambiguous. One of the mentors commented that:

'There is a broad statement about our duties and the training methods, but there is no guidance about which methods we can use to train our mentees'

Four tutors supported the mentors' comments about the lack of contact between schools and universities. Three tutors also indicated that the universities do not follow or observe the mentor's performance during the training course.

According to the Initial Teacher Training instructions, the tutors are supposed to follow the mentors' performance during the training course, but they have no formal authority to do this. Tutors indicated that the universities do not give mentors any incentive for their co-operation. All of these reasons may play a part in preventing mentors from following the training plan and instructions.

The majority of tutors claimed that there are no criteria for the selection of mentors, and no workshops or short courses to train them. The universities do not select the mentors; they are selected by the headteachers of the partner schools. Any teacher could be a mentor regardless of his or her experience and qualifications. One of the tutors commented:

'The universities do not select the mentor, and they give their attention to the place of partner schools. Therefore any teacher in the selected schools could be a mentor regardless of his or her experience or qualifications'

It is interesting to note that seven tutors agreed with the student teachers' responses and they indicated that the lack of mentors who have experience as trainers is one of the weaknesses of the course. One of the tutors said:

'There are no selection criteria for mentors. We take any mentor who is available at partner schools regardless to his experience and qualifications, and we found some mentors did not follow the training instructions and stages'

Five tutors raised the issue of the lack of workshops or training courses for mentors and the lack of incentives for mentors to give student teachers more attention. Eleven mentors during the interviews complained about the lack of training and guidance. Elliot and Calderhead, (1995) indicated that the main problems facing mentoring revolve around the following key issues:

- Understanding the nature of the mentor's role;
- Coping with a close interpersonal relationship with the mentee;
- Feeling adequately trained and befriended;
- Being realistic about the attitudes of staff not selected to be mentors;
- Accepting responsibility for making judgements and assessments, and communicating these to the trainee;
- Coming to terms with the demanding nature of the role, knowledge and emotional commitment.

The tutors recommended improving the mentoring process by creating criteria for selecting mentors and providing training courses. One tutor suggested that:

'We should send our student teachers to mentors who are qualified and sufficiently experienced in teaching by selecting them according to their professional records in teaching at the Ministry of Education'

Mentors and tutors emphasised that the universities should demonstrate clearly the instructions and training plan for the school based work, and the responsibilities for both mentors and headteachers from the beginning of the training course, to give them more time to understand their roles before they start mentoring student teachers.

In general the findings show that the participants felt that the mentors' role in the ITT is poorly defined and carried out. They attributed this to the following reasons:

1. The mentors were not familiar with their responsibilities.
2. There are no incentives for mentors as a reward for their co-operation in school-based work.
3. There are no training courses or workshops for mentors to train them in how to guide their trainees, and how to give them effective feedback on their teaching performance.
4. The majority of mentors do not hold a university degree.
5. There are no checks on the mentors' performance.

It was recommended by some tutors that the selection of mentors should be according to specific standards which depend on their performance in schools. In addition they recommended providing mentors with some training in the mentoring process.

The Mentors' Role in Supporting Student Teachers

In addition to the mentors' professional role in training student teachers for teaching, they have some social or counselling duties. They have to:

> 'Solve and facilitate any problems that the student teachers might face in their practice; and help the student teachers in any academic or non-academic activities they want to do' (Yarmouk, 1996, p. 5).

The duties of the mentors as laid down emphasise their social role in helping with social or personal problems of student teachers. The following Table 5.5 shows the student teachers' responses about the mentors' social role.

Table 5.5 indicated that for the majority of student teachers (64%) their mentors were helpful and co-operated in solving their general problems at school. The findings show that the rest of the student teachers were dissatisfied with their mentors' support. This result might be attributed to the fact that some mentors were unhappy with the universities, because they do not receive any money or incentives. Moreover, it is compulsory for them to accept and monitor student teachers. Adey (1997) indicated that the relationship between mentors and student teachers should be a friendly and trusting relationship from the early days of the student teachers' school-based experience. The mentor is a critical friend without whom effective initial professional development cannot take place.

Table 5.6 shows that virtually 60% of student teachers indicated that there is gap between mentors and tutors in their instructions and guidance. This can be attributed to the lack of meetings and collaboration between the mentors and tutors. One of the mentors commented that:

> 'The tutor never discusses with me anything related to our trainee. I did not see his comments about the trainee's performance, and he used to ask the headteachers about his daily attendance and training'

Table 5.5   The mentors role as a social supporter

Item	Agree		Disagree	
	F	**%**	**F**	**%**
My mentor helped me with my problems at school	94	64%	52	36%

F: Frequencies of the sample. %: The percentages of the frequencies.

Table 5.6   The agreement between mentors and tutors instructions

Item	Agree		Disagree	
	F	%	F	%
I find that my tutor's and mentor's guidance is always the same	60	41%	86	59%

F: Frequencies of the sample. %: The percentages of the frequencies.

The mentors emphasised that the tutors and mentors did not share their experience and information about their student teachers, and the discussions and tutorials between student teachers, tutors and mentors are held separately. Five mentors claimed that they have no plan about what and how they are going to train student teachers.

The result is that the mentors focus on their own experience in teaching and ignore new knowledge and educational theories. Tutors focus on the links between the theoretical background of the trainees and the actual practice inside the classroom, when it should clearly be the mentors who do this since they are the practitioners who know their pupils and the constraints of having a large class and a demanding syllabus.

The findings show that the supervision visits to student teachers at the partner schools was not sufficient in number and variety. Tutors used the visits to student teachers to examine rather than for formative development. The student teachers' responses indicated that the mentors did not abide by the training programme instructions, and saw mentors as unqualified for their training needs.

There is a consistency about the messages of poor relationships which is disturbing. Ambiguity of purpose, a lack of mutual respect, and a lack of real understanding gives student teachers a negative impression of schools even as they embark on their careers. They are allowed into school grudgingly. They rarely discuss the pedagogy as part of the excitement of teaching and learning, and they are sometimes made use of in an insensitive way. The experiences vary, but the overall fact is that little attention is given to the importance of the teaching practice and the needs of the student teacher within it.

Many of the school-based mentors appeared to be unqualified to work with student teachers and unfamiliar with their roles and what was expected of them. The student teachers felt that the mentors' guidance and feedback about the teaching processes was inadequate. The mentors did not use appropriate up to date methods and did not follow the training plan for the school-based work provided by the universities. There are at present no criteria for selecting mentors and a lack of training courses or workshops for mentors. Duquette's study (1994) revealed that there is a lack of ability on the part of the mentors' to explain what they are doing and why. Little seems to have changed since then. Mentors require initial in-service training and more explanation of their roles before they start mentoring the student teachers. This should be provided by the universities. In England, Her Majesty's Inspectors

(1993) reported that many mentors are still unclear how to help their trainees, and unfamiliar with the content of the trainees courses in the training institution (Dunne & Bennet, 1997). This is despite mentor training courses being provided in the UK. Hawamleh (1999) indicated that the Islamic education mentors tend to neglect some of the important activities that are needed such as giving and receiving feedback and encouraging the trainees to reflect on this. Mentors are in an ideal position to act as positive role models in these areas.

It was found that some mentors did not encourage their student teachers to link theory and practice or to try their own ways of teaching. The research has confirmed that student teachers are provided with few opportunities to be independent and to apply their own ideas, because mentors did not allow them to practise their own ways of teaching. Mentors prefer their student teachers to copy them. Mentors often reject the student teachers' opinions and are not prepared to accept any comments on their teaching from student teachers, because of their greater experience. Student teachers have few chances to discuss and apply their own ideas as generated from their university course (Owais, 1999). Mentors tend to use the 'apprenticeship' approach. This approach is the oldest approach, and although it may be appropriate for the very first stages of the mentoring process, it will not enable trainees to develop as critical, reflective practitioners.

Whilst it is clear that there are many difficulties with mentoring even in the most sophisticated systems and with experienced teachers (Vozzo et al, 2004) there is no reason to avoid addressing some major issues. We know that mentoring can make a difference (Fletcher and Barrett, 2004). Certain reforms could, therefore, be initiated.

The problem is that it takes years to develop the personnel to make a system function, however well it is planned. The actions that could be taken are clear.

The tutors should increase their supervision visits to student teachers and to give them more time for feedback and guidance. Supervisory visits to the placement schools should take place early in the teaching practice to discover the range of work which the student teachers are expected to undertake, and discuss this with the head teacher and mentor.

The communications and links between tutors, mentors and universities should be developed and enhanced to keep all informed of the student teachers' progress in their training. Sweeny (1994) emphasised that mentors must know what is expected of them and the student teachers, they should communicate frequently with ITT leaders or co-ordinators using dialogue journals, personal conferences, frequent phone calls, letters, or a combination of several of these.

Mentoring by experienced teachers is critical. For mentoring to contribute to educational reform, it must be connected to good teaching (NCRTL, 1995). Booth (1995) indicated that simply placing trainees in schools without qualified mentors and adequate mentoring support gives trainees little chance to develop their teaching skills and competencies, especially when they are looking for support in the early stages of their work in schools. Bird (1993) asserted that mentors should possess a wide range of knowledge and experience to enable a broad view of approaches and practice to be given. They should be able to introduce the theory which must underpin good practice, and to show the importance of research and its effect in the classroom. Ismail (2001) maintained that if mentors show a professional attitude, and are well-trained and competent in their field of work, it would leave a positive impression on the student teachers, which would motivate them to be more effective as teachers. Selecting mentors should be from the basis of experience and teaching competencies that would enable them to fully contribute to the success of the pre-service teacher training courses.

Mentors in Jordan should be trained how to co-operate with the student teachers and assess their performance. They also need to have explained to them their duties and responsibilities, and be given a clear description of the training stages, through documentation such as a mentor's handbook. The mentoring process needs to be organised as part of the partnership between the schools and universities. Both mentors and tutors need training related to the purposes of teacher induction, working with adult learners, the stages of teacher development, the concerns and needs of beginning teachers, clinical supervision, classroom observation, conferencing skills, teacher reflection, and fostering self esteem and self-reliance in the novice teacher.

Mentors should go beyond allowing student teachers to copy their own practices and they should encourage them to experiment with new approaches, and to try to develop their own style. They should be flexible in dealing with their mentees, and they should also value their ideas and allow them to experiment.

Organising workshops for mentors at the beginning of school-based work of ITT to train them in how to observe and analyse the observation lessons is essential. The observed trainees must be fully aware of when they will be observed, what the observer is looking for and why the observation is taking place. The observer must be fully trained and prepared for the observation, so that he or she knows exactly what is required from the observation (Rae, 1997). Learning how to observe an experienced teacher and identify the different skills that he or she is using is an achievement in itself (Adey, 1997).

References

AACTE (American Association of Colleges for Teacher Education). *Comprehensive Teacher Education: A Handbook of Knowledge*. Washington: America. ERIC-NO: ED427006.

Adey, K. (1997), 'First Impressions Do Count Mentoring Student Teachers', *Teacher Development*, vol. 1(1), pp. 123–133.

AL-Hawamleh, M. (1999), *An Evaluative Study of the Mentoring of Islamic Education Student Teachers in Jordanian Public Universities*, Unpublished M.A Thesis, University of Huddersfield.

AL-Sagarat, K. (1999), *Attitudes of Student Teachers in Mu'tah University in the South of Jordan Towards the Practical Education Programme*. Unpublished M.A Thesis, University of Huddersfield.

Balch, P. and Balch, P. (1987), *The Co-operating Teacher: A Practical Approach for the Supervision of Student Teachers*. University of Press America, USA.

Bird, E. (1993), 'Whither...? The First Year of Teaching', in E. Bird, M. Grenfell, V. Harris, B. Jones and V. Stone (eds), *Partners: A guide to School-Based Initial Teacher Training in Modern Languages*. Centre for Information on Language Teaching and Research, London, UK.

Booth, M. (1995), 'The Effectiveness and Role of the Mentor in School: The Students' View', in T. Kerry and S. Mayes (eds), *Issues in Mentoring*, Open University, London, New York.

Bridge, F. (1997), 'Exploring the Interface Between Mentor and Protégé', in S. Joan (ed), *Mentoring- the New Panacea? Mentor and Protégé*, Dereham, UK.

Bush, T., Coleman, M., Wall, D. and West-Burnham, J. (1996), 'Mentoring and Continuing Professional Development', in D. McIntyre and H. Hagger (eds), *Mentors in Schools: Developing the Professional of Teaching*, London, UK.

Campbell, A. and Kane, I. (1996), 'Mentoring and Primary School Culture', in D. McIntyre and H. Hagger (eds), *Mentors in Schools: Developing the Professional of Teaching*, London, UK.

Cameron-Jones, M. and O'Hara, P. (1995), 'Mentors Perceptions of Their Roles with Students in Initial Teacher Training', *Cambridge Journal of Education*, vol. 25, pp. 189–206.

Clutterbuck, D. (1999), *Every One Needs a Mentor: Fostering Talent at Work*, 2nd Edition, Institute of Personal and Development, London, UK.

Dagmar, K. (1992), *Supervision of Student Teachers*, ERIC, Washington, USA.

David, K., Mtetwa, J. and Thompson, J. (2000), 'Towards Decentralised and More School-Focused Teacher Preparation and Professional Development in Zimbabwe: the Role of Mentoring', *Journal on In-Service Education*, vol. 26(2), pp. 311–328.

Dunne, E. and Bennett, N. (1997), 'Mentoring Processes in School-based Training', *Educational Research Journal*, vol. 23(2), pp. 225–237.

Duquette, C. (1994), 'The Role of the Co-operating Teacher in A School-Based', *Teaching & Teacher Education*, vol. 10(3), pp. 345–353.

Duquette, C. (1998), 'Perceptions of Mentor Teachers in School-Based Teacher Education Programs', *Journal of Education for Teaching*, vol. 24(2), pp. 179–191.

Edwards, A. and Collison, J. (1996), *Mentoring and developing practice in primary schools. Supporting student teacher learning in schools*, Open University Press, UK.

Elliot, B. and Calderhead, J. (1995), 'Mentoring for Teachers Development Possibilities and Caveats', in T. Kerry and S. Mayes (eds), *Issues in Mentoring*, Open University, London, New York.

Fagan, M. and Waiter, G. (1982), 'Mentoring among Teachers', *Journal of Educational Research*, vol. 76(2), pp. 113–117.

Fletcher, S. and Barrett, A. (2004), 'Developing Effective beginning teachers through mentor-based induction', *Mentoring and Tutoring*, vol. 12(3), pp. 336–351.

Franke, A. (1996), 'Conceptions of Mentoring: An Empirical Study of Conceptions of Mentoring During the School-Based Teacher Education', *Teaching & Teacher Education*, vol. 12(6), pp. 627–641.

Gusky, T. (1986), 'Staff Development and the Process of Teacher Change', *Educational Research*, vol. 15(5), pp. 5–15.

Haggarty, L. (1995), 'Identifying the complexities of school-based teacher education', *Teacher Development*.

Hagger, H., Burn, K. and McIntyre, D. (1995), *The School Mentor Handbook: Essential Skills and Strategies for Working with Student Teachers*, Kogan Page Limited, London, UK.

Hawkey, K. (1998), 'Mentor Pedagogy and Student Teacher Professional Development: A Study of Two Mentoring Relationships', *Teaching and Teacher Education*, vol. 14(6), pp. 657–670.

Ismail, N. (2001), *The Mentoring Processes of Primary ESL Student Teachers in Malaysia*, Ph.D. Thesis, the University of Exeter, England.

Jones, B. (1993), 'How Trainers Can Help Trainees Achieve Competence', in E. Bird, M. Grenfell, V. Harris, B. Jones and V. Stone (eds), *Partners: A guide to School-Based Initial Teacher Training in Modern Languages*, Centre for Information on Language Teaching and Research, London, UK.

Jones, M. (2001), 'Mentors' Perceptions of Their Roles in School-based Teacher Training in England and Germany', *Journal of Education for Teaching*, vol. 27(1), pp. 75–94.

Jordanian University. (1996), *Practical Teaching Programme the Presents and the Future*, Faculty of Educational Sciences, Amman, Jordan. (Informal document).

Kerry, T. and Mayes, S. (1995), *Issues in Mentoring*, Open University, London, New York.

Lunenberg, M. (1999), 'New Qualifying Requirements for the Mentoring student Teachers in the Netherlands', *European Journal of Teacher Education*, vol. 242(2), pp. 159–172.

McNally, P. and Martin, S. (1998), 'Support and Challenge In Learning to Teach: The Role of the Mentor', *Asia-Pacific Journal of Teacher Education*, vol. 26(1), pp. 39–55.

Mu'tah University. (1998), *Practical Educational Programme*. Statistics on Primary Students Teachers for the Second Semester 1998/99. Faculty of Educational Science.

NCRTL (The National Centre for Research on Teacher Learning). (1995), *NCRTL Explores Learning from Mentors: A Study Update*. Office of Educational Research and Improvement (OREI), U, S Department of Education.

Oweis, F. (1999), *The Roles of the Science Co-operating Teachers in Initial Teacher Training at the University of Jordan*, Unpublished M.A Thesis, Leeds University. UK.

Rae, L. (1997), *How to Measure Training Effectiveness*, 3rd Edition, the University Press, Cambridge, UK.

Shaw, R. (1995), 'Mentoring', in T. Kerry and S. Mayes (1995). *Issues in*

Mentoring,Open University, London, New York.

Stanulis, R.N. (1994), 'Fading to a Whisper: One Mentor's Story of Sharing Her Wisdom without Telling Answers', *Journal of Teacher Education*, vol. 45(4), pp. 31–38.

Stanulis, R. (1995), 'Classroom Teachers As Mentors: Possibilities for Participation in A Professional Development School Context', *Teaching and Teacher education*, vol. 11(4), pp. 331–344.

Sweeny, B. (1994), 'A New Teacher Mentoring Knowledge Base of Best Practices A Summary of Lessons Learned From Practitioners', http://www.teachermentors. com

Tauer, S. (1998), 'The Mentor-Protege Relationship and Its Impact on teacher Education', *Teaching and Teacher Education*, vol. 14(2), pp. 205–218.

Vozzo, L., Abuson, P., Steele, F. and Watson, K. (2004), 'Mentoring retrained teachers; estending the web', *Mentoring and Tutoring*, vol. 12(3), pp. 367–381.

Wang, J. (2001), 'Contexts of Mentoring and Opportunities for Learning to Teach: A Comparative Study of Mentoring Practice', *Teaching and Teacher Education*, vol. 17(4), pp. 51–73.

Yarmouk University. (1996), *Pathway of Practical Programme*. Faculty of Education & Fine Arts, Irbid, Jordan.

Chapter 6

Mentoring in the Induction Systems of Five Countries: A Sum Greater Than Its Parts

Edward D. Britton

This chapter describes commonalities across the induction systems in five countries, as found in a recent multi-year, cross-national study. Educators around the world are realizing that helping new teachers learn more about teaching is an important investment, one that can yield enhanced instruction throughout a career lifetime.

The study team interviewed our colleagues in over a dozen countries that have participated in the Third International Mathematics and Science Study (TIMSS). Many contacts reported that weak or no teacher induction programs existed in their countries. However, they had a rapidly growing conviction of the need to strengthen the learning of their beginning teachers. In contrast, some countries are ahead of the game in providing more comprehensive teacher induction. China (Shanghai only), France, Japan, New Zealand and Switzerland became the locations for our research, which we focused on beginning mathematics and science teachers at the secondary level (both lower and upper secondary levels).

What is the relationship of mentoring and induction? The author is not familiar with a shared meaning for these terms among educators within a given country, let alone cross-nationally. For this chapter, mentoring is considered an important activity that is part of a larger induction system, as illustrated in Figure 6.1. Until the fairly recent surge of interest among many countries in empowering beginning teachers, induction often was viewed as a limited initial effort with beginning teachers, such as orienting them as new employees; in contrast, mentoring was a significant, sustained effort. In the five countries, however, the induction systems were the even larger enterprise, within which mentoring functioned as a critical, substantial ingredient.

The chapter subtitle alludes to the following crucial understanding, or disclaimer, to keep in mind throughout. For the sake of making the chapter manageable, it discusses and illustrates particular aspects of each country's induction of beginning teachers. However, the chapter space is not adequate for fully portraying how the sample particulars within a country in fact add up to a whole system. The volume *Comprehensive Teacher Induction: Systems for Early Career Learning* describes the entirety of each country's induction system (Britton, Paine, Pimm & Raizen, 2003).

In part to help mitigate this pitfall, the chapter begins with an initial description of mentoring and other induction strategies in New Zealand, providing at least

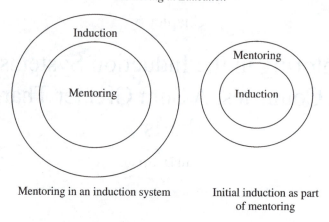

Mentoring in an induction system　　　　　Initial induction as part
　　　　　　　　　　　　　　　　　　　　　　of mentoring

Figure 6.1　Relationship of mentoring in the induction of beginning teachers

one portrait of an induction system. More importantly, this description serves as a backdrop for illustrating the central points of the chapter. A short outline of the research study behind this chapter helps one gauge the foundation of its arguments. After the study description, our conception of comprehensive teacher induction is described. The majority of the chapter addresses this question: What are the shared characteristics and strategies among the robust induction systems in these five quite different countries? Each of nine characteristics is discussed in turn, and illustrated by examples from various of the five countries.

Illustrating Comprehensive Induction: School-based Induction in New Zealand

The universal experience of beginning teachers is to encounter pitfalls at every turn. But in many New Zealand schools, beginning science teachers also find help in every direction (Britton, Raizen and Huntley, 2003). New Zealand's national Ministry of Education requires that schools give first-year teachers 20 percent paid release time, and the ministry provides the funds for it. Typically, that means new teachers are assigned four classes rather than five, which gives them three to five more free periods a week than their more experienced colleagues. In 2002, the government strengthened the induction programme by extending 10 percent release time to second-year teachers. New teachers in New Zealand are usually not assigned to the most difficult classes. In addition, all schools in New Zealand must develop an 'Advice and Guidance' program for their first- and second-year teachers (Moskowitz and Kennedy, 1997; Teacher Registration Board, 1997, 1993).

　　Beginning teachers receive help from many sources, especially within their schools but also from outside, as shown in Figure 6.2. Novice science teachers are assigned one primary mentor, usually the science department head. Department heads formally and informally observe beginners' classes, hold one-on-one meetings

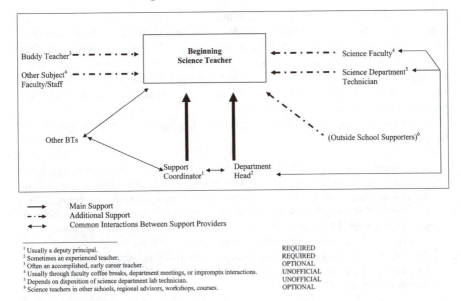

Legend:

→ Main Support
- · → Additional Support
← → Common Interactions Between Support Providers

[1] Usually a deputy principal.   REQUIRED
[2] Sometimes an experienced teacher.   REQUIRED
[3] Often an accomplished, early career teacher.   OPTIONAL
[4] Usually through faculty coffee breaks, department meetings, or impromptu interactions.   UNOFFICIAL
[5] Depends on disposition of science department lab technician.   UNOFFICIAL
[6] Science teachers in other schools, regional advisors, workshops, courses.   OPTIONAL

Figure 6.2   Support providers for beginning Secondary Science teachers in New Zealand

with them, permit beginners to observe their teaching, arrange for novices to observe other teachers, and alert them to professional development opportunities outside the school. The department head is the person in the induction system that works with beginning teachers on matters related to mathematics and science content or how to teach it.

Every school has an AG coordinator, usually a deputy principal, who is the novices' second main source of support. The administrators' flexible schedules give them the availability to meet beginning teachers for one-on-one meetings whenever the novices have free periods. Coordinators also bring together new teachers on a regular basis, typically every two weeks, to grapple with whatever practical, emotional, or other needs the teachers are facing. Thus, beginning teachers help each other through these facilitated, peer-support meetings.

Buddy teachers usually are a secondary source of support, and their roles vary. Some buddy teachers help substantively – for example, by observing novices' classes and offering advice. Other support coordinators have a quite different view of the buddy teacher's role: 'I assign a buddy teacher who lives nearby and can give them a ride if need be, bring some work home to them if they're sick, etc.'

Although not a formal part of the induction programme, other people in the New Zealand schools support beginning teachers; these include other science teachers, science department laboratory technicians, and teachers in other subjects. The most common way that other science teachers help is through informal means such as conversations at 'interval' and lunchtime. All secondary schools have a 15–20-minute interval in the morning when the entire school faculty comes to the faculty lounge for coffee and refreshments while the pupils have a recess. In our school visits, it appeared that over 90 percent of the teachers regularly show up for these collective breaks. As a result, new teachers have a chance to briefly discuss anything on their mind with virtually any other teacher. A similar phenomenon occurs at lunchtime, although less so because attendance is lower (about 50–80 percent). Beyond the school, regional science advisers and leaders of workshops or short courses at colleges and universities also aid novices.

The following comments by one second-year teacher illustrate the support found by novices in New Zealand.

> 'Four people were especially helpful last year. Dorothy [her department head] was brilliant. Any questions and I'd go straight in and ask, and she was happy to answer. I still do. The second person was Glenda [her buddy teacher], the biology teacher next door. She was the first line of attack because she was next door. I'd run across to her and she was full of advice. The third was Irene, who helped me with astronomy and geology. Mr. Hastings [her AG coordinator] absolutely was looking out for me, and the meetings he ran for all of us [beginning teachers in the school] were really valuable. Officially, Dorothy and Glenda were assigned to me by Mr. Hastings. But with Irene, it just turned out that she was a lot of help to me too.'

One aspect of the New Zealand educational system that makes beginning teacher support programmes effective is a commitment throughout the educational system to beginning teacher support. Players at all levels of the system assume that new teachers have particular needs and, therefore, that the system must pay explicit attention to addressing them. Many new teachers state that they feel free to approach most anyone in their department for advice. For example, new teachers feel they can ask other teachers to drop in to see how they teach some specific topic or activity. This strong culture of support makes it easier to implement beginning teacher support programmes and activities.

About the Study

Countries were selected for study because their induction efforts were robust, and each induction system had been established for 10 or more years. In New Zealand, for example, they have been doing this for more than 25 years. Researchers made at least three field visits per country, for at least ten days per visit. More often, visits lasted two or three weeks. Two or more researchers collected data during at least one of the field visits, which collectively constituted two to three person-months of fieldwork. Colleagues from each country informed and oriented our work, the initial design of the study and the fieldwork itself – but data analysis and writing were our own responsibility. As drafts of cases emerged, we solicited feedback from insiders within each country. The four lead researchers all work in anglophone North American research settings, in one or more of these fields: mathematics education, science education, teacher education, comparative education. However, all of them have experience conducting international research, as well as previous experience observing teaching and conducting interviews with pupils, teachers and teacher educators. In the non-English language settings of our study, case studies were led by researchers with prior experience of that country's educational system. Case leaders were also fluent speakers and readers of the relevant languages.

Comparative education has a long and not entirely illustrious history of looking beyond one's national borders at educational practices and institutions 'abroad'. As researchers, we were mindful from the start of the dangers of armchair travel, of the potential to create 'others' of those we studied, others about whom simple generalizations could be made. We were also alert to the seductive appeal of simple borrowing of practices, programs and even policies. Equally, we do not wish to pretend we were 'insiders', with both the strengths and weaknesses that that can bring.

Defining Comprehensive Teacher Induction

In the U.S., 'mentoring' has come to stand for a prevalent remedy to a problem that tends to remain unexamined. It is variously seen as insufficient experience of the practicalities of teaching, inadequate information about local practices and customs in the particular school or incomplete knowledge of various sorts of instructional practices. While the surface analyses vary somewhat, they all share the common presumption that the novice arrives lacking something, arrives equipped with a particular *deficit*: 'induction' – here, meaning the assistance of a mentor – is somehow to make up for this deficiency.

However, induction can be more than simply the filling in of gaps. Teacher induction can be – and in some places is – far more than the mere orientation of beginning teachers at the start of the school year or the provision of on-going practical support throughout the school year. Induction programmes can recognize that even fully prepared beginning teachers need to learn (and can use help in learning) more about teaching. This is so, even though they could not have learnt these things before starting to teach – hence neither they nor their teacher preparation programmes can be said to have failed in this regard. Induction can go beyond immediate teacher support and survival to assist beginners to learn more about how to: assess pupil understanding; craft a lesson; develop a repertoire of instructional practices; gain a deeper knowledge and broader awareness of subject-matter issues; work with parents; and more.

Given this claim, we argue it is important to recognize there are many possible goals for induction and we can imagine systems as being more or less *comprehensive* in their attempts to attend to them. It is but a step to imagine an underlying continuum. Figure 6.3 illustrates possible distinctions between what we have termed 'more limited' and 'more comprehensive' teacher induction.

As Feiman-Nemser (2001) has observed, induction can be seen not simply as a programme, but a phase, a period of time, a process, and a system. As a *phase*, it brings certain unique needs and opportunities. It is also a *period of time*, like

Programme Feature	Limited Induction	Comprehensive Induction
goals	focus on teacher orientation, support, enculturation, retention	also promotes career learning, enhances teaching quality
policies	provides optional participation and modest time, usually unpaid	requires participation and provides substantial, paid time
overall program design	employs a limited number of ad hoc induction providers and activities	plans an induction system involving a complementary set of providers and activities
induction as a transitional phase	treats induction as an isolated phase, without explicit attention to teachers' prior knowledge or feature development	considers the influence of teachers preparation and professional development on induction program design
initial teaching conditions	limited attention to initial teaching conditions	attention to assigned courses, pupil, non-teaching duties
level of effort	invests limited total effort, or all effort in few providers, activities	requires substantial overall effort
resources	does not provide resources sufficient to meet program goals	provides adequate resources to meet program goals
levels of the education system involved	involves some level of the system, perhaps in isolation	involves all relevant levels of system in articulated roles
length of program	one year or less	more than one year
sources of support	primarily or solely uses one mentor	uses multiple, complementary induction providers
conditions for novices and providers	usually attends to learning conditions for novices	also provides good conditions and training for providers
activities	uses a few types of induction activities	uses a set of articulated, varied activities

Table 6.1   Key features of limited versus comprehensive induction programmes

adolescence, one with boundaries that are socially and culturally constructed, but clearly marked off. Consider the construction of the concept of 'adolescence'. That term spawned a set of scholarly questions, professional associations and specialists to pursue them, and has had among its institutional consequences the creation of the modern middle and high school (or lower and upper secondary school). But, today, most lay people take the notion of adolescence for granted. It simply describe a particular period in a person's life, with its distinctive characteristics, dilemmas and needs. It is possible to see 'induction' as a comparably constructed category, equally signaling a specific phase in the life-span of a teacher, one that brings with it unique challenges, requirements and needs. Some writing in France refers to 'stagiaire' (beginning) teachers in terms of their being 'the adolescents of the profession'.

The induction *process* supports teachers' further acquisition of skill and knowledge, as well as the development of certain habits of mind – teacher learning that can only occur in the course of teaching itself, or at least alongside and in conjunction with actual day-to-day teaching. This conception situates *learning* at the center of the induction process, rather than either training or orientation. The dominant North American metaphor for induction has been one of 'support', a frame which does not necessarily involve any learning whatsoever on the part of the novice (Gold, 1996). Lastly, induction in the settings we studied is also more than a single practice, such as 'mentoring', or a loose collection of relatively unconnected practices. Induction can constitute a *system*, one that is characterized by complexity, interconnectedness, variety, coordination, responsiveness and dynamism.

Deeply addressing *all* the needs of beginning teachers requires a lot of effort, by a lot of people having different roles and expertise, using a variety of activities tailored to the novices' needs. This tall order is rarely filled around the world, even though research has long documented that novices come with a very wide range of needs. Most induction programmes tackle only some kinds of needs; common ones are improving classroom management or orienting teachers to their school's facilities and procedures. While induction systems in the studied countries also included the absolutely important kinds of support mentioned above, they go beyond support. They also launch novice secondary teachers into early career learning; for example, they offer detailed understanding of how to plan and teach lessons in their subjects, how to assess student understanding, and how to work with parents. They also promote reflection on teaching, thereby encouraging continuous learning throughout a career.

Addressing more and more diverse needs of beginning teachers requires more effort, more resources, participation by all sectors of the education system, more kinds of people, more kinds of activities, more time in the year, a longer period of time, and so on.

Commonalities of the Induction Systems

Together, these sites reflect great variation in their level of centralization, the organization of the teaching force, educational philosophies and reforms in play. Yet as we look across the sites, we note a surprising pattern of similarity. They employ comprehensive teacher induction – both in terms of what induction is intended to support and ways such learning can be fostered. The remainder of this paper highlights nine key features of comprehensive teacher induction that we gleaned from the five countries' systems.

The 'curricula of induction' are ambitious

These countries see induction as a distinct phase in a teacher's learning career, one where particular knowledge, skills and understandings can only and should best be learned. There is unusual, broad cross-national similarity in what teachers need to learn in their first several years of teaching, and the help they need to do so. Even in settings like Switzerland, where extensive teacher preparation occurs that provides a solid grounding in both subject specialization and pedagogy, there is the assumption that a beginning teacher, even one with prior classroom experience (as a substitute teacher, for example) needs opportunities to learn. The induction goals among the countries included in our study speak loudly to the importance of developing knowledge and skill in:

- effective subject-matter teaching;
- understanding and meeting pupils' needs;
- assessing pupil work and learning;
- reflective and inquiry-oriented practice;
- dealing with parents;
- understanding school organization and participating in the school community;
- understanding self and current status in one's career.

Induction benefits from variation within programmes

In New Zealand, induction involved both school-based Advice and Guidance discussions and out-of-school seminars. In France, the first year teacher not only teaches part-time in a school but also each week takes courses at the IUFM, a higher education institution designed to support teacher learning, and assists an experienced teacher in a second school. The range of options for novice teachers in Switzerland include beginning teachers practice groups, individual counseling made available to any new teacher, observation of other teachers, seminars and courses. In Shanghai, there is a menu of possibilities both in and out of school that includes demonstration lessons, school-level and district-level mentoring, teaching competitions, school orientations, district seminars, subject specific telephone hot-lines, and more. Beginning teachers, these programmes assert, need a range of different approaches – different formats and different teachers – to support the broad range of learning and development required of novices.

Multiple sources of support are articulated and coordinated

In a related point, the induction programmes in all five countries coordinated support from multiple sources. Most support in New Zealand was within-schools because there are no school districts in the country; each school interacts directly with the national ministry of education. In other countries, school districts, and/or district or regional professional development centers, and/or teacher preparation institutions also played a strong role in teacher induction.

Such induction systems are organizationally complex, requiring coordination and articulation of induction activities across multiple levels of the education system. With so many professionals involved in developing beginning teachers, the induction systems have designs that delineate the roles of different induction providers (articulation) and schedule activities in a systematic way (coordination). All systems at least specify clearly the contributions of different participants and some of the systems actively coordinate the activities, as in the case of the Advice and Guidance coordinators in New Zealand schools.

'Facilitated peer support' is a central strategy in some countries

Induction providers in these countries also created regular opportunities for novices to share, discuss, plan, investigate and vent with other beginners. Peer observation, peer reflection, joint inquiry projects all reinforce the idea that novices can learn from each other. For those unfamiliar with such strategies, the concern often arises that 'the blind will be leading the blind'. That is, how can beginning teachers have enough experience to offer productive advice to each other? One way that such concerns are addressed is by having the peer support groups facilitated by someone with experience if not training in supporting beginning teachers.

In New Zealand, the school's Advice and Guidance coordinator, typically an administrator, convenes the beginning teachers every other week. Because AG coordinators tend to keep this responsibility for several years at a time, they accumulate more and more expertise in meeting the needs of beginning teachers. Part of each meeting is spent discussing whatever pressing matters beginning teachers bring to the table. Facilitators recognize that even just venting frustrations is valuable, to let off steam, and more. When novices hear the tales of peers, it can provide tremendous validation that what they are going through is normal. They realize they are not uniquely suffering a bad fate, or that that they are a failure. Mentors and other support providers can try and reassure novices on this point, but when they hear directly from peers, it is a much more powerful comfort.

But the peer support sessions are not driven solely by whatever needs that novices express in the moment. Over the course of the year, the AG coordinator brings important topics and issues to the table. Figure 6.4 is an outline provided to the study team by an AG coordinator at one secondary school. The study team heard similar details from other AG coordinators, although the entire list of items and their timing during the school year was school specific. While this list constitutes general things that are relevant to all the novices in a secondary school, each novice also receives support from their department head for matters related to their particular school subject.

The Swiss practice groups offer the other strongest example of the attention and value given to such peer connections. In these groups, the authority for the direction of the group discussion is given to the novices themselves based on a view that,

Term 1	Term 2	Term 3	Term 4
first lesson/day/week school instructional resources staff support network homeroom duties classroom management classroom discipline detention/discipline system pupil progress reports parent/teacher meetings	school history school structure expectations for pupil behaviour roles of department heads, guidance counselors, principal outdoor education teaching in Co-Ed school	teaching grade 8/9 role of trustees arranging substitutes school-wide exams special education cultural differences sports organizations teaching controversial issues	case studies in pupil behaviour professional language relationships with pupils year in review looking ahead school finance

Figure 6.3   Sample schedule of topics for facilitated peer support meetings in New Zealand

as adult learners, they are problem solvers. However, the facilitators are freed up from some of their regular responsibilities and receive a wide range of professional development offerings to increase their leadership capacity.

There is an important distinction between the Swiss and New Zealand models of facilitating peer support. The groups of six-seven Swiss teachers are drawn from across a number of schools, whereas the New Zealand groups are novices from within the same school. The Swiss novices related that being outside their school affords the opportunity to be even more candid when sharing their experiences. Having peers from other schools also increased the richness and variety of ideas offered. As a by-product, learning about experiences from other schools helped them to realize that some situations in their school were derived from a particular school's norms, rather than being a universal standard for teaching.

Collaboration is a forte of the five induction systems

Collaborative group work is understood, fostered, and accepted as a part of teaching culture in most of the countries studied. There are shared experiences, shared practices, shared tools and language among colleagues. It is a function of the induction phase to engender this sense of group identity and treat new teachers as colleagues and cohorts. The Swiss and New Zealand peer support groups already illustrate this principle for those countries. In Shanghai and Japan, daily teaching itself is configured as a very public practice, where colleagues jointly develop lessons and discuss the delivery and impact for students in great detail. Teaches vary in their reflectiveness and ability to articulate their reasons and thinking behind their teaching. But the novice teacher has multiple opportunities both to listen and to be encouraged or pushed to develop skill and understanding.

Induction systems require self-reflection

Induction can also push beginners to look closely at their own practice by creating activities that focus on reflection and inquiry. Beginning teachers develop a reflective stance, personally and/or professionally. The year-end *Standortbestimmung* in Switzerland exemplifies the importance Swiss educators give to the personal in teacher development. The principal ongoing activity in the practice groups is to work together in an investigation of problems that are arising from their practice. Additionally, toward the end of the year, support groups collectively and individually reflect in broad ways about how they are doing as teachers, including whether teaching as a profession fits well with their personality, skills, etc.

The year-long professional memoir – a kind of action research project – typifies the French interest in teachers developing analytical and reflective skills which they can bring to bear on aspects of their own emerging practice. The memoir is to report a detailed exploratory investigation into some aspect of beginning teachers' practice, which each teacher selects in collaboration with their induction providers. At the end of the year, the novice submits a formal report, typically 25–30 pages in length. Further, the novices must present their investigation to a committee formed of their mentor, the regional inspector assigned to their school, and others. Here are examples of a memoir for a beginning mathematics teacher: Can one educate geometric perception in three dimensions? Leading pupils in grade six and seven to distinguish an object from its representation in Cavalierian perspective; and obstacles linked to the learning of cosine.

Learning also takes place outside one's own classroom

Learning can be amplified by participating out of one's primary teaching context. Thus, each system also provides opportunities for beginners to participate in activities out of school. For Switzerland, this occurs though the peer support groups (see point 4). Further, the organizers of teacher induction in a canton (a Swiss state) poll the facilitators of the peer support groups early each year to learn what patterns of issues or topics are arising. The induction system leaders then respond by quickly putting together some short modules of information that address those topics and distribute them for use by the various practice groups.

In New Zealand, teachers participate in a couple of regional sessions. For example, all the beginning science teachers in a region were convened to discuss science safety and swap ideas for science lessons. In France, beginning teachers regularly visit another teacher's classroom in a different school for several months. They also attend a day and a half of beginning teacher courses at the university. In Japan, the prefectures (Japanese provinces) require beginning teachers to attend a similar amount of classes. And Japan has perhaps the most novel extra-classroom support of beginning teachers: a national cruise ship which each year takes about 20 per cent of the nation's new teachers for a summer cruise that embphasizes cultural activities.

Comprehensive induction takes time

The total number of hours is significant: Shanghai beginners are committed to a minimum of 100 hours of induction activity, although we consistently observed novices engaged in more intensive induction. French first-year mathematics teachers, one could argue, have their entire week arranged to support induction – with a day and a half at the IUFM, solo teaching of a single class in one school throughout the entire year, developing and presenting a professional memoir, and supporting and observing weekly at another school (for some twelve weeks in a block during the year). Weekly Advice and Guidance meetings, coupled with a range of other activities, constitute 20 percent of a beginning teacher's schedule in New Zealand. In Japan, the out-of-school induction component alone involves ninety days. Also important is that any single activity is, for the most part, a sustained one. Working with a mentor, constructing a professional memoir, participating in a practice group all involve repeated interactions over a substantial period of time, affording opportunity to develop relationships, dig into a topic, consider alternative views and gather and explore data.

Adequate resources are provided

The complexity of these systems is supported by policy that is robust and authoritative. The national or regional levels of these induction systems have established requirements and provided the resources needed to carry them out. All of these changes came with some resources or required lower jurisdictions to do something that meant they would have to allocate resources. Japan mandates prefectures to provide in-service events and courses, provides a reduced load for beginning teachers and funds guiding teachers. Shanghai's Municipal Education Commission created an induction plan that requires contributions and resources – time and personnel – from both schools and districts. Switzerland's induction creates courses, counselling on demand and practice groups, specially designed for new teachers, that address problems arising from the novices' classroom experiences.

Moreover, in none of these sites is induction seen as a resource-free activity. Most major induction providers in the system have some kind of support for what they do, rather than simply being required to add another function to their existing workload. This means that induction becomes a part of their teaching, not extra to it. In Switzerland, some providers do this work full-time and are paid for it full-time. The same is true for novices: induction is, in fact, part of the core, remunerated workload of beginning teachers. For beginning teachers in France and New Zealand, a lightened teaching load creates space for induction activities. It is a fully paid part of their job as a new teacher, not something additional to it.

The Importance of Teacher Induction

Why is induction so important? There is a growing international realization that launching beginning teachers on the road to learning more about teaching is an investment that can yield enhanced instruction throughout a career lifetime, affecting the quality of what hundreds, even thousands of pupils will learn in conjunction with each teacher.

In some countries, though strikingly in only one of those we studied, an additional or alternative goal of induction programmes is to *retain* beginning teachers in the profession. For example, a phenomenon of the U.S. educational system perceived as wasteful is that large numbers of teachers who embark on this career soon quit. Interestingly, in Switzerland, teachers leaving the profession after training is seen as enriching the society as a whole and is not considered a loss or waste there.

In the five countries, the first purpose of teacher induction was early career learning, not teacher recruitment and retention. Teacher recruitment was a motivating factor in establishing the current induction approach in France, and teacher retention is an issue in some of these sites today. Yet, induction is not simply or primarily to decrease teacher turnover: instead, it stands as a key juncture of learning, growth and support. It is not primarily about fixing a problem. It is about building something desirable – a teacher, a teaching force, a profession, a kind of learning for pupils in schools. Rethinking induction, in ways that can encompass not only support and assessment but also learning, we see that a more comprehensively envisioned induction can also have more far-reaching benefits than we often hope for it.

The five countries that we studied have some of the most comprehensive teacher induction programmes in the world. They illustrate what can be done. We do not mean to suggest that many other countries have such robust teacher programmes yet. However, we do hope these five examples can promote a global trend of empowering beginning teachers to reach their potential.

References

Britton, E., Paine, L., Pimm, D. and Raizen, S. (2003), *Comprehensive teacher induction: Systems for early career learning,* Kluwer Academic Publishers and WestEd, Dordrecht, Netherlands and San Francisco.

Britton, E., Raizen, S. and Huntley, M. (2003), 'Help in every direction: Supporting beginning science teachers in New Zealand', in *Comprehensive teacher induction: Systems for early career learning*, Kluwer Academic Publishers and WestEd, Dordrecht, Netherlands and San Francisco.

Feiman-Nemser, S. (2001), 'From preparation to practice: designing a continuum to strengthen and sustain teaching', *Teachers College Record*, vol. 103(6), pp. 1013–1055.

Gold, Y. (1996), 'Beginning teacher support: attrition, mentoring, and induction', in J. Sikula, (ed.), *Handbook of research on teacher education*, Macmillan, New York, NY, pp. 548–594.

Moskowitz, J., and S. Kennedy, S. (1997), 'Teacher induction in an era of educational reform: the case of New Zealand', in Moskowitz and Stephens (eds), *From students of teaching to teachers of induction around the pacific rim* (pp. 131–168), Department of Education, Washington, DC.

Raizen, S., Huntley, M. and Britton, E. (2003), 'Collegial cooperation and reflective practice: Swiss induction programs', in *Comprehensive teacher induction: Systems for early career learning*, Kluwer Academic Publishers and WestEd, Dordrecht, Netherlands and San Francisco.

Teacher Registration Board. (1997), *Information for newly registered teachers*, Teacher Registration Board, Wellington, NZ.

Teacher Registration Board. (1993), *Advice and guidance programmes for teachers*, Teacher Registration Board, Wellington, NZ.

Chapter 7

Learning Mentorship in the Primary School

Christine Farmery

Learning Mentors were first introduced as a new workforce into schools in 1999 through the Excellence in Cities (EiC) initiative by the then Education Secretary. A package of measures totalling £350m were announced, with the introduction of Learning Mentors as one of three main strands of the Excellence in Cities programme; the aim of the programme was outlined as addressing low expectations prevalent in England's inner-city comprehensive schools. By 2001 the School Standards Minister was acknowledging the success of the initiative, stating that the learning mentors '... are helping to change inner city pupils' attitudes to schooling.' and announcing an extension to the initiative; the recruiting of nine hundred Learning Mentors to work in primary schools.

My involvement in Learning Mentorship in the primary school began when these first Learning Mentors were employed, as the school in which I was Deputy Head was allocated the equivalent of two full-time Mentors. Interestingly, we found from the outset that the role was not clearly defined and thus not easy to implement in practice. This was contrary to expectations as it was clearly stated that the strand was so successful that it was being expanded and introduced into the primary sector. However, the DfES in 2001 accepted that the role in practice was not clearly understood and recognised that this lack of understanding had been one of the key barriers to its successful implementation in schools. As the role developed in the school in which I was employed the schools' collective lack of understanding was addressed through a piece of research into Learning Mentorship in practice.

A lack of understanding of the role may be considered surprising in view of the amount of money dedicated to developing Learning Mentorship in schools – £100m in 2003/2004 – and indeed to the long tradition of *mentoring* as a technique for developing skills and knowledge, as described well by Klasen & Clutterbuck (2001). When introducing the initiative in 1999 the Secretary of State described learning mentorship as an adult offering '... individual pupils advice and guidance ... to encourage young people to stay in education.' This described the desired outcome of the strand but did not address the process of Learning Mentorship, thereby distinguishing it from other types of mentorship, although Roberts reported in 2000 that there is generally a '... lack of consensus as to what constitutes mentoring' and concluded that it is best described as a *process* (p. 162). It may therefore not be so surprising that the specific role of a *learning* mentor is also not either easily definable or plainly understood, but merely reflects the general lack of understanding regarding the role of the mentor in general. It must then be questioned that if the role is not understood then how can it be effectively implemented and evaluated. It was this question that led to a piece of research into the role as it had evolved in one primary school.

The school at the heart of the research is a large primary school in the North of England, in an area designated by the Local Education Authority (LEA) as one of high social deprivation. As noted earlier, the Excellence in Cities initiative funded the equivalent of two full-time Learning Mentors; this was later supplemented by the school's budget to employ four part-time Learning Mentors, each working within specific Year Groups. The initial allocation, made through the Local Authority, was based on the school's location; the school's size; the provision of free school meals and the percentage of EAL (English as an Additional Language) pupils. The most recent data (2004) shows that:

- The school is much lager than the Authority average, having over 100% more children throughout school.
- Eligibility for free school meals at 34.1% is also greater than the Authority average of 20.2% and the National average of 17.3%.
- The percentage of EAL pupils, 9.7%, is more than double that of the Authority average but slightly below the National average of 11%.

The comparison made at the time of the expansion of the Learning Mentor initiative was similar to this latest comparison and so indicated that a significant number of pupils could be expected to require specific help to engage in the school and its curriculum; thus mirroring the Government's interpretation of the outcome of the role and leading to the initial allocation being made.

The school's intake is mainly from local authority-owned housing, although there is some private housing in the area. Many of the families have an above-average number of siblings within either non-nuclear families or single parent families. There are often low aspirations for the children. This may be due to the area experiencing third generation unemployment or to the lack of education of the parents; indeed it is recorded by the Authority that 43.4% of the adult population in the school's traditional catchment area have no formal qualifications. Although the school operates an open-door policy for parents, many are reluctant to engage in their children's school life; this is an area that is currently being addressed by both the school and the Local Authority who is promoting family learning within its schools. The designation of the area in which the school operates as socially deprived reflects well the impoverished nature of many of our pupils and their home lives; the drab Victorian school building with very limited outdoor space is in keeping with the local area and therefore serves to reinforce some of the pupils' (and their parents') low aspirations and, in turn, their expectations of behaviour.

Although the school was allocated Learning Mentors at the beginning of the expansion of the initiative, and I had had some involvement in the development of the role in school, it was later as Acting Head at the school that I initiated a review of the work of the Learning Mentors that led to the piece of research into the role in practice. At this time I believed that the role in practice could be more effective in the school than it had been, although this was an almost instinctive belief as my knowledge of the role was based purely on an introductory course I had attended earlier and on the previous Head's interpretation of the role. Indeed, I found it quite difficult at this stage to articulate all my concerns but the review, involving the school's Learning Mentors and the LEA Link Learning Mentor, enabled me to verbalise and clarify my thoughts and those of the Learning Mentors themselves. We concluded that the approach being used was not the most effective use of the mentors for various reasons:

- Mentors worked within only four of the seven Year Groups;
- It therefore did not ensure access for *all* children who may develop a need for mentorship;
- Mentors were often used to carry out teaching assistant roles rather than carrying out mentorship;
- There was little opportunity for the Mentors to share ideas, strategies, successes and problems.

The third point was most important, as it was obviously a result of the lack of understanding of the role by the teaching staff that led them to direct the Mentors to carry out tasks related to the responsibility of a teaching assistant rather than to mentorship. The review thus indicated clearly that there needed to be a shared understanding of the role across school, a change in focus to promote equal access to mentorship for all children and an approach that facilitated cooperation and sharing between the Mentors themselves. This identification of school needs led to the LEA Link Learning Mentor aiding in identifying a new approach to Learning Mentorship within the school, based on the team approach that is already in use in many secondary schools but is much less common in primary schools. The identification of the Team approach was the critical incident that led to the recognition that research into the role of the Learning Mentor within the school was both indicated and necessary to the development of the role in practice.

The review as a whole indicated to me the need for three associated courses of action to be carried out:

1. A review of relevant literature about Learning Mentorship;
2. An agreement on how the role would be carried out within the school the following academic year;
3. A piece of research into Learning Mentorship in practice within the school.

These associated courses of action would develop my own knowledge of Learning Mentorship which could then be shared with the staff, would establish a fairer system of Learning Mentorship for the children and would, in time, evaluate this approach to the role.

The Next Step

My starting point was to seek out further information about both the background to the initiative and the role in practice. At the time of the research, I found little documentation available. There is much more information available currently, including a collection of case studies on the DfES standards web site, dedicated mentoring websites and the publication of new books (Cruddas, 2005; Roberts & Constable, 2003) The lack of documentation at the time of the review was unfortunate as I believed it essential to provide an informed interpretation of the role in practice in order to move forward within the school. At this stage I could only speculate on the reasons for this lack of information – that it may not be written about, that it may not be available or that it may not even exist. Following an extended period of reading and trying to locate the information needed I contacted the DfES to request the information that I considered to be essential at this time but even this direct approach proved to be fruitless. I could only therefore continue my search for the relevant background information whilst exploring the general concept of mentoring, in order to reflect on why the approach may have been considered appropriate to pupils in the primary school, and indeed to speculate why the title *learning mentor* was deemed fitting to this new workforce.

Although there is a wealth of writing about mentoring in practice in many contexts (Wilkin, 1992; Zachary & Daloz, 2000; Fletcher, 2000) there remains a generalised and accepted confusion about a definition of the role itself. This is clearly explained by the National Mentoring Network (www.nmn.org.uk), who state that the lack of a universally accepted definition is due to the range of activities that mentoring may encompass, that it is responsive to need and is thus dependant on *why* mentoring is being used, *where* it is being used and *with whom* it is being used. This explanation may appear to suggest that a definition of mentoring and, in turn, *learning mentoring*, may never be arrived at, but it actually aids in defining the role in individual situations. If it is accepted that the definition is based on 'why, where and with whom' it is being used, it can begin to be appreciated why the term *learning mentor* was used, in that the initiative was introduced to enable all pupils to access the curriculum, in other words, to learn, as if they had not been doing so before. The function of the learning mentor would thus be to support identified children to engage in learning, again mirroring the government's aims for the introduction of the role into schools as if teachers were not enough.

The reading into the role and the background to the initiative reinforced my knowledge of the responsibilities of a learning mentor; indeed it is stressed that the Learning Mentor has two overriding areas of responsibility:

1. To improve attendance

2. To remove a pupil's barrier to learning

   (www.standards.dfes.gov.uk/sie/eic/ eiclearningmentors)

Barriers to learning are described as problems that a pupil faces due to difficulties at home, bullying issues or general disaffection. The barriers are thus pastoral concerns that may result in feelings such as anxiety, depression or anger; these feelings are cited by Goleman (1995) as those that render pupils unable to learn, as they are powerless to concentrate or take in new information. By addressing such problems, the Learning Mentors therefore enable the pupil to engage in *learning*, thus indicating why the term Learning Mentor is appropriate to their work.

The reading also introduced a description of the mentoring process that became key to the approach to Learning Mentorship to be adopted and, in turn, aided in identifying the focus for the research:

> ... the support given by one person for the growth and learning of another ... and the .... integration into and acceptance by a specific community. (Malderez, 2001, p. 57)

The Team Approach suggested by the Link Learning Mentor merely suggested a means of working together. Interpreting this in practice needed much more thought but a further incident influenced this approach in practice; indeed this additional incident directed its development.

My Acting Headship, within which the review of Learning Mentorship in the school at the heart of this study was carried out, arose through the unexpected leaving of the Head of the school. The effects of his sudden departure from school were immediate, with staff, parents and children becoming unsettled and uncertain about the future. Behaviour across the school generally declined and it was quickly realized the effect the Head had had on behaviour management. It was clear that he shouldered the full responsibility for behaviour management across the school, thus disempowering and deskilling many of the staff and, perhaps more importantly, the children. For the overwhelming majority of the pupils this was not an issue that could be unresolved, but for a significant minority (around 5%) it proved to be a very de-stabilising event in their lives.

It was during the time following the Head's departure that many members of the school staff became increasingly concerned about the decline in standards of behaviour and believed that the Leaning Mentors should be used to manage this behaviour, as evidenced by a later questionnaire for teachers into the role of the learning mentor. One teacher recorded that:

> I spend a lot of time in my classroom refereeing behaviour instead of teaching and I have never had any support from the Learning Mentor Team.

Another teacher also alluded to behaviour management as a role of the Learning Mentor, stating:

In my class and Year Group there are many issues of behaviour. It isn't possible for one Learning Mentor to cover all of them regularly.

A third teacher recorded that the Learning Mentor's responsibility towards behaviour management was limiting the support she had for other children in her class:

The children who exhibit barriers to learning due to behaviour are well supported by the Team. However, I have other children who are identified for other reasons and are not supported adequately.

These comments again reinforced the staff's collective misunderstanding of the role of the Learning Mentor as it is clearly recorded that Learning Mentors should not be used merely to deal with misbehaviour across the school (DfES, 2001). The review we had carried out centered on the inappropriateness of allocating the learning mentors to specific Year Groups and yet this seemed to be the model that the staff welcomed, even noting that one Learning Mentor per Year group was not sufficient for the behaviour problems being managed. Although I was mindful of the staff's views, I continued to question the school's interpretation of the role and believed that it could be improved, and indeed could address a range of behaviour issues through a more structured, proactive approach. It was this belief that shaped the Team approach within the school.

Focus of Research

The research was therefore to be school-specific, focusing on the newly agreed approach to Learning Mentorship within the school. However, we acknowledged at the review that this new approach might not prove to be worthwhile, particularly in view of the context of the school. I believed that a small-scale piece of research into the approach would both document the evolution of the approach and draw conclusions regarding its effectiveness; thus indicating a case study of the setting. My biggest influence here was Bassey (1999) who described three categories of case study; I initially categorised my research as one aimed at evaluating and developing practice, rather than one of testing or seeking a theory. It was an open-ended piece of research whereby the natural evolution of the role in practice would be documented rather than a system imposed that would then be tested to ascertain its worth. My aim for the study was concerned with much more than an evaluation of what was already in place. Such an evaluation would form only a small part of the research. It therefore became the *telling of the story of a setting*, telling the story of how the Learning Mentorship approach was developed in the school, how it evolved and how it worked in practice. This clearly indicated the need to collect data from various sources, with background and contextual data being as important to building up a picture as data to be collected from the participants in the research. The data collection centred on two sets of related data, one involving a range of contextual data regarding the role of the Learning Mentor in theory, both locally and nationally, and one regarding the role in practice within the school. One specific consideration here was that the research would use data collected from children. Greig & Taylor (1999), West, Hailes & Sammons (1997) and Watts & Ebbutt (1987) provided direction here in order to devise data collection instruments that would yield data useful to the story being told.

Again using Bassey's view (1995, p. 56) that the purpose of research is to '... understand, evaluate and change.' the change expected was the establishing of a workable, effective system of Learning Mentorship that would ensure access for all pupils needing help to overcome barriers to learning that would, without intervention, lead to the failure to become engaged in school life as a whole and a failure to meet expected attainment levels within the curriculum. In view of the number of pupils in the school now displaying difficulty in accepting and engaging in the routines of school life, I identified this *engagement* as the specific focus for the research. Taking Malderez' description of mentoring (2001, p. 57) as the '... integration into and acceptance by a specific community.' and the dictionary definition of socialization (Dictionary.co.uk) '.... the adoption of the behaviour patterns of the surrounding culture;' justified this focus. At the time, in addition to the significant minority of pupils displaying overt rejection of the school rules and routines following the departure of the previous Head, another layer of pupils were identified who were unsettled at the inevitable changes that a change in leadership at the school brought. The changes served to change the nature of the school society and so it became important to the research that the school was considered in terms of a society and explored the effectiveness of the Learning Mentor approach in the socialisation of both the pupils showing overt rejection of the school society and those who were unsettled within this changing society. The central theme of the case study then became the engagement in school life of an identified group of mentored pupils.

The Baker's Dozen

Once the focus had been identified, the cohort of children to be involved in the research needed consideration. There was an obvious dilemma between making the cohort size manageable for such a small piece of research yet large enough to ensure that the data they would provide would be adequate for the research findings to be judged *significant* (Anderson and Arsenault, 1998). Reading other research reports aided me in deciding that a group of twelve children would be manageable yet fruitful.

Further considerations included age, gender, ethnicity and ability, together with the two groups of pupils identified – one showing overt rejection of the school's rules and routines and one showing signs of being unsettled within the school society and in danger of both rejecting the school as a society or simply not accessing the curriculum due to their disquiet. With this in mind, I identified a group of children that I believed reflected the overall pupil population at the school. Since this identification process produced a pair of twins both were included in the research and so the group of children became known as the Baker's Dozen.

Age: All children were in key stage 2, to ensure the pupils could understand questions posed and could give meaningful answers.

Gender: The school population has slightly more boys than girls yet the number of children displaying either overt rejection of the school's rules and routines or signs of being unsettled within the school society were predominantly boys. The research group reflected this imbalance of gender by including two girls and three boys, rather than reflecting the school population as a whole.

Ethnicity: The school population includes a ten percent ethnic minority group. To reflect this, one child of ethnic origin was included.

Ability: Four of the research group were considered to be of less than average ability and three of above average ability.

In addition to the above breakdown of the group characteristics, three pupils were displaying overt rejection of the school's rules and routines; indeed within the research period they spent an extended time away from the classroom environment in order to meet both their own needs and the needs of the class. Following a period of teaching and mentoring within a small group made up of disaffected pupils they did return to the classroom. The rest of the research group had begun to display signs of being unsettled within the school society. These signs included increasing misbehaviour, disrespect towards adults and a reluctance to engage in classroom activities. Many of the group was also known to have unsettled or non-conventional home backgrounds, five children in total.

The Team Approach

Following the acceptance that the team approach to Learning Mentorship was the way forward for the school, the practicalities of how it would work in practice needed to be determined. It was quickly agreed that:

- A central area for the Learning Mentors was needed.
- A Team timetable was to be devised.
- All learning mentor records would be shared documents.
- An initial cohort of pupils requiring Learning Mentorship to be identified.
- Drop-in sessions for parents established.
- Drop-in sessions for pupils, in order to self-refer.
- A staff briefing to be arranged to inform staff of the practicalities of the Team approach.
- Parents and pupils to be informed of the service provided by the Mentor team.

The Learning Mentor room was deemed most important to the Team approach, as it was here that the Learning Mentors would be seen to work as a team and would carry out the proactive work that we believed was vital to effective Learning Mentorship within the school.

I had been introduced some time earlier in my career to the notion of Nurture Groups (Bennathan & Boxall, 2002), having visited an established Nurture Group within a smaller primary school. I was profoundly influenced by the work of the group. The children were catered for within the Nurture group because they found difficulties in accessing a mainstream classroom and it was clear that the Nurture Group environment promoted sharing and learning from each other and from the adults. Cooper et al (2001) describe this environment as not only a pleasant setting in which the children work, but a holistic approach of ethos that is important and effective. It was this holistic approach to children's needs that influenced my thinking when considering the use of a dedicated Learning Mentor room. I believed that an approach based on the Nurture Group ethos would contribute towards the socialisation of pupils into the school environment. Such an adaptation was acceptable to the principles of a Nurture Group, as Bennathan & Boxall (2002) report that groups are being established in many schools throughout England in many forms, and provide a checklist of criteria for the effective Group This checklist was used to ensure the Learning Mentor room adhered to the guidance.

It was important that the Nurture Group environment was structured and predictable and emphasized the key aspects of home and work surroundings. In practice, the Learning Mentor room was set up to have:

- A quiet area for reading and music, furnished with sofas;
- A dining area;
- Tables for completing class work;
- Play area;
- An office area.

The Nurture Group checklist sets out a series of responsibilities of the staff within the Group; these reflect well the principles of Learning Mentorship in practice, most notably the need for staff to:

- Model good relationships;
- Develop relationships whereby children can begin to trust adults and to learn;
- Provide support for the children's social, emotional and educational development of each child.

The Nurture Group ethos, together with the adoption of the team approach to Learning Mentorship, thus centered on pupils being exposed to appropriate relationships and attitudes. They would access the service in both the Learning Mentor room and in the classroom, through carrying out curriculum activities and activities designed to raise self-esteem and develop an awareness of the rules and routines of the school. Staff were made aware of the new arrangements through a staff meeting and were invited to refer pupils requiring intervention by the mentors – it was from the staff and my referrals that the research group of pupils were selected. Parents and pupils were introduced to the new service through meetings, assemblies, letters and leaflets. In turn, parents and pupils were encouraged to self-refer to the service. Finally, a timetable was issued showing allocated times for drop-in sessions, work in class, specific and targeted circle times and all other Learning Mentor activities; the timetable remained flexible to allow for urgent response by the mentors if needed. In time other activities were introduced into the timetable, including an after school craft club for targeted children, visits out to reward developing attitudes towards school and lunchtime invitations to reward appropriate engagement in school activities. Most important to the Team approach was the sharing of all records and the sharing of involvement with the pupils.

The Findings

Research data was collected over one academic year, from the establishing of the Team approach to Learning Mentorship at the beginning of the school year through to a final evaluation at the end of the year. It included contextual data about the school, the changing nature of the school society, the learning mentor initiative itself and the first thoughts about learning mentorship at the school from Learning Mentors, teachers and the identified group of children.

Mid-way through the year an interim review of the Learning Mentor approach was carried out, again involving participants in the research; a final review was carried out at the end of the school year. In addition to this data, the pupils completed attitudes and behaviour questionnaires at the beginning and end of the research period, to identify any changes made and to identify which, if any, were in response to the children's access to Learning Mentorship. As one of the two over-riding responsibilities of the Learning Mentor is to remove barriers to learning to enable a pupil engage in learning, a consideration of attainment was needed. This focused on Literacy and maths, using SATs data (from optional and statutory SATs) to make a comparison between attainment at the beginning and end of the research period.

The findings were a mixture of what was expected and what was unexpected. The Learning Mentors worked hard to establish the Team approach and the Nurture Group ethos and were justifiably pleased with both their efforts and the successes of the approach. Below are just a few of their comments that sum up their reflections:

> 'We've got flexibility. It's a bit like being the SAS if you like. You've got the core things that you do on your timetable, but you're still available to mentor a child that's having a difficult day, to come out of class to deal with any situation. We've got that flexibility that you can't have as a class teacher because their responsibility is to their whole class whereas, because we now work in a team, one person can leave the Mentor room.'

'Personally I think it seems easier because we're sharing, we're working together, we're bouncing off each other.'

'I found it quite hard, working separately, even though we're a whole school and we do talk about things with each other. To work as a team is easier. We can bounce of each other and you don't feel as isolated. We know that if a child comes to you with a particular problem or they're upset, we know that anyone of us could deal with it. If you're in a particular Year group or class, you're the only one that has that problem given to you. You feel that you can deal with it if you can share it with someone else. That's what we've done.'

'It's a fantastic back up system because if you work with one child and something happens to you, obviously the team before was aware of bits of it, you are more aware of it now and it would not be such a disruption now you are working as that team. That's got to be more beneficial to the child and to the school.'

'Its not good practice I don't think for them to be reliant on one person. We're not here to be a prop. And that's how it was last year.'

'Its given us a chance to work holistically with children. It's not just Literacy or numeracy, everything can be brought in for that child. We're looking at the whole child. Social skills, peer mentoring, all sorts of things we can use to get them to get on together.'

I firmly believed in the new approach and the research justified this belief. It demonstrated that the approach was workable, proactive and resulted in improving the engagement of the targeted pupils in the work of the school. I was particularly pleased that, following the initial review and the sharing of our ideas about Learning Mentorship, it was the Learning Mentors themselves that led the new approach, thus taking ownership of it and ensuring its success in practice. We knew that the approach we were intent on adopting in the primary school was a radical idea at the time and that there was a mixture of opposition and surprise amongst the staff at what we were doing but we believed, and the research findings demonstrated, that we were right to introduce it. The LEA Link Learning Mentor supported this view.

The data collected from the children also reinforced the beliefs. The attitude and behaviour scales showed clearly that the pupils' attitude improved; they were happier in school and in the classroom. They were happier with their own behaviour in general and, in particular, their behaviour at break times.

One of the most surprising findings came about when interpreting interview data gathered through group interviews with the children towards the end of the research period. Although the children agreed that the Learning Mentors helped them to behave in school, they appeared apathetic to the questioning. My first thoughts were that we had not only enabled the children to overcome their barriers to learning but that we had taken away their individuality, what I termed their *spark*.

They seemed particularly surprised at my questions about their involvement with the Learning Mentors and were much less positive about the support the Learning Mentors provided. This was an unexpected and unwanted side effect of the Learning Mentorship and I continued to be confused by their responses. I then interviewed the children individually and found similar responses to those given during the group interviews. However, on further discussion with the children, I interpreted their apparent apathy as indifference due to their reduced need for access to Learning Mentorship. I remembered that the Learning Mentor guidance recommended that mentorship should be offered for one to three terms followed by a period of re-integration into class and staged withdrawal from Mentorship. We had not offered this and yet the children themselves had recognised their improvement in socialization within the school, had withdrawn from Learning Mentorship and began to access the classroom fully. This indicates the success of the approach developed by the school, as the pupils were able to take the lead themselves in recognising that they no longer exhibited barriers to learning related to the schools rules and routines.

Following the success of the new approach to Learning Mentorship provided by the school, based on the Nurture Group ethos, it was decided to develop the use of a Nurture Group for the delivery of the team approach to Learning Mentorship, particularly for younger pupils displaying barriers to learning.

The understanding of the concept of Learning Mentorship across the staff as a whole developed throughout the research period. This was due to the raising of awareness through meetings and through the research itself. The staff became able to refer to barriers to learning, began to appreciate the proactive role we were trying to develop and understood the pastoral nature of the role than the purely academic role of aiding pupils with their learning. Although more work is needed to ensure all staff in school appreciate the full nature of the role the research has demonstrated the effectiveness of the school's interpretation of Learning Mentorship.

References

Anderson, G. and Arsenault, N. (1998), (2nd edn) *Fundamentals of Educational Research*, Falmer, London.

Bassey, M. (1999), *Case Study Research in Educational Settings*, Open University Press, Buckingham, Philadelphia.

BBC, (1999), *Blunkett Targets Urban Comprehensives*, http://news.bbc.co.uk/1/hi/education/300358.stm.

BBC, (2001), *More Mentors for City School Children*, http://news.bbc.co.uk/1/low/education/1132949.stm.

Bennathan, M. and Boxall, M. (2000), (2nd edn) *Effective Intervention in Primary Schools: Nurture Groups*, David Fulton, London.

Cooper, P. (2001), *We Can Work it Out: What works in alternative provision for children with social, emotional and behavioural difficulties*, Barnardo's, London.

Cruddas, L. (2005), *Learning Mentors in Schools: Policy and Practice*, Trentham Books, Stoke-on-Trent.

DfES, (2001), *Good Practice Guidelines for Learning Mentors*, DfES, Nottingham.

DfESa, *The Standards Site*, www.standards.dfes.gov.uk/sie/eic/eiclearningmentors

DfESb, *The Standards Site*, www.standards.dfes.gov.uk/la/case_study_13.pdf

DfESc, *The Standards Site*, www.standards.dfes.gov.uk/sie/eic/eiclearningmentors/ LMCaseStudies

Dictionary.co.uk, http://www.dictionary.co.uk

Fletcher, S. (2000), *Mentoring in Schools: a handbook of good practice*, Kogan Page, London.

Goleman, D. (1995), *Emotional Intelligence*, Bantam Books, New York.

Greig, A. and Taylor, J. (1999), *Doing Research with Children*, Sage, London.

Klasen, N. and Clutterbuck, D. (2001), *Implementing Mentoring Schemes*, Butterworth Heineman, Oxford.

Malderez, A. (2001), 'New ELT professionals', *English Teaching Professional*, vol. 19, pp. 57–58.

Roberts, A. (2000), 'Mentoring Revisited: a phenomenological reading of the literature', *Mentoring & Tutoring*, vol. 8(2), pp. 145–170.

Roberts, M. and Constable, D. (2003), *Handbook for Learning Mentors in Primary and Secondary Schools*, David Fulton, London.

Watts, M. and Ebbutt, D. (1987), 'More than the Sum of the Parts: research methods in group interviewing', *British Educational Research Journal*, vol. 3(1), pp. 25–33.

West, A., Hailes, J. and Sammons, P. (1997), 'Children's Attitudes to the National Curriculum at Key Stage 1', *British Educational Research Journal*, vol. 23(5), pp. 597–613.

Wilkin, M. (ed) (1992), *Mentoring in Schools*, Kogan Page, London.

Zachary, L.J. and Daloz, L.A. (2000), *The Mentor's Guide: Facilitating Effective Learning Relationships*, Jossey Bass Wiley, San Francisco.

Chapter 8

'Sitting with Nellie'? Subject Knowledge and the Role of the Mentor

Dina Al-Jamal with Cedric Cullingford

Introduction

Whilst the role of the mentor has a long and ambiguous history, it is a strategy that is continually invoked and constantly tried. This chapter explores attempts in Jordan to use a particular type of mentoring to support the teaching of English as a foreign language. Great hopes have been placed on the success of the model. The question remains whether these hopes are justified.

The idea of the mentor sounds attractive and sympathetic, although it needs a substantial amount of training for the mentor. The traditional role of the mentor as a perfect example of good practice can become debilitating as well as enabling. It can be as narrow as the derided concept of 'Sitting with Nellie'. This is not a model that works well in subject specific circumstances, and, where the student is still developing, subject expertise.

In all the studies on mentoring the stress has been on the need to understand generic pedagogy and how to convey it. Less attention has been paid to the mentor as a supporter of subject knowledge. When we look at some models of mentoring, as in Arabic countries, we see that there are many tensions between the traditional role of the model from whom good practice will be learned and the critical friend. Teaching a subject like English as a foreign language brings this tension to the fore, since it clarifies the ambiguity between teaching by example and the need to give specific inputs.

Drummond (1998), Al-Hawamleh (1999) and Owais (1999) have pointed out that, despite the investment, mentoring in Jordan has not fulfilled its objectives and that mentoring has proven to be less than ideal. Programmes of mentoring were implemented in 1996 with too little conceptual understanding, with unrealistic expectations, and with poorly thought out implementation strategies. As Zeichner (1986) indicated, a teaching practice programme is a significant occasion in a teacher's education for acquiring new knowledge, skills and dispositions. The essential problem was that the role of the mentor was never clearly defined, and the consequences of this on teacher education are many. Whilst this chapter concentrates on the experience in Jordan it has implications for any mentoring programme, particularly in a subject such as second language learning, and particularly where the emphasis includes the acquisition of subject knowledge.

This chapter highlights some of the complexities of the role of the mentor in a particular circumstance. This is when the subject itself entails an awareness of the content as well as an awareness of the process of its delivery. One may assume that the EFL mentor 'should' be proficient in the language *per se* as well as being aware of the process of acquiring the basic capabilities and aptitudes necessary to begin teaching. This puts the EFL mentor in a difficult position if s/he is supposed to follow, criticise and supervise the linguistic as well as and teaching performance of student teachers.

The teaching of the English language has grown in importance world-wide not only because English is a language of international communication, but because it is also the language of science and technology (Abbott 1998). English is formally introduced in Government schools in Jordan in the fifth class (at the age of 10–11), and is taught over the rest of the school years up to the 12th class (at the age of 18). On average, there are five to six contact class periods (45 minutes each) a week. The pupils' contact with the English language is very limited since it is virtually non-existent outside the classroom. Khamis and Scharer (1990) point out that communicative textbooks, which were introduced in Jordan in 1988, placed great emphasis on the use of English {as opposed to the mother tongue (Arabic)} in the classroom. Such an approach places more pressure on teachers than in the past to use English easily and fluently in the classroom.

Teachers following the communicative approach are not merely expected to initiate sets of responses from their pupils (as was often the case with earlier, audio-lingual, structural based materials) but also to initiate a wide range of natural and spontaneous utterances from pupils and to respond to them. This, in turn, requires teachers continually to adjust their speech to an appropriate level of difficulty (Mitchell, 1988). As Marton (1988) suggests, the communicative strategy requires teachers to be prepared for any linguistic emergency. They are also expected to handle genuine reading texts, often posing cultural as well as linguistic difficulties. In short, communicative materials and methodologies demand of the teacher a high level of proficiency in English, and the confidence to use it over an extended period in the classroom.

Teaching English as a Foreign Language and Mentoring

Drummond (1998) pointed out that the objectives of the EFL teacher mentoring in Jordan do not appear to have been met. The objectives of such programmes were assumed to be self-evident, that is, '*to practice being a teacher*' (p. 5). When introduced into the Jordanian educational system in 1996, teaching practice was presented to schools as a set of general guidelines without paying attention to the crucial role of the mentor. According to these guidelines mentors were asked to focus on general aspects which were of particular interest to their student teachers. However, neither the context nor the content of these guidelines was explained in detail.

Martin (1994) claimed that a successful mentoring programme requires a conceptual understanding of the mentoring role. In order to be effective in training EFL student teachers, mentors need a vision of the goal and the likely stages of development.

It is therefore necessary to articulate what mentoring consists of so that those involved have the confidence that they possess the skills necessary to fulfil these expectations.

Savignon (1983) introduced the idea of communicative competence to foreign language teaching. She originally defined communicative competence as the ability to function in a truly communicative setting- that is, in a dynamic exchange in which linguistic competence must adapt itself to the total informational input, both linguistic and paralinguistic, of one or more interlocutors. She argued it is only through performance that competence can be developed, maintained, and evaluated. It is, also, context-specific. The communicatively competent language user knows how to make appropriate choices to fit the situation in which communication occurs.

This knowledge of the linguistic system and rules (as in structural approaches) does not by itself ensure effective communication. This puts EFL mentors in a difficult position when they mentor the linguistic performance of the student teachers. Should mentors embark on communicative skills or not? The societal contexts can help the individual person in what, when, and how to speak with people in a particular situation (Hymes, 1977; Romaine, 1994), but does a mentor need to take this on board or is essential linguistic knowledge enough? Accounts of English language teacher education in Jordan often indicate how the language improvement component tends to be neglected (Ahlawat and Belleh, 1996; Drummond, 1998). This puts extra pressure on Mentors.

Robles (1998) maintained that fostering student teachers' awareness of the learning process becomes a way of fulfilling two needs: paying attention to the process, and catering for individual needs. He placed great emphasis on the language component in English language teacher training. Before being able to teach the language, student teachers must be competent in the language. The EFL teacher trainee, for whom English is a foreign language, is learning to do something much harder than native-speaking trainees (Medgyes, 1986). S/he is trying to establish communication in a foreign language with students who share their own mother tongue. Non-native trainees have to develop and mature not only ideas about the nature of language, but also what it means to use a language in order communicate meaningfully.

Mentoring Models

It is possible to identify three different models of mentoring: the apprenticeship model, the competency model and the reflective practitioner model (O'Hear, 1988; Hillgate Group, 1989). There is a long tradition that some skills, including many that are difficult, complex and of high moral and cultural value, are best learned by the emulation of experienced practitioners and by supervised practice under guidance. In the case of such skills, apprenticeship should take precedence over simple instruction even if it is thought of in terms of 'collaborative teaching' (Burns, 1992).

Some argue that learning to teach can best be understood as a form of apprenticeship while others advocate a competency-based approach. For those in this camp, learning to teach involves practical training on a list of pre-defined competencies. The mentor takes in the role of a 'systematic trainer', observing the trainee, perhaps with a pre-defined observation schedule, and providing feedback. They are in effect coaching the trainee on a list of agreed behaviours that are, at least in part, specified by others.

What is argued about the competency approach is that after an initial period of collaborative teaching, trainees benefit from an explicit programme of training following a routine of observation and feedback. In the competency model, one common problem, according to the Hillgate Group (1989), indicates that once students have taken control, once they have established routines that work for them, they can stop learning – they have hit a plateau. At this point the mentor therefore needs to 'remove the structure' of support and to change his/her role further regarding teaching styles and strategies. Just because trainees are ready for more explicit training in relation to their own performance it does not mean that the benefits of modelling through observation and collaborative teaching are over. The foundations for an extended repertoire continue to be best laid by working alongside and observing experienced teachers. In other words, it is not appropriate to think of these phases of mentoring as discrete entities; rather, they are progressive generally leading to what is currently widely advocated as 'the reflective practitioner model'.

In this final stage, trainees need to be encouraged to switch from a focus on their own teaching performance to focus on the pupil's learning and how they can make it more effective. To achieve this switch means more than the trainee simply extending his/her repertoire of routines. To focus on pupil's learning demands that trainees move beyond routines and rituals; they need to develop a deep understanding of the learning process; thinking through different ways of teaching and developing their own justifications and practical principles from their work (Calderhead and Gates, 1995).

Maynard and Furlong (1993) argue that trainees are unlikely to be ready for this form of reflection on their own practice until they have gained some mastery of their teaching skills and in this case their linguistic skills. They need to be ready to shift their focus from their own teaching to the pupils' learning and that cannot come until they have gained some confidence in their own ability and command of what they are teaching, not just delivering subject matter but using it. To facilitate this process mentors need to be able to move from being a model and instructor to being a co-enquirer. Those other aspects of their role may continue but in promoting critical reflection a more equal and open relationship is essential. This relationship is strained unless there is mutual confidence, including confidence in the subject being taught.

Methodology

The purposes of this research were to map the field and to obtain an in-depth understanding of the mentoring process integrated with a language development component. The methodology, therefore, was a mix of qualitative and quantitative measures reflecting a simple one-shot survey design.

The nature and aim of the research questions influenced the decision to use the following methods of data collection: self-completion questionnaires and semi-structured interviews. Triangulation of methods was intended to supplement and complement each other and provide useful data for the study under investigation. In this study, the qualitative data provided by the interviews have been triangulated with the quantitative provided by the survey questionnaire during the training process. The views on these elements were elicited from 381 participants in Jordan (306 mentors and 75 student teachers). These views were also obtained from 19 interviewees (nine mentors, 10 student teachers). In these interviews, student teachers were asked to talk about how they felt about their teaching practice, how they perceived their mentor's role, and what they perceived as weaknesses in their current practice.

The mentors were asked about their attitudes towards their roles as mentors while taking into consideration the chief areas of guidance and feedback student teachers may need.

Samples of EFL mentors as well as EFL student teachers were targeted where the selection procedure tried to include a spread over a wide geographic area all over the Jordanian Universities which are spread all over the country. Mentors who responded to the questionnaires were chosen by random sampling. Each member of each population under the study had an equal chance of being selected. This method of sampling involved selecting at random from a list of the names of the population (EFL mentors as well as EFL student teachers) which required a number of subjects for the sample. This procedure of sampling is representative of the population and generally acceptable. The mentors and student teachers who were also chosen for the interview from those that responded to the questionnaire had indicated that they would agree to be interviewed.

Two types of self-completion questionnaires were developed for EFL mentors and the EFL student teachers. The main objective of these questionnaires was to obtain information about the training process from a large number of English language mentors and their student teachers. Basically, the first step in constructing the questionnaire was to review the objectives of the study and the intended function of the questionnaire within it.

Research Questions

For the purpose of this research, the questionnaire was considered to be the main instrument because it gave an opportunity to elicit the perceptions of EFL mentors as well as EFL student teachers regarding the teaching practice programme.

In short, the major questions the questionnaire intended to investigate were:

1. What are the attitudes of mentors as well as their student teachers towards the teaching of 'English' as a foreign language? And what are their attitudes towards the mentoring process in general?

2. How do foreign language mentors in Jordan actually perceive their student teachers' command of language skills vocabulary, reading, listening and structures?

When going over the participants' responses to the questionnaires, one should bear the above questions in mind in order to articulate what mentoring is about in Jordan, how EFL mentors perceive their roles as teacher trainers, and most importantly, what their role as mentors implies.

Findings

Attitudes and competencies

Deming (1982) remarks that the trainer's attitudes, both towards his or her role in the training process, are important. To Deming, attitudes can be negatively affected by prior experience in an educational system. When the mentors are not aware of the training requirements of their role as mentors, they tend to establish a sense of helplessness and a low level of self-esteem and self-image.

When asking one EFL mentor about her feelings towards the training process, she stated that she did not enjoy her role as a mentor because of her overloaded timetable. To her, the training process was not an inspiring experience since her personal involvement was minimised. Another mentor emphasised that the more positive feeling the mentor has, the better the mentor will be. One may argue that knowledge of the training subject matter may affect how the trainer feels about the process or visa versa.

Positive feelings regarding the training and the trainees may form an indication of the quality of the training, simply because the trainer will be more keen on developing the student teacher's skill and knowledge base.

The findings of this study showed that EFL mentors tend to have negative attitudes towards the profession of teaching English as well as towards the mentoring process. Table 8.1 presents evidence on the mentoring process in Jordan where EFL mentors are portrayed as impulsive and ingenuous. The majority showed no interest in teaching the language (English) in the classroom (Question 1), or in working as English language teachers' trainers (Question 2), or even worse, in encouraging student teachers to become English teachers in the future (question 3).

The issue of negative attitudes may raise two major interrelated issues which are relevant. The question of being English teachers themselves in the first place is not fully welcomed. 50.3% of the mentors in Jordan strongly disagreed with the statement that teaching English is interesting. Furthermore, 65% were not intending to encourage their student teachers to become English teachers. It is the role of this

Table 8.1   Mentors' attitudes towards the teaching of English and the mentoring process in Jordan

Question No.	S.A %	A. %	U.D %	D.A %	S.D.A %	Mean scores	St. D	Respond No.
1. I find teaching English in the classroom interesting.	00.0	00.0	08.7	41.5	50.3	1.58	0.64	306
2. I am enthusiastic towards my role as an EFL mentor.	00.0	00.0	07.0	47.7	51.6	1.49	0.51	306
3. I encourage my STs to join the profession of teaching.	05.2	01.0	03.3	65.0	25.5	1.95	0.89	306
4. I think the University courses have been relevant to the STs' actual teaching in schools.	07.2	18.3	07.5	45.1	21.9	2.44	1.22	306
5. I welcome my STs additional classroom support.	00.0	00.3	03.6	49.7	46.4	1.58	0.58	306
6. I feel my STs' classroom language does not match the pupils' level.	11.1	33.7	21.2	24.8	09.2	3.13	1.18	306
7. I know the language skills that my STs may need.	00.3	01.6	13.4	49.7	35.0	1.83	0.74	306
8. I think my STs have enough skills to enable them to cope with teaching.	00.3	00.7	24.8	57.5	16.7	2.10	0.68	306
9. I think my STs should develop their vocabulary.	00.3	02.3	19.0	62.7	15.7	2.09	0.68	306
10. I think my STs should pay more attention to spelling.	00.3	18.0	29.1	31.0	21.6	2.44	1.03	306
11. I think my STs should pay more attention to speaking.	03.9	31.1	12.1	29.1	41.8	2.68	0.98	306
12. I think my STs should pay more attention to grammatical knowledge.	00.3	08.5	30.1	49.7	11.4	2.37	0.81	306

Table 8.1   *Continued*

	S.A	A	U.D	D.A	S.D.A	Mean	St.D	N
13. I think my STs should pay more attention to pronunciation.	00.0	02.6	27.1	55.2	15.0	2.17	0.71	306
14. I think my STs should pay more attention to writing.	00.3	03.3	32.7	44.4	19.3	2.21	0.80	306
15. I feel that I need training as a mentor.	00.7	18.0	20.9	39.9	20.6	2.38	1.02	306
16. I adhere to tutor's comments about the student teacher's professional development.	00.3	01.3	10.1	39.2	49.0	1.65	0.74	306
17. I feel upset whenever the STs misses his/her training by being absent from school.	10.5	22.2	10.1	32.7	24.5	2.61	1.34	306
18. I am willing to model lessons in order to demonstrate a certain technique.	00.7	00.7	03.9	46.7	48.0	1.59	0.66	306

*S.A {Strongly Agree}; A.{Agree};U.D.{Undecided}; D.A {Disagree}; S.D.A {Strongly Disagree}.

*St.D: Standard Deviation. *ST: Student Teacher.

'mentor' to train EFL student teachers to become English teachers. 51.6% of the EFL mentors were hesitant regarding their roles as teacher trainers. Perhaps that EFL mentors tend not to be 'enthusiastic' towards the training process because they do not know what the role implies. Perhaps they are not 'interested' in being English teachers in the first place, because they are not proficient themselves in the English language. Such negative views may be related to the low status of the teaching profession in Jordan in general (Ahlawat and Bellah, 1996) and mentors' low proficiency in the target language {English} (Drummond, 1998). Such negative views could be relevant to the lack of recognition of mentors' effort and time by the government, or even to the lack of training for mentors (Al-Hawamleh, 1999; Owais, 1999).

Trust needs to be highlighted when talking about the role of the mentor. If the mentor is uncertain about his or her subject knowledge (English), how can s/he mentor student teachers? This study questioned mentors' confidence in their language before posing any further questions regarding how to mentor EFL student teachers.

Mentors reported that they were not satisfied with their work as mentors, firstly because of the lack of reward for what they were doing and, secondly, from their overloaded timetables. One mentor maintained that:

I see myself being demoralised by the sheer hard work of it all. I have to work very hard and already that's becoming a bind.

The findings, shown in Table 8.2, indicated that 49.3% of the EFL student teachers in Jordan strongly disagreed with the statement 'I find teaching English in the classroom interesting' (Question 1).

Student teachers have the same sort of feelings towards teaching English which is similar to that of the mentors. Such attitudes, by the mentors as well as by the student teachers, may be derived from their low proficiency levels in the language. Dissatisfaction with the level of students' language is articulated by the mentors and the student teachers themselves.

As outlined in Table 8.2, the majority of the EFL student teachers in Jordan disagreed with the statements 'I find my mentor interested in the mentoring process' (Question 2) and 'My mentor encourages me to join the teaching profession' (Question 3). Mentors tend to pass negative attitudes to their student teachers regarding training as well as teaching the language. These perceptions are highly distressing to the student teachers who are looking forward to maximising the benefits of school-based training.

49.3% of the student teachers, strongly disagreed with the statement 'I find teaching English in the classroom interesting' (question 1) which reflects the impact of the attitude of the mentor on their perception of the task. Mentors 'should' help student teachers learn how to be teachers of the language with a full range of EFL procedures at their command. Thus, mentors 'should not' help student teachers to perceive the teaching of the language (English) as a nuisance or a fruitless task.

Eight EFL student teachers out of ten in the interview seemed worried about their teaching practice. One major role of the mentor is to support the practice of the student teacher, motivate the student teacher, and enhance his/her skills as a potential teacher. In this regard, one student teacher said that:

I need to express my feelings about my lesson with my mentor, I need to talk with her about how I felt like and what can be improved.

From this typical remark, one may derive what sort of roles the mentor 'should' fulfil. The mentor needs to act as communicator, counsellor, coach and advisor. The mentor is required to encourage a two-way exchange of information, help to interpret and clarify 'the lesson', give interpersonal feedback and serve as a third party, provide information, options and suggest appropriate strategies (Williams and McLean, 1992).

Table 8.2   Student teachers' attitudes towards teaching English and the mentoring process in Jordan

Question No.	S.A %	A. %	U.D %	D.A %	S.D.A %	Mean scores	St. D	Respond. No.
1. I find teaching English in the classroom interesting.	00.0	00.0	13.3	37.3	49.3	1.64	0.71	75
2. I feel my mentor is enthusiastic towards his/her role.	00.0	00.0	00.0	57.3	42.7	1.57	0.50	75
3. My mentor encourages me to join the profession.	02.7	01.0	05.3	62.7	28.0	1.88	0.79	75
4. I think university courses have been relevant to my actual teaching in school.	09.3	24.0	10.7	38.7	17.3	2.69	1.27	75
5. I feel my mentor welcomes any additional classroom support I make.	00.0	00.0	04.0	57.3	38.7	1.65	0.56	75
6. I feel my classroom language does not match the pupils' levels.	14.0	29.0	20.0	28.0	08.0	3.15	1.22	75
7. I feel that my mentor knows the language skills that I may need.	01.3	01.3	17.3	56.0	24.0	2.00	0.77	75
8. I feel my mentor thinks that I have enough skills, which enable me to cope with teaching.	01.3	01.3	24.0	58.7	14.7	2.16	0.74	75
9. My mentor thinks that I should develop my vocabulary.	00.0	01.3	21.3	58.7	18.7	2.05	0.68	75
10. My mentor thinks that I should pay more attention to spelling.	00.0	17.0	36.0	36.7	16.0	2.55	0.96	75
11. My mentor thinks that I should pay more attention to speaking.	01.3	34.7	12.0	34.7	14.0	2.59	0.93	75
12. My mentor thinks that I should pay more attention to grammatical knowledge.	00.0	06.7	32.0	52.0	09.3	2.36	0.75	75

Table 8.2 *Continued*

	S.A	A	U.D	D.A	S.D.A	Mean	St.D	ST
13. My mentor thinks that I should pay more attention to pronunciation.	00.0	02.7	28.0	56.0	13.3	2.20	0.70	75
14. My mentor thinks that I should pay more attention to writing.	02.7	02.7	32.0	49.3	13.3	2.32	0.84	75
15. I feel that my mentor needs training.	02.7	14.7	25.3	38.7	18.7	2.44	1.04	75
16. I feel that my mentor adheres to tutor's comments about my professional development.	00.0	02.7	05.3	42.3	49.3	1.64	0.82	75
17. My mentor feels upset if I miss training by being absent from school.	08.0	26.0	10.7	29.3	25.3	2.63	1.33	75
18. My mentor is willing to model lessons in order to demonstrate a certain technique.	00.0	01.3	08.0	56.0	34.7	1.76	0.65	75

*S.A {Strongly Agree}; A.{Agree};U.D.{Undecided}; D.A {Disagree}; S.D.A {Strongly Disagree}.

*St.D: Standard Deviation. *ST: Student Teacher.

Does the 'Sitting by Nellie' model therefore lead to successful training? The model of mentoring which seems to operate in Jordan is one in which those being mentored merely copy their mentors. This is hardly beneficial:

> You find yourself standing in the shadow of that woman (mentor) and doing the same type of teaching the pupils are used to that, and that's the safest thing for you to do. I think there is a danger that you tend to become almost a clone of the mentor you are with on teaching practice.

Clearly, copying how the mentor teaches is never one of the goals of the teaching practice.

Student teachers' limited knowledge of the subject matter is highlighted by this research. Sadtone (1991) indicated that the trainers should have knowledge of the content of training materials and the skill of translating this knowledge into practise. Morris (1993) argued that teacher development might not take place unless the student teacher has expertise not only in the training material but also in the material on which the content is based.

The majority of EFL mentors perceived their student teachers as not being quite competent to cope with the subject matter in teaching. 33.7% of the mentors agreed with the statement 'I feel that my student teachers' classroom language does not match the pupils' levels' (Question 6). The mentors considered the student teacher's competence as a source of weakness, particularly in speaking where 31.1% of the EFL mentors expressed their concern that student teachers should pay more attention to it. The EFL mentors stress communication.

The question is whether mentors are competent in using the language in general and in performing the skill of speaking in particular. If they are not confident whether they really enjoy themselves as English teachers or as trainers for English language student teachers, how can they be certain that the skill of 'speaking' is what these students need? Is it the context of using the language that undermines the competence of the mentors as well as the student teachers when they 'speak' and establish 'communication' in the target language?

Obviously, many tensions regarding the linguistic knowledge base of the mentors are apparent before discussing the linguistic knowledge base of the student teachers themselves. This is why more and more attention should be made to subject matter knowledge (language per se) when it comes to mentoring.

When asked about the student teachers' competencies, six EFL mentors (out of nine) reported that student teachers do not have adequate knowledge of the subject matter. One mentor put it plainly by explaining how unhappy she is with the students' language competencies. She says:

> Student teachers tend not to use appropriate vocabulary, or even know how to communicate with pupils.

Similarly, the EFL student teachers felt unhappy with their competence in using the target language (English) in the classroom, in the sense that it did not seem to match the pupils' own level of understanding. 29% of the EFL student teachers stated that their classroom language does not match the pupils' levels (Question 6). One may need to highlight the importance of classroom language when training the EFL students to develop communication skills in the classroom.

Student teachers reported a number of problems such as substantial difficulties with the subject matter (English) and coping with the wide ability range of teaching skills as well. One of them says:

> I feel I have no ability (in English) whatsoever. I know you have to be good at it so that the pupils learn it right.

In this regard, what can the EFL mentor in Jordan do in order to deal with student teachers' language? The mentor may work collaboratively with the student in a variety of ways to improve their command of classroom language. The mentor can provide help for student teachers and act as a frequent discussant; listening; responding; probing and encouraging the student; helping the student teachers to learn how to organise the practice of English and explain its working. This puts the mentor into the position of a teacher, having to add to subject development rather than reflective practice.

The EFL students in Jordan perceived the relevance of university courses to their teaching practice experience as essential (see Table 8.2). Student teachers probably perceive that their teaching in school should correspond to what they learn through university courses. If this is the case, why do they consider their language as not being 'good' enough to cope with teaching? This may create tensions that may undermine the content of EFL student teacher education at the university and consequently question the delivery of courses related to classroom language. These tensions are relevant to the sort of courses they are currently studying, or the sort of courses they 'should' study in order to enhance their learning of the language. It can be argued that university courses tend to disregard the student teacher's classroom language development. This may be a crucial insight into what is needed in EFL teacher education.

Surveying the attitudes towards the mentoring process indicated patterns of empirical evidence that constantly point to the attitude-oriented concerns and perspectives of mentor training in Jordan. The EFL mentor does not know actually what the role involves where s/he gets no training. Mentors do not have a code of practice. The training operates in a manner which allows the trainees no option but that of copying the practices of the trainer, without paying special attention to developing any required teaching skill or, more importantly, any needed language skill. The pattern of mentoring, here, is the 'apprenticeship' model but it is, in fact, apprenticeship to a teacher of languages rather than a developer of teaching skills.

Trainees need first-hand experience of real teaching situations, classroom strategies and subject matter. In the early stages of their training, the purpose of that practical experience is to allow them to start to form conceptual schemes of the process of teaching. But in order to 'see' what they are doing, trainees need an interpreter. They need to work alongside a mentor who can explain the significance of what is happening in the classroom. The problem is that attention has to be paid to competence in the delivery of subject matter, rather than the learning that takes place. It is as if in 'Sitting with Nellie', Nellie is a distraction from the task rather than a support.

The reason for the dominance of the apprenticeship model in Jordan is not because it is the best form of mentoring. It is the lack of confidence in students' actual command of the English language, which makes mentors fall back on the simplest of models. Instead of concentrating on pedagogic techniques or different teaching methods the mentors are themselves struggling with the subject matter. This, of course, is disabling. They find it hard to be constructive. Such a lack of confidence, which tempts any teacher to play safe, and to avoid exploring all the challenging possibilities of new approaches, is not a good model to follow.

Conclusions

EFL mentors in Jordan tend to adopt an apprenticeship model where the student teacher merely copies his or her mentor. EFL mentors in Jordan are not aware of the training roles allocated to them as teacher trainers. EFL mentors' performance in Jordan was perceived as not satisfactory.

The results indicated that mentors have negative attitudes towards the mentoring process and, even more, negative attitudes to the teaching of English as a foreign language. The functions of the mentor, encompassing essential components such as nurturing, caring and encouraging, were never met (Anderson 1993).

Mentoring has recently been regarded as a key component in the 'reform' of teaching. Wildman et al (1992) maintained that direct involvement of mentors in the training process could help student teachers develop an awareness of the teaching/learning process. Mentoring has been identified as a complex, intellectually challenging process which makes new personal and professional demands on the person undertaking that role (Moon, 1994; Martin, 1994; Tomlinson, 1995; Goodlad, 1998). All this is very well but the reality is somewhat different.

Field and Terry (1994) suggested that there are certain skills (competencies) necessary at the beginning of a career in teaching which develop as the teacher grows in professional understanding and maturity. It is the skills of beginning teachers that mentors must have in mind as they guide the practising students towards professional competence. Because of its very practical nature, McIntyre (1993) stressed that mentoring introduces certain difficulties, which complicate the task of its effective delivery. One of the causes of these difficulties is the wide range of learning and teaching activities associated with the mentor.

The results of this research demonstrated that EFL mentors fully supported any moves to intensify or expand the language of the student teachers in terms of the skill of speaking. Given the role of the language in moulding the confidence of the successful non-native English teacher in developmental educational contexts, it is high time language improvement is afforded proper status in Jordan. That is, EFL mentors should be confident about their own language which in turn should be incorporated whilst training the EFL student teachers. Yet the study highlighted tensions regarding EFL mentors' language which question their roles as teacher trainers. So what can be expected from them? In this regard, Holec (1985) maintained that to teach the learner to learn, that is to carry out the various steps which make up the learning process, is the best way of ensuring that learning takes place (p. 264).

One element of EFL teacher mentoring which has been reletively neglected is the actual methodology of training itself. It is significant that EFL mentors are not concerned about the language improvement component during the training process in the same way as the teaching practice component. The training should only not be about 'practise being a teacher' but rather to 'practise being an English teacher'. The familiarity of classroom language and routines would maximise the effectiveness of trainees' own language training. While there is a current focus on the training process, the study has frequently pointed out the methodology of teacher training has a major impact on what is of concern to EFL student teachers: the development of their language skills. For non-native English teachers, language proficiency will always present the bedrock of their professional confidence.

This puts the role of the mentor into a different perspective. The mentor is being asked to make up for previous deficiencies, thus fundamentally changing the nature of the relationship with student teachers and provoking a sense of old fashioned interference rather than the more constructive possibilities of the role. The dissatisfaction evident here might be more common in mentoring generally, even if hidden.

References

Abbott, G. (1998), *Conformity and Variety in the Global Diffusion of English*. PhD Thesis, University of Manchester.

Ahlawat, K. and Billeh, V. (1996), *Educational Reform in Jordan: An Analytical Overview*, NCHRD, Amman, Jordan.

Al-Hawamleh, M.S. (1999), *An Evaluation of the Mentoring of Islamic Education Student Teachers in Jordanian Public Universities*, M.Ed Dissertation, University of Huddersfield.

Anderson, J. (1993), 'Is A Communicative approach Practical for Teaching English in China? Pros and Cons', *System*, vol. 21(4), pp. 471–479.

Bell, J. (1993), 'Doing Your Research Project', *2nd Edition, Buckingham, Open University Press*.

Burns, A. (1992), 'Teacher Beliefs and Their Influence on classroom Practice', *Prospect*. vol. 7(3), pp. 56–66.

Burroughs, G.E.R. (1971), *Design and Analysis in Educational Research*, Educational Review, England.

Calderhead, J. and Gates, P. (1995), *Conceptualising Reflection in Teacher Development*, Falmer Press, London.

Cohen, L., Manion, L. and Morrison, K. (2000), *A Guide to Teaching Practice*, 4th ed, Routledge, London, New York.

Deming, M.S. (1982), *Evaluation Job-Relating Training: A Guide for Training the Trainer*, American Society for Training and Development, Washington, D.C. and Prentice-Hall, Inc. Englewood Cliffs, New Jersey.

Dewey, J. (1904), 'The relation of theory and practice in education', in *The Third NSSE Yearbook, Part 1*, Bloomington, III, Public School Publishing Company.

Drummond, O. (1998), *Teaching Practice*, Report Published by NCHRD, Amman, Jordan.

Edge, J. (1988), 'Applying Linguistics in English Language Teacher Training for Speakers of Other Languages', *ELT Journal*, vol. 42(1), pp. 9–27.

Field, B. and Terry (1994), *Teachers as Mentors: A Practical Guide*, Falmer Press.

Gardner, R.C. (1985), *Social Psychology and Second Language Learning*, Edward Arnold, London.

Goodlad, S. (1998), *Mentoring and Tutoring by Students*. Kogan Page, London.

Hillgate Group (1989), *Learning to Teach*, Calridge Press, London.

Holec, H. (1985), 'Taking Learners' Needs into Account in Self-Directed Learning', from 'Aspect of Autonomous Learning', in P. Riley (ed), *Discourse and Learning*, Longman, London.

Hymes, D. (1977), *Foundations in Socio-linguistics: An Ethnographic Approach*, Tavistock Publications.

Khamis, M. and Scharer, J. (1990), *Training EFL Teachers. A Handbook for Training the Jordanian Teachers of Basic Education Stage*, Ministry of Education, Jordan.

Martin, S. (1994), *The Mentoring Process in Pre-Service Teacher education*, School Organisation, vol. 14(3).

Marton, W. (1988), *Methods in English language Teaching*, Prentice Hall, New York.

Maynard, T. and Furlong (1993), 'Learning to Teach and Models of Mentoring', in D. McIntyre, et al (eds), *Mentoring: Perspectives on School Based Teacher Education*, Kogan Page, London.

McIntyre, D. (1993), 'Theory, Theorising and Reflection in Initial Teacher Education', in J. Galderhead, and P. Grates (eds), *Conceptualising Reflection in Teacher Education*, Falmer, London.

Medgyes, P. (1986), 'Quires from a Communicative Teacher', *ELT Journal*, vol. 40(2), pp. 107–112.

Mitchell, R. (1988), *Communicative Language Teaching in Practice*, Centre for Information on Language Teaching and Research, London.

Montgomery, M. (1995), *An Introduction to Language and Society*, Routledge, London.

Moon, Jayne (1994), 'Teachers as Mentors: a route in-service development', *ELT Journal*, vol. 48(4), pp. 347–355.

Morris, J.E. (1993), 'Evaluation of In-Service Teacher Training', in R.C. Burgess, et al (eds), *Implementing In-Service Education and Training*, Burgess Science Press, Basingtoke.

O'Hear, A. (1988), *Who Teaches the Teachers?*, a contribution to public debate of the DES green paper, London, Social Affairs Unit.

Owais, F. Peters, R. and Schnare, G. (1976), *Variables that Determine the Effectiveness of Teacher In-Service Workshops*, Final Report to the National Institute of Education, Washington.

Robles, A. (1998), 'Reflective Learning: Why and How', *Modern English Teacher*, vol. 7(1), pp. 43–46.

Romaine, S. (1994), *Language in Society: An Introduction to Socio-linguistics*, Oxford University Press, Oxford.

Sadtone, E. (1991), *Issues in Language Teacher Education*, SEAMEO Regional Language Centre.

Savignon, S.J. (1983), *Communicative Competence: Theory and Classroom Practice*.

Addison-Wesley Publishing Company, Menlo Park, CA.

Tomlinson, P. (1995), *Understanding Mentoring*, The Open University Press and Buckingham, Philadelphia, London.

Wildman, T.M., Magliaro, S.G., Niles, R.A. and Niles, J.A. (1992), 'Teacher Mentoring: An Analysis of roles, activities and conditions', *Journal of Teacher Education*, vol. 43, pp. 205–213.

Williams, B. and McLean, I. (1992), 'Someone to trust', *Nursing Times*, vol. 88(38), pp. 67.

Zeichner, K. (1986), 'The practicum as an occasion for learning to teach', *The South Pacific Journal of Teacher Education*, vol. 14(2).

Chapter 9

Mentoring in the Academic World

Ulla Lindgren

The notion of mentoring has many interpretations and these have changed over the years. It is only recently that the concept has been so highly charged, as it has become systematic and imposed rather than an informal and individualized practice. Mullen and Kealy (1999) argue that mentoring is a relevant up-to-date method for development suitable for the actual needs of modern life. In the United States mentoring has become widespread as a common practice within organisations and local governments. One of the reasons for this is that mentoring is seen as a new form of working practice. It gives the possibilities for change and development through the opportunity to discuss new ways of thinking, understanding and interpreting problems. Ingrained opinions and behaviour can become more apparent in an organisation and the result of this is that there can be a better climate for changes in fixed routines or old methods of working. This in turn can contribute to new developments that influence and improve the internal structure and environment of organisations (Kram, 1998; Lucas, 2001).

Another reason for the interest in mentoring is that rapid social development has created a strongly increased demand for more professional staff in specialist positions, a development that is international. Mullen and Kealy (1999) typically point out that the perceived fast changes in society make more strenuous and particular demands on the experienced practitioners. Greater changes of practice and changes of job make existing expertise more, rather than less, valuable.

Despite the demands in society, and the increase in vocational degrees, there are few courses in academic institutions that concern social competence, individual maturity, ability in relationships and professional development. It is, therefore, the student's own responsibility to develop these abilities. This reality has been noticed and lamented, e.g. by Hulbert (1994): 'I am concerned that we in higher education are not doing a very good job of guiding and nurturing the next generation.' (p. 261).

Stalker (1994) has observed that within the academic world mentoring can be seen as an important part of the students' social development and that it can, to a degree, contribute to their personal development. In that perspective, mentoring, as a unique form of education, can be a seen as necessary, like a bridge or affective door, for the understanding of professional life. The mentor/mentee relationship does not have teaching as a goal; it is built upon openness and confidentiality, where the mentor is an experienced, judicious person interested in supporting a less experienced individual (Brooks & Sikes, 1997; McGee, 2001).

As mentoring contains both discussion and reflection it starts a dynamic process, where the mentor is not the person who solves problems but the one who listens, who through analyzing questions, makes it easier for the mentee to come to his or her own decisions. To help the mentee to progress professionally the mentor also has to act as a good role model (Lucas, 2001; Mullen & Kealy, 1999).

Mentoring can also be seen as a democratic process, where the mentee and his or her development will be the central focus. Mentoring is not supposed to be simply a means by which the mentor can achieve his or her personal goals through the mentee. Neither is it supposed to indulge and expose the mentor's own ideas or activities. Instead, the idea is that the mentor, transferring his or her competence and experiences, should be a disinterested support for the mentee, so that he or she gets confidence and the encouragement to grow as an individual (Freire, 1997).

According to Bourdieu (1992) even symbolic capital, with the aims both to understand and be a part of the norms and values of an organization, its language and behaviour, can be transfered through mentoring. This transfer of symbolic capital, also referred to as the 'reproducing concept', is a form of learning that is of great importance for both professional and personal progress. Aryee et al (1996) state that social reproduction is possible through the mentoring process, where norms, valuations, language, and societal behavior are transferred from one person to another. At the same time there is a need for an awareness that old traditions and values should not be transferred without critical reflection (Gilbert & Rossman, 1992; Cullen & Luna, 1993).

When mentoring is successful it is a dynamic, developing process as well as powerful method of learning about human dynamics (Lick, 1999). Alfred and Garvey (2000) stress that a special goal of mentoring is to contribute to a process where the mentee as the learner is optimally engaged and powerful. By true engagement and a consciousness about the aim of the mentoring as well as the mentor's role and tasks, mentoring can contribute to the mentee's developing constructive self-insight and enterprise (Lick, 1999; Alfred & Garvey, 2001).

However, for personal as well as professional development, it is important that the participants initially have a realistic view of what can be achieved through mentoring (Dedrick & Watson, 2002). The mentees must be able to express themselves and critically reflect in discussions with their mentors, in order to facilitate their professional development (Alred & Garvey, 2000). Moreover, the mentoring process also needs to have a clearly stated purpose that will be in proportion to the particular mentee's assumptions and needs for effective contribution to professional development (Allsop & Benson, 1997). It should not be forgotten that mentoring can also be seen as a potential for development of the mentors since the questions, values and acts of the mentees give possibilities to reexamine what they have taken for granted (Vliet, 1993). The synergy effects of mentoring depend to a high degree on the cooperative actions between the mentor and the mentee (Lick, 1999).

Mentoring – A Name for Different Teaching Methods?

In the literature about mentoring within higher education the difficulties of clearly defining the nature of mentoring is apparent. What makes mentoring difficult to define are the many existing interpretations (e.g., Jacobi, 1991). Some examples of the lubriciousness of the term are as follows. In the United States the term mentoring can be applied to tutoring, peer groups or supervision. Some distinctions should be made.

In 'tutoring' students are placed together in small groups, consisting typically of 6 to 8 individuals. It is generally seen as a complement to regular teaching. The group's assignment is to take responsibility for learning themselves through joint discussions that can lead to a satisfactory solution of a practical problem. The group can either have a 'staff tutor', another tutor other than the course leader, or a 'student tutor', a student who has recently taken the course in question. The tutor meets the group several times a week to discuss the current problem. The purpose of tutoring is for pupils to develop critical thinking in a meaningful context and consequently improve their own knowledge. It has been shown that a 'student tutor' can perform better than a 'staff tutor' at this type of teaching, as they themselves have recently done the course and can identify with the difficulties and use a vocabulary closer to that of the students (Graesser & Person, 1994; Moust & Schmidt, 1995).

Research in the US has shown that tutoring has the potential for discussing and solving problems in a completely different way than classroom situations, where time and possibilities are limited (Moust & Schmidt, 1995). It is also evident that students who have taken part in tutoring perform much better than students who have only received traditional forms of educational delivery. The advantages made apparent in tutoring is that it offers social, cognitive and pedagogical possibilities that make it easier for the students to understand and take control over their own studying and learning process (Schmidt, van der Arend, Kokx & Boon, 1995).

'Peer groups', which involve dividing students within the same class into smaller groups, occur very frequently in the US. These groups work with learning based on problem solving and the students have to come to various possible solutions through discussions and deliberation. More experienced students are used as helpers for younger students in programmes sometimes called 'peer mentoring'. These programmes provide support for pupils who need extra help in their learning process (Keim & Tolliver, 1993).

The teacher instructing the group supplies assignments and has the responsibility of following up the work in progress, even though the group works independently. A formal or informal leader for the group usually becomes apparent, to make sure that the work progresses. This is based on the presumption that the students are active and can take responsibility for their own studies, express opinions, listen, draw conclusions and explain. The students are also encouraged to think critically and answer questions through converse arguments and supplementary questions. It is taken for granted that the students act as mentors for one another, as there is no adult present in the group. As a consequence of this technique, the results of the students have been seen to improve (McKeachie, 1994).

'Supervision' is a well-known phenomenon in many educational situations but it can have different meanings, as between the supervision of doctorates or the supervision of experiments or teaching practice. Supervision can also to be a form of teaching (e.g., Salander & Salander, 1989). It usually makes clear where the expertise and the responsibility for decisions lie (Delamont et al, 1999).

Research supervision has old traditions and is a well-known occurrence in the academic world. A supervisor is supposed to support the dissertation and to contribute to the development of a doctoral student's knowledge and intellectual techniques in their area of expertise. At the same time the supervisor has a key role in guiding and encouraging the doctoral students in their process of becoming independent researchers (Hagman, 1994; Dedrick and Watson, 2002). Although the aim of the doctoral student is clearly decided and a deadline is set, there is a lack of formalized criteria for how the supervision should be given. The characteristics of the research topic, the attitudes of the supervisor and the doctoral student and their relation to the research work influence the planning of the supervision. The supervisor's function as a judge and a reviewer can result in a dependent relationship, where the student is reliant on the supervisor's decisions on when to give positive support (Elvin-Nowak & Dahlberg, 1992).

Some important differences between supervision and mentoring

Even if mentoring and supervision can seem to be alike there are differences between them. Three important differences are:

- While supervision is included as a paid task in a researcher's work, mentoring is voluntary.

- A supervisor is chosen according to his/her subject knowledge while a mentor is usually recruited from an area of expertise that lies beyond the one of a mentee.

- As opposed to a supervisor, a mentor has no appraisal or reporting obligation. What the mentor and the mentee talk about is not shared with anyone else.

Some of the criteria that are involved in the two phenomena are illustrated in Figure 9.1.

The most important difference between supervision and mentoring is that whist supervision always involves dependence, mentoring is free from judging, and as a result of that, creates an independent relationship. Because of that it is impossible that mentoring should be seen as similar to, or just a new name for, supervision.

To highlight the similarities and disparities in tutoring, peer groups, supervision and mentoring the following compilation has been made (Lindgren, 1997). The compilation is made from criteria put forward in literature. Table 9.1 makes clear the qualities that are characteristic for the different categories.

At first glance, the different categories of mentoring, supervision, tutoring and peer groups, seem to have similar implications. However, it is evident from the

	Specific research areas
	Instructions and directions
	Subject concentrated
Supervision	Influence
	Compensation, salary
	Judging
	Dependence
	Personal or professional development
	Increased self-confidence
	Listening and advising
Mentoring	Voluntary, honorary task
	Discussion partner
	No judging
	Independence

Figure 9.1   Differences between supervision and mentoring

table that mentoring, which aims at personal development, differs from the other categories. While supervision, tutoring and peer groups are mostly concerned with improving performance in academic terms, mentoring concentrates on giving self-confidence and developing the personality of the mentee. From a methodological point of view, the mentor is more of a listener than teacher or adviser. Supervision, tutoring and peer groups usually concern a subject that has been decided upon in advance and with certain goals to attain, while mentoring starts out from the mentee's personal situation and wishes. Because of that, the subject matter can vary from one meeting to another. The purpose of mentoring particularly, is to increase the mentee's awareness about him/herself and his/her own situation.

The greatest difference between mentoring and supervision, tutoring and peer groups lies in the fact that mentoring is founded on an independent relationship between mentor and mentee. However, it must not be overlooked that even supervision, tutoring and peer groups can inspire increased self confidence, better self-knowledge and personal maturity among the students, even if this is not the prime intention of these activities. In contrast to mentoring, these activities are meant to give support for studying; where the primary aim is to improve exam results. According to Boethius (1995) supervision has neither the same content nor the same aim as mentoring and similar conditions also seem to imply for tutoring and peer groups.

Table 9.1   **The distinguishing characteristics for peer groups, tutoring, supervision and mentoring**

	Peer groups	Tutoring	Supervision	Mentoring
Teaching	x	x	x	
Occurs in groups	x	x	x	
Dependency status	x	x	x	
Needs subject knowledge	x	x	x	
Subject concentrated	x	x	x	
Included in employment		x	x	
Those more experienced		x	x	x
Occurs privately			x	x
Honorary assignment				x
Personal maturity				x
Personality development				x

Results from some Mentoring Projects

Mentoring female students

In Sweden, natural science at a higher educational level is a field of study where female students are in the minority. It is therefore not uncommon for women graduates to get positions at work places dominated by men. With the aim of supporting female science students and to facilitate their stepping into professional life, mentoring projects have been carried out at Umea University since 1997. Twelve or thirteen mentor/mentee couples have participated in the project every year. The mentees were studying their second or third year of undergraduate or postgraduate programmes. All mentors were female leaders from business or industry or the public sector.

The major purpose of the mentoring projects was to give female students the opportunity to get support in their personal and professional development, to increase their confidence and develop their self-esteem. The projects provided work placements as well as information about the professional world. Another purpose was to establish co-operation across the dividing-line between the universities and industry and the public sector. The mentors and mentees acquired awareness about each other's field of knowledge.

Every mentor/mentee couple regularly met once a month during the year. A series of structured workshops were scheduled. These workshops focused on attitudes, skills, employment interviews, job searching and professional responsibilities that ensure success in working life. At the end of the mentoring project an evaluation followed. The mentees set personal goals in collaboration with their mentor. The evaluations had two categories:

Personal development

One of the project's goals was to support the mentees´ personal development. All of the mentees could give examples of how they felt they had developed. Their statements have been divided into three categories *Improved self-confidence, Increased self- awareness* and *Increased risk-taking*. Five examples under each category are made below:

Improved self-confidence

- During this year I have discovered qualities I did not know I possessed.
- I have got a more positive picture about myself now.
- Now I am able to better reflect on an opinion and create an own understanding.
- That we had to create our own opinion in different questions has been very developing.
- I have developed mainly thanks to support and confidence I have received from my mentor and the other novices.

Increased self-awareness

- I have realized the importance of how I am using my language.
- I have got a better awareness about myself and how I react to things.
- I know my opinions, my abilities and myself a lot better now.
- Above all the meetings with my mentor have given me awareness about my own possibilities now and in the future.
- My personal development has really progressed, mainly thanks to the project, the mentor and the meetings in particular.

Increased risk-taking

- I am not afraid of meeting challenges, also not afraid of regretting things I have done.
- Now I believe in myself and can tell others when I think something is wrong.
- I am less uncertain about things now and I have got a much better self-confidence.
- I feel strengthened to finish my education and in a satisfying way as well.
- That we had to create our own opinion in different questions has been very developing.

Recognizing your own development is not always easy nor is it obvious, and therefore it must be seen as positive that all of the mentees were able to give examples of how they experienced their own development.

Professional development

The other project goal was to prepare the novices for professional life. General issues related to work, together with leadership, were the normal subjects of discussion at the separate mentor/mentee meetings as well as at the common meetings. Every mentee stated between one to three examples on how they could see their professional development. Their statements have been divided into three categories.

Increased awareness of their own possibilities

- I have got a totally different approach to working life.
- I have realized that I am a strong individual, who can manage most things.
- I have a better self-confidence and can handle setbacks in a constructive way.
- I have learnt to think in a broader perspective and to see things in different perspectives.
- By learning to know oneself and being proud of who you are, you will get far both individually and in industry.

Improved preparedness for working life

- I much better analyse my immediate surroundings.
- I have got an understanding on how to manage different situations that will appear in the working life.
- I have learnt that I individually can decide how I should spend my time.
- I have become more objective and learnt not to involve feelings in different situations.
- I have got a glimpse on what the working life is and the pitfalls which are to be considered.

Increased knowledge of the meaning of gender in working life

- I have learnt that you can always learn a lot from people with experience.
- Different things and occurrences, which I only thought were clichés, do exist. It feels safe to be a bit prepared for what could happen to me.
- It is tough to be a woman trying to make a career.
- It is good to have female role models who show that it is not impossible nor is it strange to progress on a workplace.
- I have got a deeper insight into being in a manager's position, what is to be considered and how to combine working and private life.

All of the novices stressed awareness of their own abilities. They felt that they had developed professionally since they were better prepared for professional life and for leadership. The evaluations make clear that the mentoring had been good for the students. By meeting female role models they had acquired increased confidence and positive self-concepts and their knowledge about the world of the professions had been widened.

Mentoring High School Students

Since 2001 mentoring programmes for high school students have been carried out at Umea University. The number of the participants has varied during the years. Between 20 to 50 students from the Department of Science and 40–50 pupils from high schools in Umea and its surrounding areas have taken part. Since the interest to participate in the programme on the part of the high school pupils was large, some of mentors had two novices each. Because of that the number of mentees is a little bit higher. The aim for the mentees was to get an idea of what university studies would be like, thereby becoming more aware of their coming choices. The aim for the mentors was to learn how a mentoring programme can be created and carried out as a preparation for working life.

In the programmes, which lasted 6 months, individual mentor/mentee meetings, mentor meetings as well as joint mentors/mentees meetings were included. The programme was a 3-credit course for the mentors, and some obligatory tasks such as literature seminars and a written final examination were included.

Every programme was evaluated through an inquiry in which the experiences of the mentees were collected by their mentors through a short interview. The result presented here is from the first programme, which started 2001 and involved 22 mentors and 39 mentees.

The relationship

The mentors met their mentees an average of six times during the programme. The meetings took place mostly within the University. In these separate meetings the mentors were all available as a resource for discussing homework and special work assignment with their respective novices. In addition to these meetings the mentors had e-mail and telephone contacts with their mentees. A total of 32 novices' points of view were reviewed. The reason that not all of the 39 mentees participated in the evaluation was said by some of the mentors to be difficulties of getting in touch with the mentees at the end of the semester because they were busy finishing their high school studies.

All of the 32 novices experienced their participation in the programme as positive. Their motivation and determination to continue their studies at a university were increased, even though not all novices were going to apply for the Science Faculty. Even if some mentors thought that their mentees had had a low engagement with the programme, all the mentees thought that they had increased their knowledge about what university studies can involve. The talks between the mentors and the mentees

Table 9.2   The mentors´ experiences of the talks with their mentees

Experiences	Number of mentors
Interesting, giving, very diverse, relaxed	14
Slow in the beginning – better at the end	4
Both mentees were uninterested	1
The mentees were just interested the first time	1
One mentee was only a bit interested to study further	1
Difficult to meet both mentees at the same time	1

have been central in the relationships. Table 9.2 shows how the mentors experienced the talks with the mentees.

Most of the mentors thought that the talks with their mentees had worked well. The few difficulties that are named were because some of the mentees lacked interest in continuing their studies and the difficulties of having talks with two mentees at the same time.

The programmes planning

Most of the mentors' meetings and the mentors/mentees' meetings were scheduled after the end of the school day and never lasted more then 2 hours.

It is evident that all of the mentors thought that the way the programme was planned worked well (see Table 9.3).

Experiences of the programme

The mentors' attendance at the joint meetings was high and it was uncommon for any one of them to be absent. All of the mentors carried out the duties which were included under the programme.

None of the mentors had previous mentorship experiences. Accordingly, they did not know in advance what was expected of their participation. From their experiences it can be concluded that the mentors saw the programme as developmental (see Table 9.4). Whilst the mentors had been trained to take responsibility for other people and to be open for their needs and desires, the mentees had taken part in the university

Table 9.3   The mentors' experiences of the programme

Experiences	Number of mentors
Very good	8
Well balanced between individual and joint meetings	5
Good planned structure	7
Time duration was just right	2

culture, which gave them possibilities to discuss questions about further studies. They had also participated in different activities typical of the university world.

Conclusion

With the aim of supporting the autonomy of the individual and supporting induction into working life, modern mentoring is distinguished from the old forms of mentoring

Table 9.4   The mentors' experiences of their participation in the programme

Experiences	Number of mentors
Positive and developmental	11
Had own large engagement	3
Have mature has a person	2
Learn to take bigger responsibility	2
Will recommend others to participate next year	2
Got a wider perspective in my own studies	1
Developed my social competence	1

and from the various descriptions of mentoring as a teaching method. However, there is a need to be aware that mentoring is not the only thing of importance for development. During the mentoring period the mentees will meet a lot of other people and experience different situations in their private as well as their professional lives. Even if participation in mentoring generally has positive effects, other factors of influence cannot be excluded (Lindgren, 2000).

People learning from each other and from a variety of sources will be increasingly necessary in the future. To make mentoring more efficient there is a need to define the nature of mentoring and clarify existing interpretations. The special goals and motivations as well as the results and the effects of mentoring need to be highlighted.

Even if the key components are not specified, it is clear that mentoring is a unique method for personal development. Mentoring, when characterised as interactive and reflective individuals, stimulates and facilitates the learning process. Through this a 'learning society' can be created and supported. The challenge for twenty-first-century researchers is to contribute to an increased awareness about the possibilities with mentoring. An important question for future research is how to get mentoring to be seen as something natural and central, with people learning from each other in a mutual lifelong ongoing process rather then simply being taught.

References

Allsop, T. and Benson, A. (1997), *Mentoring for sciences teachers*, Open University Press, Buckingham.

Alred, G. and Garvey, B. (2000), 'Learning to Produce Knowledge – the contribution of Men toring', *Mentoring & Tutoring*, vol. 8(3), pp. 261–271.

Aryee, S., Wyatt, T. and Stone, R. (1996), 'Early career outcomes of graduate employees. The effect of mentoring and ingratiation (management development)', *Journal of Management Studies*, vol. 33(1), pp. 95–118.

Bergenheim, A. (2001), *Inspirationskälla, föredöme, tränare och kollega. Forskarhandleres visioner och verklighet*, [Source of inspiration, model, coach, and colleague. Supervisors' visions and reality.] Umea University, The University's Centre for Staff Education, Umea, Sweden.

Boethius, M. (1995), Mentorskap. Hur och för vem? [Mentoring. How and for whom?] Utbildningsförlaget Brevskolan, Stockholm.

Brooks, V. and Sikes, P. (1997), *The good mentor guide*, Open University press, Buckingham.

Bourdieu, P. (1992), *Kultur och kritik*, [Questions de sociologie.] Daidalos, Göteborg.

Cryer, P. and Mertens, P. (2003), 'The PhD examination: support and training for supervisors and examiners', *Ouality Assurance in Education*, vol. 11(2), pp. 1–8.

Dedrick, R.F. and Watson, F. (2002), 'Mentoring Needsof Female, Minority, and International Graduate Students: a content analysis of academic research guides and related print material', *Mentoring & Tutoring*, vol. 10(3), pp. 275–289.

Delamont, S., Atkinson, P. and Parry, O. (2000), *The doctoral experience. Success and failure in graduate school*, Falmer Press, London.

Freire, P. (1997), 'A response', in P. Freire (ed), *Mentoring the Mentor*, Peter Lang Publishing, New York.

Jacobi, M. (1991), 'Mentoring and undergraduate academic success: A literature review', *Review of Educational Research*, vol. 61(4), pp. 505–532.

Gilles, C. and Wilson, J. (2004), 'Receiving as well as giving: mentors' perceptions of their professional development in one teacher induction program', *Mentoring and Tutoring*, vol. 12(1), pp. 87–106.

Graesser, A.C. and Person, N.K. (1994), 'Question asking during tutoring', *America Educational Research Journal*, vol. 31(1), pp. 104–137.

Hulbert, K.D. (1994), 'Gender Patterns in Faculty-Student Mentoring Relationships', in S.M. Deats and L.T. Lenker (eds), *Gender and Academe: Feminist Pedagogy and Politics*, Rowman & Littlefield, London.

Keim, N. and Tolliver, C. (1993), *Tutoring & Mentoring*, Resource Publications, Inc, San Jose.

Kram, K.E. (1988), *Mentoring at work: Developmental relationships in organizational life*, University Press of America, New York.

Lick, D.W. (1999), 'Proactive Comentoring Relationships: Enhancing Effectiveness through Synergy', in C.A. Mullen and D.W. Lick (eds), *New Directions in*

Mentoring: Creating a Culture of Synergy, Falmer Press, London.

Lindgren, U. (2000), *En empirisk studie av mentorskap inom högre utbildning i Sverige*, [An empiric study of mentoring in higher education in Sweden.] Umea University, Department of Swedish and Social Sciences, Umea, Sweden.

Lindgren, U. (2003), 'Mentorship to support female engineering students – A complement to traditional education', Paper presented at the European Conference on Educational Research in Hamburg, Germany, 17–20 September.

Lucas, K.F. (2001), 'The Social Construction of Mentoring Roles', *Mentoring & Tutoring*, vol. 9(1), pp. 23–47.

McGee, Ch.D. (2001), 'Calming Fears and Building Confidence: a mentoring process that Works', *Mentoring & Tutoring*, vol. 9(3), pp. 202–209.

McKeachie, W.J. (1994), *Teaching tips. Strategies, reaserch and theory for college and university teacher*, D. C. Heath and Company, Lexington.

Moust, J.H.C. and Schmidt, H.G. (1995), 'Facilating small-group learning: a comparison of student and staff tutors´ behavior', *Instructional Science*, vol. 22, pp. 287–301.

Mullen, C.A. and Kealy, W.A. (1999), 'Lifelong mentoring: The creation of Learning Relationships', in C.A. Mullen and D.W. Lick (eds), *New Directions in Mentoring: Creating a Culture of Synergy*, Falmer Press, London.

Schmidt, H., Arend van der, A., Kokx, I. and Boon, L. (1995), 'Peer versus staff tutoring in problem-based learning', *Instructional Science*, vol. 22, pp. 279–285.

Stalker, J. (1994), 'Athene in academe: women mentoring women in the academy', *International Journal of Lifelong Education*, vol. 13(5), pp. 361–372.

Webb, N.M. (1989), 'Peer interaction, problem-solving and cognition', *Evaluation in Education*, vol. 13(1), pp. 21–39.

Chapter 10

Mentoring New Academic Staff in Higher Education

Gillian Trorey and Chris Blamires

Mentoring, especially the introduction of more formal mentoring schemes, has become increasingly widespread in higher education over the last decade (Blackwell and McLean, 1996a; Garvey and Alfred, 2000). However, Morton (2003) reports that the quality and purpose of such schemes has been variable. Where they work well, the mentoring relationship has been seen as a 'cornerstone' of both professional and personal development. Morton also states that the least successful outcomes for mentees have usually been experienced where mentors have been appointed as part of formally established institutional schemes. This clearly has implications for higher education institutions which are planning to establish or revise such schemes.

This chapter examines the use of mentoring in higher education. Using empirical evidence collected from one institution – a 'new' university in the north of England – it attempts to identify the nature of support required by newly appointed staff, in order to inform the development of mentoring schemes that meet the needs of both the individual and the institution in a more effective way.

The literature on the theory and practice of mentoring is vast, ranging from scholarly articles to 'how to' manuals. The importance of mentoring has long been recognised in many aspects of working life, and therefore the bulk of the literature has come from the world of business and management. In recent years the term has become more widely associated with education, with the mentee being seen as 'an adult learner who has consciously undertaken a developmental journey' (Cohen, 1995, p. 2). Thus the wider field of management and education literature is used here for a discussion of the meanings of mentoring and the characteristics of effective mentoring relationships, before moving on to consider the more specific arrangements for mentoring in higher education.

What is Mentoring?

The classic portrayal is of an older and wiser individual influencing the personal and intellectual growth of a younger protégé. However, many varied definitions exist. Dodgson (1986) for example argues that the definition of a mentor is 'elusive and varies according to the view of the author' (p.29). Clutterbuck (2001) agrees that there is some confusion over the term, pointing out that there is a marked difference between the way it is applied in Europe and the USA. In the USA, mentors tend to be perceived as 'sponsors' or authority figures:

'a mixture of parent and peer... a transitional figure in a man's development' (Levinson, 1978, quoted in Clutterbuck, 2001, p. 2).

This view is reinforced by Mathews (2003), writing in Australia, whose 'sample of mentor definitions' (p. 314) all refer to the mentor as being higher ranking, more experienced or influential. She uses the terms *mentee* and *protégé* interchangeably, to refer to 'the person receiving the help guidance and support of a more senior, experienced staff member' (p. 332).

The presumption here is that the (usually) older, wiser mentor has undergone the relevant learning experiences that have enabled him or her to adapt to the culture of the organisation and to work successfully within it. Such mentors can provide advice and support, based on their experience, that will facilitate the development of the individual, and by so doing, will result in benefits to the organisation (Kram, 1985).

However, Morton (2003) warns that there is a problem with this, and questions:

'when does advice and suggestion become instruction, to be followed through without thinking?' (p. 4)

She argues that this is more likely to happen if the mentor is more senior, going further to suggest that, in some schemes imposed by organisations, mentors with seniority may be used to ensure that the scheme meets the needs of the organisation. Morton argues that it is experience, not seniority, that is the essential attribute for a mentor, and points to a number of successful peer mentoring schemes that are in operation.

A widely quoted definition is that of Clutterbuck (2001):

'Off-line help by one person to another in making significant transitions in knowledge, work or thinking'. (Clutterbuck, 2001, p. 3)

'Off-line' refers to the mentor having no line management responsibility for the mentee. Megginson, in an early attempt at a definition, also refers to this:

'Mentoring is an essential aid to staff development... This requires a level of trust missing from the judgemental line management relationship where discipline has to be maintained and performance assessed'. (Megginson, 1979, quoted in Parsloe and Wray, 2000, p. 77)

Although the focus of the mentoring relationship tends to be on career development, many writers agree that personal development plays an important part. Levinson, for example, says that mentoring is:

'one of the most complex and developmentally important relationships a man can have in early adulthood'. (Levinson, 1978, quoted in Clutterbuck, 2001, p. 2)

Cohen (1995) also writing from the USA, considers that mentoring can help adults achieve their educational and career goals:

'Mentoring as a behavioural activity refers to the one-to-one relationship that evolves through reasonably distinct phases between the mentor and the adult learner... to develop, separately or in combination, his or her personal, educational or career potential'. (Cohen, 1995, p. 2)

Collin (1979), in a collection of definitions of mentoring, presents one with an essentially humanistic viewpoint. Mentoring is:

'a protected relationship in which learning and experimentation can occur, potential skills can be developed, and in which results can be measured in terms of competencies gained rather than curriculum territory covered'. (Collin, 1979, quoted in Clutterbuck, 2001, p. 3)

This definition is particularly relevant to the current climate in higher education, with new staff expected to undertake certificate programmes in teaching and learning in higher education. Many are new to teaching, and these programmes encourage participants to experiment with innovative methods of teaching and learning, and are usually based on the achievement of learning outcomes rather than a set curriculum.

The Role of the Mentor

Cohen (1995) shows that there is general support for the view that the role of the professional-as-mentor (in adult learning) is composed of six interrelated behavioural functions:

- Relationship emphasis – to establish trust
- Information emphasis – to offer tailored advice
- Facultative focus – to introduce alternatives
- Confrontive focus – to challenge
- Mentor model – to motivate
- Mentee vision – to encourage initiative.

He provides detailed mentor behaviours for each function; those of relevance to this study are likely to be:

- responsive listening
- using open-ended, probing and hypothetical questioning
- giving non-judgmental responses
- re-statement of issues to ensure factual accuracy and interpretive understanding

- presenting multiple viewpoints
- focusing on likely strategies for meaningful change
- emphasising the value of learning from unsuccessful or difficult experiences
- providing a direct, realistic assessment of positive belief in the mentee's ability to pursue attainable goals
- encouraging reflection on present and future educational, training and career attainments

Morton (2003), looking specifically at mentoring in higher education, explores the idea of the mentor being a 'sounding board', someone to 'bounce ideas off' (p. 4), encouraging the mentee to think things through in order to reach their own conclusions. She points out that at a time of change – undertaking a new job or new role – learning and experimentation is likely to take place which may be challenging. The mentor should be able to work with the mentee to reflect on these experiences and learn from them. She also suggests that mentoring can involve elements of coaching, although this is not essential to the mentoring role. She concludes by saying that mentoring is not about:

> 'championing the mentee's cause, or solving their problems or telling them what to do'. (p. 14)

Mentoring in Higher Education

In an academic environment, there will be marked differences between the mentoring needs of new staff in different disciplines. In some areas, notably sciences and psychology, recent PhD graduates may be appointed who could be entering their first employment. Other areas, such as law and the health professions, will appoint staff who have been working in their profession for many years, but may still be new to teaching. Different faculties also exhibit diverse subcultures, which will affect the nature of the mentoring relationship, especially in terms of its formality.

Fullerton (1996) points out that many of the roles now formally identified as mentor/mentee relationships have existed in HE for many years; these are now being recognised, and given status and value. In addition, institutions are now planning and actively encouraging mentoring relationships which would not have occurred naturally (Cohen, 1995), usually by the introduction of formal mentoring schemes. However, Blackwell and McLean (1996b) point out that the stimulus for this may be the increasing pressure to ensure that new staff become productive as quickly as possible.

Cunningham (1999) agrees that reasons for the introduction of a mentoring programme in higher education institutions include helping staff to adjust to the workplace and acquire skills and experience that enable them to contribute more effectively. Mathews (2003) also points out that:

'Socialization, job competencies, clarification of roles, future career prospects, satisfaction and understanding of organisational culture can be enhanced through mentoring'. (p. 329)

Fullerton (1996) states that there is no 'recipe' for mentoring schemes; each institution must find its own solutions. However, whatever system is adopted, it must be relevant to the culture and values of the institution. Griffiths and Magee (1996) agree that it is important for mentors to fully understand and value the system involved. Blackwell and McLean (1996b) make a case for a formal mentoring scheme, centrally organised, with 'written rules and prescriptions, formal training and monitoring ... on the grounds of consistency and equity' (p. 25). However, in reporting surveys of mentoring schemes at two universities, they show that most mentees prefer informal arrangements 'so there's no pressure to meet when there's no need to meet' (ibid.). However, where problems exist, increased formality is not necessarily the solution. They conclude that 'a light framework of rules' with a minimum of regulations regarding the purpose of the scheme is most appropriate for staff in higher education. Separate further guidance could be made available for those who wish it.

Evaluating Mentoring Programmes

Megginson and Clutterbuck (1997) point out that relatively few mentoring schemes are systematically evaluated. Evaluation raises a number of difficulties, such as a possible breach of confidentiality and trust within the mentoring relationship, as well as its essential informality. Cohen (1995) provides detailed scales for the self-assessment of mentors, but not for mentoring programmes. Clutterbuck (2001) suggests that attempts to measure programmes only become unacceptable when:

- a mentor is expected to report on a mentee's performance to a third party
- a mentor's opinion is linked to a reward for the mentee
- the content of discussions are disclosed.

He considers that a certain amount of measurement can help a mentoring relationship to grow, as well as enable scheme co-ordinators to improve the operation of the scheme – including training. He points out that there are three main reasons for evaluation:

1. to 'troubleshoot' individual relationships
2. to provide information for quality improvement of the mentoring programme
3. to demonstrate (to senior management) that the investment in mentoring has been worthwhile.

Clutterbuck presents a model or 'measurement matrix' (see Figure 10.1):

Relationship	Processes	Outputs
Programme	Processes	Outcomes

Figure 10.1   Measurement matrix for mentoring scheme (Clutterbuck, 2001)

Relationship processes are:

• how often does the pair meet?
• have they developed sufficient trust?
• does the relationship have a clear sense of direction?
• do they have concerns about their own or each other's contribution to the relationship?

Programme processes are:

• how many mentors and mentees attended the training?
• how effective was the training?

Relationship outcome is:

• have the mentor and mentee met the goals they set?

Programme outcomes are:

• have we increased retention of key staff?
• have we raised the competence of mentees in critical areas?

It can be seen that Clutterbuck's matrix is mostly concerned with individual relationships. Evaluation of some of the processes in the above model is unlikely to be acceptable in Higher Education, being likely to raise concerns regarding possible value judgements and intrusion into an essentially private relationship. However, some points are relevant to the 'whole scheme' evaluation intended in this study, such as frequency of meetings and the effectiveness of mentor training. Programme outcomes either require data collection at the institutional level, or are integrated into a mentee's individual performance review, which again is confidential.

Clutterbuck (op.cit) reports the findings of one company evaluation, that of BP Chemicals, which audits its mentoring scheme annually. The main findings were that mentoring works best when:

• the new staff member meets his or her mentor shortly after arrival

- early meetings are regular
- mentors appear purposeful and confident
- the relationship feels 'real'
- the mentor and mentee are on the same site but in different parts of the company
- both have a positive attitude towards the concept of mentoring
- the mentor is not a line manager to the mentee ('off-line')
- mentees use 'diary notes' to discuss what they have been doing since the last meeting.

This review of the literature has identified definitions of 'mentoring' and issues relevant to mentoring in the higher education context, selected an appropriate model for the mentoring role and considered methods of evaluating mentoring schemes. This is used as a framework for the research that follows.

Background to the Research

One aim of this study was to determine whether the existing university mentoring scheme is achieving its aims. At present, only staff attending the Postgraduate Certificate in Professional Development (PCPD) are routinely allocated a mentor. Each mentor is a member of the same department or faculty, selected by the relevant department. Although mentors receive training, their practice is essentially managed by their academic department.

The philosophy of the PCPD programme, as stated in the course handbook, is 'firmly located in professional experience and your day to day activities as an HE practitioner'. Kolb's Experiential Learning Cycle is used as a model (Kolb, 1984), together with the notion of the 'reflective practitioner' (Schoen, 1987). Course participants are expected to reflect on their experiences in order to 'generate concepts which link into existing theories.... which provide ....the conceptual framework with which to plan and tackle new situations effectively'. Participants are encouraged to discuss their experiences with others, both formally and informally. This includes tutors and mentors and other members of the participant's department or faculty.

Informal feedback from course participants suggests that a range of mentoring practice currently exists, but there had been no formal evaluation of the mentoring arrangements and whether these are meeting the needs of new staff. In addition there is not a consistent policy across the institution regarding the provision of mentors. Hence newly appointed staff who are already 'teacher trained' and not required to attend the PCPD programme may not be given a mentor, despite the fact that they may come from a background of teaching in schools or further education and still require induction to, and support in, the higher education environment.

Research Methodology

The first part of the study involved an analysis of the various documents related to the PCPD programme, in order to determine these aims, and how clearly they are presented to participants. This is in accordance with the view that mentors must fully understand the system with which they are involved (Griffiths and Magee, 1996). As Fullerton (1996) points out, any mentoring system must be relevant to the culture and values of the organisation. Key organisational policies such as the University Strategic Plan and Human Resources Policy were also examined in order to establish organisational expectations.

The second part of the study involved a questionnaire to current and past PCPD participants. Initially, the choice of a questionnaire for this type of research may be a surprise. A study of the experiences of people in different contexts suggests a naturalistic approach rather than the more positivistic stance that questionnaires usually represent. However, it was recognised that the main constraint for the respondents in this study, as new lecturers with full teaching loads, was the availability of time to take part. It was considered unethical to request interview time in view of these pressures. However, a well-designed, relatively short questionnaire was considered acceptable, especially if presented by Email, with the opportunity to respond by the same medium. This also meets Clutterbuck's (2001) suggestion that any evaluation of mentoring schemes must be 'unobtrusive', 'timely 'and 'easy to apply'.

The questionnaire was based on nine closed questions, prescribing a range of responses selected from the researcher's experience and from the literature on mentoring, in order to obtain information about how the current mentoring scheme operates in practice, and whether it has met or is meeting participants' needs. This was followed by four open questions intended to explore the preferred nature of mentor support. For ethical reasons, the questionnaire only ventured into the pragmatics of the mentoring relationships rather than the evaluation of individual relationships. For convenience, the questionnaire was presented by Email, but with the option of printing off and returning in the internal mail if anonymity was required. Confidentiality was assured for all participants.

The first nine questions were of the 'mark the response that most closely applies' or 'mark as many that apply' type. Simple frequencies and percentages were recorded for each item, and used to identify any patterns. The open ended questions that followed were subject to a basic 'content analysis'. Content analysis is usually used as a method of 'quantifying' qualitative data (Miles and Huberman, 1994; Cohen, Mannion and Morrison, 2000), but here it is used to identify any clusters of responses and emerging themes.

It was intended that some in-depth interviews with new staff engaged in successful mentor/mentee relationships might be used if the questionnaire responses did not provide adequate qualitative information, but in the event this was not considered necessary because of the quality and detail of the responses obtained from the open-ended questions.

Analysis of Key Documents

An analysis of key policy documents was undertaken in order to determine what has been written (and therefore established as 'strategy' or 'policy') by the university, relating to the support and mentoring of new staff. The university's approach to its staff is perhaps best summarised by the following quote from the Strategic Plan:

> 'University staff must be able to contribute fully to its operation, its development and their own development through policies and procedures for human resource management that maximise organisational integration, improve flexibility and adaptability, improve quality, enhance staff commitment and encourage contribution to the professions'.

This reflects the notion that any mentoring scheme would be expected to benefit the organisation, with mentors expected to focus on their mentees taking responsibility for their own professional development, and being encouraged to adapt to new and more flexible ways of working. However, mentoring is only mentioned once in the Strategic Plan, and then only in respect of research:

> 'When appointing new staff, the university will take into consideration their potential to contribute to research.... Best practice will be disseminated by mentoring and mutual assistance'.

It is only in the Staff Development Policy, under *Plans for enhancing training and development*, that the provision of mentors, for both new staff and new managers, is mentioned:

- 'providing a mentor/buddy for all new staff and for those who move posts
- developing and documenting an integrated induction process

This suggests that the writer(s) of this policy may see mentoring as having purely a 'training and development' function, rather than a wider supportive and developmental role.

The PCPD Course Handbook, however, provides detailed guidance on the role and responsibilities of mentors, their appointment and the management of their role. In contrast, this sees the mentors' role as being:

- 'essentially supportive and developmental
- providing subject based advice and .... academic/pastoral support'.

This suggests a lack of co-ordination amongst the various documents at the different levels within the institution. It is apparent that the current approach to mentoring is that of 'bottom up', arising from the PCPD course. Following the course philosophy, the focus is on the needs of the individual.

Questionnaire for New Staff

The questionnaire was presented by Email to 45 current and past PCPD participants. There were 12 responses to the first round, one of whom was unable to complete the questionnaire because his mentor had left and not been replaced. A second request resulted in six further responses, a total response rate of 40%. This low level of response was expected, due to the many other demands on respondents' time. No respondent exercised the option of anonymity.

Arrangements for mentoring relationships

All the mentors were experienced lecturers, more senior than their mentees; this is as expected, in order for mentees to be able to benefit from the mentors' experience. However, three mentors also had line management responsibility for their mentee. This practice is not recommended, as it may affect trust and confidentiality – a mentee is less likely to want to confess to doubts or shortcomings if their mentor has a monitoring or assessment role, or is in a position of power.

Just over half of the mentees selected their own mentor, with the rest having their mentor selected by their line manager. Where the individual selected their own mentor, the reasons for their choice, and the numbers selecting each option were:

someone they thought they would relate to (9)
someone from the same subject area (6)
a manager who would 'point in the right direction' (4)
an experienced researcher/international research reputation (2)

Only one chose the person with whom he or she worked most closely. Other reasons given were 'someone I felt comfortable with discussing my shortcomings and concerns' and 'someone competent'.

The most positive responses in this survey were undoubtedly about relationships where the mentee had made their own choice of mentor. Clearly, if this is to happen, it cannot take place immediately, as time will be needed to get to know relevant colleagues. Therefore it is likely that the induction phase for the new staff member will be managed by others, perhaps a line manager.

Only three mentors/mentee pairs had fixed meeting times, of twice per month, once per month and once per semester respectively. Two relied on the mentor arranging the meetings, while the majority were at the request of the mentee, two thirds of which were on the basis of 'immediately or as soon as the mentor is free'. Two had 'informal meetings in the corridor' in addition. Most meetings (15) took place in the mentor's office, two pairs met in a teaching or meeting room and two 'in a café/pub. off campus'. Frequency of meetings is one of the criteria used by Clutterbuck (2001) to evaluate mentoring relationships; in this survey, meetings appear to mostly be taking place according to the mentees' needs, rather than meeting when there is not felt to be a need. This accords with the findings of Blackwell and McLean (1996b), that staff do not want to feel pressurised to meet when there is no specific need. Meetings that took place 'immediately or as soon as the mentor was free' were particularly helpful, especially where a 'crisis' had arisen for the mentee. The question arises as to whether more senior staff are usually in a position to be available for their mentees at such notice – or is it more likely to be a matter of prioritisation, with 'good' mentors immediately making themselves available?

Two thirds of mentors/mentees kept either notes or minutes of the meetings, with half agreeing action points arising from the meetings. Of those that kept documentation, this was usually kept by the mentee (7) and in three instances, by both. Just one mentor kept the documentation only, which could suggest less ownership of the process on the part of the mentee.

Seven pairs had verbal agreements about the nature of their mentoring relationship, and nine pairs did not. One pair had discussed having an agreement and felt it was 'unnecessarily formal'. The 'light framework of rules' recommended by Blackwell and McLean (1996) would appear to be operating here. However, Cohen (1995) considers that having a formal system in place provides the necessary structure, a point also made by one of the respondents:

'[Mentor's name] is someone I think I would always feel I could turn to for advice in any case, but the mentor system legitimises that slightly and makes me feel more comfortable about doing it on a regular basis'.

Matters discussed with mentors

A list of 18 possible matters was presented, with participants being invited to tick as many that applied to them. Each item is presented in rank order with the number selecting each item in brackets:

Reflecting on and evaluating your own performance. (13)
Your PCPD portfolio/reflective commentary. (13)
New ideas for teaching your subject. (12)
Ways of teaching your subject. (11)
Issues to do with your professional development. (11)
Resources for use in your teaching. (9)
How to manage student tutorials, coursework etc. (8)
Personal issues. (8)
How your Department/School operates. (8)
Assessment of students' work. (7)
Planning your lectures, tutorials, student assignments etc. (7)
Managing your time. (5)
Ideas for research. (5)
IT support e.g. use of Email etc. (5)
Student 'discipline' type issues. (4)
How the University is structured. (3)
Administration – how to do. (2)
Possible publications/commenting on your draft publications. (0)
Other (please state). (0)

Clearly, it is the issues to do with the professional development, especially in teaching and learning that were discussed most frequently, with administrative and organisational issues of lesser importance. Personal issues also featured highly, the importance of which is perhaps understated in the literature.

The benefits of having a mentor

On being asked what were the 'best things' about having a mentor, access to advice from experienced practitioners was most frequently mentioned, followed by support, guidance, and the ability to talk ideas through (or act as a 'sounding board'). This may suggest that in the early stages, new staff may value specific advice from experienced lecturers rather than having a mentor who helps plan ways through issues and problems. It suggests the mentor taking a 'coaching' rather than a 'mentoring' role. This could in part be due to the increasing demands on new staff and the expectation that they will be 'up to speed' in ever shorter periods of time. However it could also reflect the traditional view of the mentor (Levinson, 1978), as suggested by one participant:

'Being able to access someone with a great deal of experience and position of responsibility'.

Mentees also valued feedback on their teaching, and general encouragement:

'The feedback on my actual practice was particularly helpful in both building my confidence up a little and yet directing me to areas which needed improving. One of the main things that my mentor is good at is offering reassurance that my lecture/seminar plans are good ones and that I can stop [over]preparing'.

Motivation and inspiration also feature:

'It is working very well. I always feel inspired after seeing him'.

These comments reflect Clutterbuck's (1995) mentor model – the mentor as motivator, – but interestingly, specific references to motivation as a benefit of mentoring are otherwise rare in the literature. It could perhaps be considered to be an implicit part of the relationship.

One member of staff was particularly happy with his mentor:

'I am 100% happy with my mentoring relationship. I had been at the university for about 4 months before I had to chose my mentor and so was able to pick someone who I knew I got on with but would be very honest with me/critical of my teaching. I don't think I could have asked for more and – compared with new lecturers at other universities I know – consider myself very lucky!'

The ideal personal and professional qualities for a mentor

Mentees again identified knowledge (of both subject and teaching and learning) and experience as the most important professional qualities for a mentor (mentioned by 12 participants), together with being available, willing and having the desire to help and give advice and guidance:

> '....prepared to offer advice to be used or considered without expecting it to be used every time in an obvious way'.

This raises an interesting difference between a mentor and line manager, as a manager would clearly expect advice to be followed, while a mentor is less likely to expect this.

The desired personal qualities mentioned most frequently were 'friendly', 'approachable' and 'easy to talk to' (8):

> '....approachable and easy to talk to, knowledgeable and giving good advice that can save you time'.

Other qualities were 'humour', 'patience', 'sensitivity', 'honesty', 'flexibility' and 'trust'. Being 'non-judgemental', 'open to learn themselves', 'a good listener', 'logical' and 'an effective problem solver' were also mentioned:

> 'For me the main things I value about my mentor are (1) her honesty and (2) her sensitivity. This means she gives me detailed critical feedback on my practice but in a way that is constructive and easy to accept. I also appreciate the professional/serious attitude she takes to the role.... My mentor takes any issues I have seriously and deals with them very well!

Cohen (1995) also identified 'responsive listening' and giving non-judgmental responses as important 'mentor behaviours':

Respondents also identified the need for mentors to be able to support their mentees' development during the PCPD course:

> '....ideally someone who has experience of writing reflective commentaries, who has a lot of teaching experience – using different methods'

There were just two instances where mentees felt that some aspects of the relationship was not working so well, and in both cases these were where the mentor was not familiar with the PCPD course or did not support its aims or the notion of reflective practice. This points to the need to select mentors carefully, especially in terms of having shared values. Information about the philosophy and structure of the PCPD programme is provided during the mentor training sessions, but unless the mentor identifies with the aims of the programme and is committed to the development of teaching and learning, this developmental support may not be forthcoming.

Conclusion

It is clear that the majority of the respondents were very satisfied with the existing mentoring scheme, with a number of mentors receiving very positive comments. In the two instances where the relationship was not working well, this appeared to be because the mentors were not fully aware of their role in supporting the mentee in engaging in reflective practice. The scheme appears to have achieved a good balance between the formal, structured scheme and the 'light framework of rules' recommended by Blackwell and McLean (1996b), the latter being more appropriate to higher education. On the whole, the mentor training currently provided is also enabling mentors to fulfil their role in supporting their mentees.

The findings of this study demonstrate that the investment in the mentoring scheme has been worthwhile. At present, only staff attending the PCPD course are routinely provided with a mentor. As this model has been shown to be effective, it could undoubtedly be extended to include all new academic staff and those changing roles. This would enable the current *Plans for enhancing training and development* in the Staff Development Policy to be implemented using a tried and tested mentor model, where the relationship is seen to be developmental and supportive, rather than taking a narrow, 'training and development' approach.

The provision of effective mentor support for all new academic staff can only result in a more effective induction and integration into higher education. Such an approach will have benefits both for the individual, in terms of their 'comfort' and perceptions of their new employer, but also to the institution, in terms of a more rapid 'bringing up to speed' of the staff member, together with enhanced pedagogical effectiveness and overall contribution to the academic community. Increased job satisfaction and scholarly productivity are advantageous to both.

When designing a formal mentoring scheme, care should be taken to ensure that the scheme 'works for the mentee' (Morton, 2003 p.13). Schemes that focus on the needs of the organisation may not benefit the mentee (and presumably, in the longer term, will not be advantageous to the organisation either). Thus, the desired outcomes for both the institution and the individual should be clearly stated at the start of any mentoring programme. The roles of both mentors and mentees should be clarified, as well as how the programme will be structured and how it will be evaluated (Mathews, 2003).

The responsibility for the success of the mentoring relationship does not rest solely with the mentor. As Mathews (2003) points out, both mentor and mentee must accept responsibility for ensuring a beneficial and effective relationship, and be committed to making it work. In high quality mentoring relationships, both will derive considerable benefit.

Mentors must be chosen carefully. New staff require experienced and knowledgeable mentors who are approachable and can find sufficient time, often at short notice, to help through a 'crisis'. They prefer mentors who possess particular personal qualities, such as honesty, approachability, sensitivity, patience and flexibility. The question is, how can we ensure that all mentors possess these qualities? Morton (2003) suggests that certain interpersonal skills can be improved through training. However, she points out that, because of the time involved, a mentor training scheme cannot *develop* such skills, but only explore how the skills can be applied in a mentoring relationship. Many of the desirable attributes are either innate or develop over a number of years. Thus mentors should be chosen with care, with consideration of the skills and personal qualities they already possess. Ideally, institutions should recognise, foster and reward the staff who possess the skills and personal attributes to work effectively in this role.

Only with a well designed scheme and effective mentors can new academic staff be provided with successful mentoring support that will enable them to develop both personally and professionally at this 'critical and formative' stage in their HE careers (Fullerton, 1996, p. 12).

References

Blackwell, R. and McLean, M. (1996a), 'Mentoring new university teachers', *International Journal of Academic Development*, vol. 2, pp. 80–85.

Blackwell, R. and McLean, M. (1996b), *Formal Pupil or Informal Peer?* in H. Fullerton, (ed), Facets of Mentoring in Higher Education 1. SEDA Paper 94, pp. 23–32.Staff and Educational Development Association, Birmingham.

Clutterbuck, D. (2001), *Everyone needs a mentor: fostering talent at work.* CIPD, London.

Cohen, L., Mannion, L. and Morrison, K. (2000), Research Methods in Education. 5th edn. Routledge Falmer, London.

Cohen, N. (1995), *Mentoring Adult Learners: a guide for educators and trainers*, Krieger Publishing Company, Malabar, Florida.

Cunningham, S. (1999), 'The nature of workplace mentoring relationships among faculty members in Christian higher education', *Journal of Higher Education* vol. 70(4), pp. 441–63.

Dodgson, J. (1986), 'Do women in education need mentors'? *Education Canada* Spring 1986, pp. 29.

Finnegan, R. (1996), 'Using documents', in R. Sapsford and V. Jupp (eds), *Data Collection and Analysis.* Sage/Open University Press, London, pp. 138–51.

Fullerton, H. (1996), 'Introduction', in H. Fullerton (ed), *Facets of Mentoring in Higher Education 1.* SEDA Paper 94, pp. 7–12. Staff and Educational Development Association, Birmingham.

Garvey, B. and Alfred, G. (2000), 'Educating Mentors', *Mentoring and Tutoring*,pp. 113–126.

Griffiths, M. and Magee, R. (1996), 'Being Mentored', in H. Fullerton (ed), *Facets of Mentoring in Higher Education 1.* SEDA Paper 94, pp. 15–20. Staff and Educational Development Association, Birmingham.

Kram, K. (1985), *Mentoring Network: Developmental Relationships in Organisational*

Life, Scott Foreman, Glenview, Illinois.

Kolb, D. (1984), *Experiential Learning*, Prentice-Hall, UK.

Lincoln, Y. and Guba, E. (1985), *Naturalistic Enquiry*, Sage publications, Beverly Hills, USA.

Mathews, P. (2003), 'Academic mentoring: enhancing the use of scarce resources', *Educational Management and Administration*, vol. 31(3), pp. 313–334.

Megginson, D. and Clutterbuck, D. (1997), *Mentoring in action: a practical guide for managers*, Kogan Page, London.

Miles, M. and Huberman, M. (1994), *Qualitative Data Analysis* (2nd. edn) Sage publications, Beverly Hills, USA.

Morton, A. (2003), *Mentoring*. Learning and Teaching Support Network Continuing Professional Development Series No. 2, York.

Parsloe, E. and Wray, M. (2000), *Coaching and Mentoring: practical methods to improve learning*, Kogan Page, London.

Robson, C. (1996), *Real World Research*, Basil Blackwell Ltd, Oxford.

Schoen, D. (1987), *Educating the Reflective Practitioner*, Jossey Bass, San Francisco.

Chapter 11

Mentoring On-line: Rethinking the Tutor/ Student Experience

Val Tarbitt

The purpose of this Chapter is to describe and discuss through my personal experiences the meanings given to on-line mentoring relationships with mature women students. Most of the published work about Internet-enabled distance learning tends to emphasise the virtues of providing on-line high quality courses and the difficulties of students learning from them. Students' expectations of on-line learning are high but, according to Salmon (2001), some become disillusioned and disengaged. She goes on to say that the support and actions of the on-line tutor, more than the function of the technology in use, can really make the difference between disappointment and highly productive learning.

The Chapter will examine the phenomenon of E-mentoring from an interpretative perspective in the way that Taylor and Bogdan (1984) describe as capturing the process of interpretation through which individuals define their worlds. My study about E-mentoring takes into account the significance of gender and as a feminist researcher I have concern for the ethical implications of research about women where the emphasis is on empowering them and transforming patriarchal social institutions through the research process. Mentoring as a current, high focus form of development intervention is used in education, as well as other work environments, to facilitate the development and learning of an individual on a one-to-one basis at a specific stage of development or transition. Translating the traditional face-to-face mentoring relationship into a highly immediate, interactive, visual electronic resource, in which the learner might want the learning to be: *Just in time, just for me, just a keystroke, just for now*. (Spender, 1995. p.45) is the idea on which I have based my research.

My research is concerned with exploring E-mentoring when it is set against the traditional form of face-to-face mentoring. I explore my experience of supporting women learners on-line. In doing so my aims are to discover:

- If it is possible to recognise a shift from E-tutoring to E-mentoring.
- What impact this has on the relationship
- What impact there is on the original tutor/student relationship

New technologies and their implications have a major impact on almost all aspects of people's lives at the level of the individual, the household and the workplace.

Computer technologies have opened up education, training and information opportunities and in doing so are affecting the nature of human interaction and social behaviour. Interactive and virtual technologies, remote networking and the Internet have changed the scope of the geographical and social boundaries of communication. Within this debate it is important to note the significance of gender and the centrality of consciousness-raising as a methodological research tool in order that the emphasis on empowering women and transforming patriarchal institutions through research can continue.

There is the need, according to Megginson (2000), to examine the benefits [and potential threats] posed by these changes and to explore the impact of technology on mentoring. He theorises about the notion of the boundaryless career, which creates the possibility of the virtual Mentor, someone who is outside the organisation of the Mentee and who rarely meets the Mentee face-to-face. This in some way again retraces our steps back to that ancient, historical perspective of the Mentor in which Athene hid her true identity in order to make the contract with Odysseus' son work.

'The Times Higher' [01.09.00] suggested that *Virtual Mentoring is the new buzzword*. However, there is a growing attention to the situation of teachers/tutors faced with the need to adopt the new technologies to use in the classroom. There is also widespread belief that students might often have a greater command of the technology than those who teach them. This potential anxiety combined with the advent of computer aided learning for students and on-line INSET and CPD for teachers/tutors has lead to the belief that opportunities for networking with and learning from other teachers/tutors has been reduced and a feeling of professional isolation rather than professional innovation is in place. In this case therefore the support given to the on-line learner is crucial. Many advocates of computer-mediated distance education emphasise its positive aspects and play down the kind of communicative and technical capabilities and work required by students and tutors. At this stage, according to Fennell (1997), it is important to listen to women's experiences as challenges to theory and the key to the transformation of theory.

Published papers and systematic analytical studies of students and tutors who have experienced new technologies in Higher Education are few. Karen Murphy, of Ohio State University, in 'The Times Higher' [02.02.01] argued that although technology would appear to be a blessing to students and tutors because of its instant access to a universe of information on any conceivable topic her research revealed that students found computerised text less interesting than paper text simply because it was computerised. Her research has implications for educational practice if computerised texts present additional hurdles for less competent readers. The implications are there, too, for tutors engaged in a distance learning programme. According to Spender (1995) the transitional generation, of which Murphy's (2001) students are a part, have grown up with print but are living in an electronic world and feel secure when surrounded by books. For them, books may be a reassuring backdrop against the electronic world in which they live. Glazer (1990, p. 338) reiterated the importance of studying women's work in education from their own perspective: *Changing the lens in how we study the professions is the first step in this transformation.*

Universities are able to implement distance learning education to reach more diverse populations and provide learning environments 24 hours a day, 7 days a week. Besser and Donahue (1996) and Rahm and Reed (1998) have examined the difficulties for tutors in developing distance learning courses. There are however, the beginnings of evidence that some technology users are rebelling against the spectre of information overload.

According to Lewis (2001) most of us are becoming victims of *information fatigue syndrome* and in 'The Guardian G2' [20.06.01] in his article 'Post Modern', Burkeman declares: *It's great to have an infinite number of connections, but that's the problem – you have an infinite number of connections.*

This argument was carried on in 'Straw Poll', [BBC Radio 4, 25.08.01] where there was agreement among the panel that for most users of new technology there was *no hiding place*.

For the on-line tutor supporting the distance learner the implications are complex. If students find the use of technology difficult or obtrusive then their relationship with their tutor will be affected. Distance Learning students and on-line tutors do not normally 'see' each other unless they have access to a video link. They might experience anxiety if they are unable to determine each other's expectations. Communicative confusions are a by-product of limited social cues such as gestures and facial expressions that are in evidence in a face-to-face Mentoring relationship. According to Hara and Kling (2001) students experienced frustration if they did not receive prompt feedback from the tutor. Interaction and feedback are fundamental to the effectiveness of distance learning programmes in the same way they are to a traditional Mentoring relationship.

The modern, currently accepted concept of Mentoring has positive connotations. Megginson and Garvey (2001) recognise that there might also be shadowed aspects, 'the dark side of Mentoring' according to Hay (1995). This is illustrated perhaps by the fact that in Homer's story Athene hid her true identity in order to make the relationship work. This 'hidden identity' might also be a powerful component of E-mentoring. Jones (1990, p. 32) notes that:

> The impact of gender on roles and organisational behaviour has been and will continue to be a topic of much interest and research.

The 'information age' or 'knowledge society' has brought with it the realisation that the paternalism of the past might not be an appropriate paradigm for unlocking individual potential. Neilsen, as far back as 1990, considers seeing women rather than just men in centre stage. Cook and Fonow (1990) supported this view and went on to assert that research should involve defining women as the focus of analysis. Aburdene and Naisbitt (1993) describe ways in which women are overturning centuries of male domination within organisational environments and how women's inspirational leadership in business will replace outdated management hierarchies.

My own research builds on these concepts. Taking the stance advocated by Fennell (1997) by studying the work of women through their own experiences of E-mentoring the interest in transformation and empowerment will add to the greater understanding of gender. Aburdene and Naisbitt (1993) believe that the fact that:

- there are more women in public life
- there are more women entrepreneurs
- there is more networking
- the expectations of girls and women have changed

will have direct relevance to the future of mentoring. They believe that as women expect to create structures and institutions where collaboration and partnership is the norm, the critical mass of women will change the norm. Increasing female entrepreneurship will change the nature of mentoring. Mentors used to the 'old order' will become obsolete because acquiring typically male approaches to functioning in a competitive hierarchy will no longer apply. According to Hay (1995, p.11) Mentors will not be *older, white, male mentors* nor will they be:

> those women who have succeeded in the corporate world by adopting the male characteristics which created the competitive hierarchies in the first place.

Again, according to Hay (1995, p. 11) women will want role models:

> Who can demonstrate the effectiveness of women's values, who can function as Mentors in a style which encourages self-development, collaboration and genuine connectiveness and who operate as equals when Mentoring.

The body of practice around mentoring on-line is seen to be as specialised and as particular as that of a face-to-face mentoring relationship and therefore in the same way needed to be fully and specifically contracted into.

Technology has potentially expanded women's access to mentoring and according to Packard (2003) technology – supported mentoring complements and extends what can be achieved by face-to-face mentoring. Intensive relationships such as tutor/student can often be portrayed in an idyllic manner but according to Earwalker (1992) tutors in their support role have to cope with a range of ambiguities, tensions and conflicting responsibilities. It is the institutional context that sets limits on the nature of the relationship. A tutor and a student may 'belong' to the same institution but they 'belong' there on different terms. The balance of power is shown in the unequal status of tutor and student.

If this relationship is then translated on-line and that on-line tutor/student relationship changes to a mentoring relationship, then there are issues to consider for all those involved in, or around, that relationship.

The literature around mentoring and technology reveals debates surrounding the nature and magnitude of the 'digital divide.'

One of the greatest strengths of e-mail is its ability to break down socio-economic, racial and the other traditional barriers to the sharing and production of knowledge. (Herring, Johnson and Di Benedetto, 1992)

However, Spender (1995) and Carli (1994) are both concerned that in order for women to play a vital part in cyberspace, they have to take on the 'new culture':

Designers, particularly female designers, need to get directly involved in the experience of the NET – they need to get involved in large numbers if they intend ever to play a role in shaping the form or the content of the Metaverse in a significant way. (Carli, 1994, P. 27)

According to Devins et al (2003) various groups [women, ethnic minorities, white working class males, refugees and asylum seekers] have been identified as being at risk of further exclusion if they do not have access to the Internet. The virtual reality is a long way removed from the ideal reality that was predicted when the Information Technology revolution began. There are still barriers to women's participation. One of the most obvious is the actual financial outlay required to buy a computer, get involved in training and buying time on the NET. Because of the financial discrepancies between the buying power of men and women, women can be disadvantaged, and by not being able to access this medium, women's disadvantage is compounded. Conefrey (1993) argues that although electronic media are available to everyone the reality of economics might subvert open access for many women whose career paths can be delayed anyway. Mills (1989) talks about 'editing women out of the organisational frame' by signalling to females that they are not regarded as full organisational members. As women can be found in low paid, low status work and where that work is defined traditionally as women's work and men are in a numerical minority men can still be found in the senior positions of power and are therefore the gatekeepers to women's advancement. As long as women have less access to computers they are denied full membership of cyberspace. Spender (1995) declares that without a voice and a vote in the creation of the technology culture there is no hope that things will improve for them.

Keisler et al (1997), in one of the first pieces of research that looked at the consequences of using the Internet, set up a field trial whose purpose was to understand people's use of the Internet at home. The trial's philosophy was to reduce barriers to use so that a diverse sample of people using the Internet for the first time could be monitored. Currently, interpersonal communication via e-mail and information search and acquisition via the World Wide Web, are the dominant uses of the Internet. The participant sample in the Keisler et al (1997) project had positive attitudes towards the Internet before they actually used it but their vague knowledge and beliefs made it difficult for them to get started. Even after a year's experience with the Internet, participant's initial computer skills still constrained their Internet usage.

The Internet is a complex and multi faceted social phenomenon. Continued research into the social and professional benefits brought about by the greater level of user use has implications for education. Teachers are faced with the need to adopt the new technologies. Education applications have accelerated and computer-mediated learning is no longer confined to the majority of self-aware and enthusiastic technology pioneers.

A Government statement (Wills 2001) quoted by Smithers (2001, p. 2) in Education @ Guardian [20.03.01] warns us that: *Technology is a fast moving field and we don't necessarily have all the answers.*

There is no doubt that the Internet is the electronic educational hub in current learning activities. For teachers and students to be able to meet and work in cyber collaboration provides an attractive concept. Linking up in cyberspace is there at the touch of a keyboard. However, when the 'digital divide' is again taken into account Rossman (1992) points out that anyone not wired up will be disadvantaged and not part of a collective intelligence. For the full time Undergraduate student the simulated classroom is a reality. For the part-time mature woman student becoming part of the learning society, at any hour of the day or night, by plugging into the library, at home or in the workplace has exciting possibilities and distinct advantages providing they are not disadvantaged by lack of access.

On-line tutors and Course planners need to take into account that many of the students for whom they are planning have grown up in an environment saturated with technology and that the use of interactive technologies can affect their social and moral development. Such technically mature students have the ability to interact with others from many different social and cultural backgrounds and they can engage in a wide range of virtual experiences that would not be normally possible or accessible in their real life environment. It might be that, according to Willard (2001), such students are often more adept and comfortable in interactive technology environments than the tutors they might meet in an on-line learning environment. However, there are certain issues that need to be recognised when planning computer-mediated distance learning. Willard (2001) is adamant that tutors and planners need to take into account the perceptions, their own and those of their students, of how electronic discussion compares to traditional class discussion in respect of the attitudes developed towards other students, tutors and the Institution delivering the on-line learning.

The evolving technologies used within an on-line learning environment present important challenges to both tutors and students. An on-line course might offer participation in a mixed-age on-line learning community. Course planners need to recognise that this can affect the quality and level of communication. The on-line discussion gives the learner the opportunity to develop, according to Willard (2001), a 'public voice' and the ability to speak out. There needs, therefore, to be recognition of the cultural traits and learning styles of on-line learners and language differences and cultural conflicts between student and tutor need to be addressed. In my own recent experience this has been the case particularly in tutoring on-line those students from Mainland China and from India.

Tutoring on-line requires tutors to have a wide range of expertise. Benjamin's (1994, p. 49) optimistic view of teaching and learning where:

Every learner can, at his or her choice of time and place, access a world of multimedia material – immediately the learner is unlocked from the shackles of fixed and rigid schedules, from physical limitations – and is released into an information world which reacts to his or her own pace of learning

is still not universally shared or universally welcomed.

According to Salmon (2000) the Open University, with its well-established distance learning methodologies, still includes some face-to-face sessions. Some Courses have a small proportion of on-line working based on e-mails only. Others have a Website with online exercises and study guides. Salmon (2000) is adamant that any significant initiative aimed at changing teaching methods or introducing technology into teaching should give the online tutor training and support. This, in my opinion, is the point at which I became interested in what was happening on-line between my Distance Learning, mature women students and myself.

Because on-line tutoring is a new approach to teaching and learning there are few on-line mentors around, so on-line tutors need to be supported if they find there is a shift in expectations when tutoring on-line.

In addition to actual training Salmon (2000) warns that the contentious issue of how much time an on-line tutor can be expected to work on-line must be addressed by the Organisation embedding teaching and learning within technology. Also, negotiated boundaries need to be part of the on-line tool kit.

Uniting mentoring with e-mail results in expanded opportunities for mentoring. While E-mentoring remains a relatively new phenomenon with little in the way of written research to support its claims, its use has expanded quickly within a brief time frame. Most writing and discussion, however, centres on the technicalities rather than issues around the relationship and how it compares with the traditional face-to-face meeting.

Single and Muller (2001, p. 68) define E-mentoring as:

a relationship that is established between a more senior individual [Mentor] and a lesser skilled or experienced individual [Mentee], primarily using electronic communications, that is intended to develop and grow the skills, knowledge, confidence, and cultural understanding of the Mentee to help him or her succeed, while also assisting in the development of the Mentor.

From this definition we can see that nothing much has changed in terms of defining a power situated, traditional experience. Because the connections are asynchronous, scheduling a meeting is no longer the obstacle it is, or can be, for face-to-face mentoring pairs because the Mentor relationships are not bounded by geographical constraints. Bennet et al (1998) point out that E-mentoring can readily flourish as long as both Mentor and Mentee have access to the Internet. The nature of an electronic relationship can also provide an additional advantage beyond that experienced within a face-to-face mentoring relationship. Where Mentoring exists between employees of different status within an organisation [or between a tutor and student], according to Frierson, (1997) this unequal relationship which exists during the initial stages of the mentoring relationship might lead to a lack of openness. E-mentoring, however, might help to overcome those initial feelings of discomfort because the status differences might not be so readily identified. Palloff and Pratt (1999) outlined that while potentially problematic for anyone not comfortable with the technology, E-mentoring does enable equality in the Mentoring relationship. A mentoring relationship is a reciprocal one. Eisenman and Thornton (1999) highlighted this when discussing how mentor and mentee benefit from the relationship. Price and Hui-Hui (2003) further expanded this in their discussion about the benefits of E-mentoring:

- It can be conducted across vast distances.
- There is flexibility of access regardless of time and place.
- It provides greater accessible resources and support [information is just a link away].
- Can create a community of sharing and problem solving.
- It increases collaborative opportunities in which there is a dialogue between learners.
- It can adopt a range of communication methods.

According to Price and Hui-Hui (2003, p. 109):

Because E-mentoring can be a private medium or a public one the rich environment and the flexibility that E-mentoring generates are both its most appealing benefits.

For Hawkridge (2003) mentoring has had a key role in the Open University's intricate education system for more than thirty years but it has changed substantially as technology has changed. Gibbs and Durbridge (1976) published papers illustrating the important characteristics of successful tutors and from their findings an Open University guide for tutors was drawn up. Salmon (2000) then developed this into an E-mentoring model in which the Mentor became an electronic friend to each student, though they rarely saw each other. This model is grounded in constructivist learning theory as well as practical experience. Just as in my own experience and practice, where face-to-face mentors aim to meet, motivate and get to know their Mentees, Salmon's E-mentoring model emphasises:

- Access and motivation.
- On-line socialisation.
- On-line exchange of ideas.
- On-line knowledge construction.
- On-line challenging and construction of meaning.

Although, according to Hawkridge (2003), there are differences between face-to-face and on-line mentoring, when tutors are on-line the best methods from traditional face-to-face mentoring need to be encompassed.

For those who have spent years building the skills for face-to-face mentoring the use of e-mail might seem a totally alien concept and an intrusion in the Mentoring relationship. According to Harrington (1999) there might be those who support the fact that e-mail is too 'lean' a medium to support the deep exchanges necessary for developmental relationships or 'alliances' (Hay, 1995), others evolve special techniques for establishing mutual understanding.

Within my own experience, part-time mature women students strive to develop, or continue to develop, a sense of career-related identity. This developmental process is supported by the tutor/student relationship in which, according to Kram (1983), the student's transition to professional moves through career, academic, psychological and role modelling functions. Ragins (1989) and Cotton (1991) have highlighted that mentoring is regarded as crucial for women's career development but that women may perceive and experience greater barriers to establishing mentoring relationships. This theory was supported by the findings of Linn and Kessel (1996) and Seymour and Hewitt (1997) when they were investigating women who pursue non-traditional careers, particularly in Science and Engineering. They found that many interested and capable women were deterred by the fact that they had little access to women mentors. With few women in these professions it was difficult to provide women with the very resource, a mentor, that research indicates could keep or attract women in these under represented scientific fields. The focus, then, should be to develop innovative ways to provide access to much needed female mentors even if they are geographically dispersed and inaccessible locally. There is also perhaps a need to consider men, or other professionals, as potential mentors because, according to Lee (1999), people from different demographic dimensions could offer important mentoring functions to women. Sosik and Godshalk (2000) state that cross gender and cross race Mentoring is successful so it is important to facilitate access to a large pool of potential Mentors despite perceived barriers. E-mentoring makes this possible.

According to Packard (2003) 'technology-supported' mentoring increases access in terms of expanding the realm of who can mentor and be mentored. A further argument could be that a face-to-face mentoring programme could have the disadvantage of restricting mentees to the mentors available in their local vicinity (Packard, 2003). Translating this into the environment of Higher Education, an E-mentoring programme is flexible and unconstrained by time restrictions (Sanchez and Harris, 1996). It can be difficult for mentors and part-time student mentees to participate in mentoring programmes during the working day if the relationship has been set up outside the remit of the mentee's working environment. E-mentoring, therefore, makes participation less of an intensive time commitment.

The intensive traditional mentoring model can often be portrayed in an idyllic manner emphasising the transformative power of the relationship for both parties (Healy and Welchert, 1990). Many E-mentoring initiatives are designed with the traditional Mentoring model in mind but using e-mail to facilitate contact. Some feminist researchers (Blackburn et al, 1981; Powell, 1999) refer to the traditional model of mentoring as male 'grooming' designed to replicate existing cultures and it is because of these 'warnings' that alternative forms of mentoring, of which E-mentoring is a major, emergent domain, needs to be researched further.

Mentors in a traditionally male dominated business world, as I discussed earlier, are usually selected because they have a track record that is seen to be appropriate and they have succeeded in an area in the organisation in which the mentee aspires to follow them. However, in Hay's (1995) 'alliance', mentors are perceived as guides rather than gurus and their aim is to facilitate growth in the mentee rather than pass on the lessons of their own experience in order that the patriarchal culture of the organisation can be easily absorbed. Learning is therefore at the heart of the relationship and mentors in an 'alliance' will need to understand the processes of learning. By being involved in such a relationship the mentees will have an awareness of the process by which they have undergone change and they will play an equal part in what is happening. Mentor and mentee will work in partnership to increase the mentee's openness to the learning that is taking place. Alongside this must also be the recognition of the learning that is taking place for the mentor.

Extracting the essence from this last statement I apply it to my own learning situation as an on-line tutor in Higher Education, responsible for developing Distance Learning Mentoring Courses. I visualise my learning as a series of cycles, like a set of Russian dolls, all interconnected. My role as tutor is the outer casing and the 'inside' dolls are my roles of Mentor, Mentee [sometimes], on-line tutor and most recently, on-line Mentor. It is the role of on-line tutor/on-line Mentor that I have put under the spotlight.

The Mentoring Courses I developed have always been 'Supported Distance Learning'. Students were required to come together as a group to meet the Course Team face-to-face in three Workshop settings during a minimum learning schedule of thirty weeks. Tutor contact continued until the student submitted work for assessment. This continued contact was negotiated and relied on face-to-face meetings, telephone tutorials or e-mail. The model was well defined and the ground rules observed. However, the Course team began to notice changes in the way students chose to operate. The availability of networked computers at home and at work, particularly in the private sector, had grown rapidly and was beginning to make an obvious impact on student learning styles.

Salmon's (2000) findings support my observations that the use of the Internet and the World Wide Web has created opportunities to use it for teaching and learning. So, in what I originally called a 'Supported Distance Learning Course' the support factor needed to be reassessed in the light of new technological trends. These trends impacted on the way students began to see the opportunities for them to contribute to a learning community, based on common objectives, rather than their own geographical location. The significant factor in the Course analysis was that the impetus for review was student driven. The initial face-to-face Workshops enabled the students to form peer support groups and then for them to decide how to keep tutor contact. E-mail was the predominant method and it was interesting to monitor the discussion around this during the Workshop sessions. Women students in particular were very proactive in setting up support groups, often basing them on clear geographical guidelines for ease of meeting to complement e-mail discussion.

For me, as tutor and Course Leader, the best practice within a mentoring relationship has always been a focus for the way in which tutor/student support would be offered. E-mail is a relatively mature technology [c.1969]. It is personalised, spontaneous and interactive. The content of a particular message is usually tailored to the recipient and will take into account prior interactions. Keisler et al (1997) found that e-mail was popular and sustaining and its use was stable over time, [albeit their survey was conducted in 1997]. Their findings supported the Course team in its discussions around tutors' electronic availability and the ground rules that could be set up to support ongoing tutor/student dialogues and relationships. E-mail support, for all of us within the Mentoring Course, offered on-line networking and in some cases on-line socialising. We used the technology that had created the opportunity. In this way it could be said, as cited in Salmon (2000), that we were building on Durkheim's explorations around the social power of ideas stemming from their development through the interaction of minds.

Sci-fi author, William Gibson [who coined the word 'cyberspace'], in an article in The New York Times Magazine [14. 07. 96, p.6] described the Web as a *'procrastinator's dream'* that offered the added advantage:

People who see you doing it might even imagine you're working.

This certainly was a concern for several women students, in particular, in those early days of communication transition when their negotiation centred on the frequency of e-mail contact permissible within their own work environment. If, for whatever reason, one of the women students changed her job it could mean that she lost her e-mail contact and therefore her contact with her peer support group. A significant development of this, perhaps, is that I am now observing some women students using a male partner's e-mail and address facility to contact me rather than one of their own.

Students who enrol on the Mentoring Course volunteer an e-mail address as part of their official enrolment details. This raised their expectations that they could, and would, be contacted through that medium. As Hara and Kling (2001) recognised, the issue about on-line teaching and learning is to understand how people work with their innovations in practice without censoring that which is problematic. The Course Team was being driven by the technology without the kinds of guidelines that would help all the participants work together harmoniously. As Course Leader I was aware that changes in our negotiated work pattern were necessary. In order that I could bring a more informed judgement to the discussion I have reflected on specific relationships with on-line students and it was from these observations that my research developed. I have explored the on-line relationships I have shared with six mature women students.

These relationships began as on-line tutor/student relationships and during four of them there was a recognisable shift in the form the relationships took. I discuss the findings of my study from my reflective diary and an e-mail trail. My research is concerned with exploring E-mentoring when it is set against the traditional form of face-to-face mentoring. I used my evidence to explore my own experience of supporting women learners on-line. My aims were to discover:

- If it is possible to recognise a shift from E-tutoring to E-mentoring.
- What impact this has on the relationship.
- What impact there is on the original tutor/student relationship.

The data produced combines this evidence with my interpretation of how I located myself, as on-line tutor, within the on-line relationship of tutor and student. This is a subjective interpretation which will I hope contribute to new knowledge though I recognise Griffith's (1995) belief that knowledge is situated in the 'knower' and therefore my subjective position re-enforces a feminist perspective.

Case Studies

Six women students are my focus group. I have reflected on the on-line tutor student relationship I developed with them. In grounding my reflections in women's experiences of on-line mentoring I was conscious of not wanting to universalise my experiences of on-line mentoring to all women.

Within my reflections about on-line mentoring I have been very conscious about the fact that my role as tutor, and therefore assessor, is a dominant factor in my relationship with my students. As a feminist I recognise the power that can be exercised over women. However, I believe that the 'in-dwelling' method I have used for my data production emphasises the validity of the power of personal experience within the research process. Locating myself as an actor in the research process (Maynard and Purvis, 1994) has helped me to fully recognise the power of the relations in which I am located.

All of the women had enrolled on one of the Mentoring Courses and had therefore met me, but not each other, face-to-face at the Workshops. Our tutor/ student relationship would normally continue on-line after that.

My relationship with Student A experienced a negotiated 'shift'. I suggested that I could support her through her professional crisis. We decided we could 'lift' our new on-line mentor/mentee relationship out of the original on-line tutor/student relationship for a negotiated time. My relationship with Student B also experienced a negotiated 'shift. She asked me to be her mentor to support her through a new academic experience and to help her make sense of it.

In both relationships we agreed that a set of ground rules were necessary but both women felt comfortable with this because we had originally met face-to-face.

> I am enthusiastic about this Val, because I know you will offer me clarity of purpose and because we have worked together face-to-face I am confident our relationship can develop on-line. [Student A.]

Salmon (2000) found from early Open University research that an influential discovery was the impact of the lack of non-verbal and visual clues in on-line interaction. Some participants find that this can result in a sense of depersonalisation and consequently negative feelings result. Had these two mentoring relationships begun on-line then Student A and Student B might have felt that negativity.

So, armed with positive responses to 'meet' on-line and comfortable in the knowledge that we would re-negotiate boundaries and review the relationships at stages in the months ahead, we began.

Student A and I and Student B and I wanted to operate effectively in this changed mentoring world. I was conscious of Hay's (1995) reminder that we will want to do things in ways that are ethical and responsible even though we have stepped outside the traditional mentoring procedures. In both 'new' relationships the initial step was to recognise the reason for embarking on them and to agree a framework in which we could operate.

Student A

In my relationship with Student A, because I had initiated the change in the relationship and had taken the role of mentor, I decided my first e-mail would be welcoming and reassuring but that it would also clarify the issues that had moved us from the tutor/student relationship. Throughout the discussions about my findings I have used a Mentoring Guide (see Figure 11.1) I devised and which is based on Hay's Stages of an Alliance (1995, p. 42). I have revisited the stages the relationships might need to pass through in order that there could be benefits.

The 'success' of my relationship with Student A would be a job change (her aspiration) so I was careful to remind myself that Hay (1995), allowing for individual differences, maintained that a 'typical' job change for a professional could take two or three years. Because of the 'newness' of E-mentoring as a support/development tool and the lack of other research material to support my findings I had to recognise that my relationship with Student A might be shorter, sharper and more like a 'quick fix'.

Our relationship developed by exploring Stages 1 and 2 (Figure 11.1). We exchanged some short, cheerful e-mails which seemed to satisfy our need for contact:

Dear Val
Thanks for your 'letter'. I had my first meeting with my new Mentee yesterday so have some good stuff to reflect on. Must go. Have plane to catch. Off to Italy for a few days but taking some books which will help me with my essay. No movement on the job front. Regards.

Mentoring Guide

This method of 'mixing' the tutor and mentor relationship continued until there was a real need for Student A to face up to the difficulties she felt she was encountering at work. I was very aware that my e-mails needed to maintain their supportive 'sound' but that I now needed to challenge her into exploring the situation at work and to begin to visualise the options open to her. I remember always writing my 'letter' to her in hard copy first in order to get the language 'right'. At that point I was aware that the technology might defeat me if I did not and that I might 'click' the wrong icon before I was sure my 'letter' was ready to send. This is a luxury not open to those in a traditional face-to-face mentoring relationship.

In February 2001 Student A's mood changed. Her anxiety about company reorganisation and the lack of opportunity for promotion within the new structure made her angry. Her e-mails to me were more frequent, soul searching and were often sent in the early hours. Salmon (2000) advises several short e-mails rather than one long one if several topics are to be included. Initially I disagreed with this advice when I was replying to her. Short messages might convey curtness or the idea that the mentoring relationship was becoming an intrusion. I had to weigh this against the fact that I was first and foremost her tutor. I began to feel that tension.

Again, in February, she began to face the situation and we reached Stages 7 and 8 (Figure 11.1):

Val
I am trying to lose myself in my essay. Sorry about the panic at the weekend. I had lost all my hand written work and then realised after a frantic search that I had screwed it up and that it was in the waste paper basket. I have decided that I will work to finish the Mentoring Award. This will hopefully give me some alternatives after reorganisation.
Regards.

Then later:

Val
There seems to be nothing for me other than this boring job dealing with schools. It's not a promotion but at least I will have a job so perhaps I need to calm down and as you say think about some alternatives once the new structure is in place.
Regards.

During this time, Stages 9 and 10 (Figure 11.1), when Student A was beginning to 'accept' the situation and was exploring the range of options open to her I knew I would have to be encouraging. I found myself sending: *Great to hear from you. Will get back later today* messages. I recognise that this tactic gave me a breathing space but it also meant that I could devote some discrete time to consider my reply. In this way E-mentoring has a quality not enjoyed by traditional face-to-face mentoring when visual clues can cause misunderstanding and instant responses are required.

Things felt problematic at this point. Communication was frequent, disjointed and despairing. Analysing my own responses I felt remote from the reality of the relationship. I was able to, and did, detach myself in a way that would not have been possible for me were we meeting face-to-face. I was also aware that I was working in isolation and was conscious of Hay's (1995) stipulation that mentors need ongoing support in the same way that Counsellors and Social Workers have Supervision. This is rarely in place for mentors and is one of the issues in my relationship with Student B and with Student D that will be discussed later. Support, therefore, for on-line mentors is another area which requires analysis and research.

Suddenly we reached Stage 13 (Figure 11.1). Student A was offered a new job with enhanced status. When we reviewed the process together she was sure that spending time analysing the options available had given her a new confidence that had been recognised by her Line Manager. The time scale in which we reached a conclusion was short but we had worked unknowingly inside a time/opportunity framework driven by the company. We had not been caught unawares by the relationship reaching this positive conclusion. Hay (1995) and Clutterbuck (1992) both advocate recognising in the early stages of the mentoring relationship that it will end possibly in the form it has been contracted. We had done this when we drew up our boundaries. Our relationship subsequently passed into an agreed new phase, social e-mailing, in addition to the tutor/student relationship that existed on-line at the beginning. Student A successfully completed the Mentoring Award.

My changing relationship with her, recognised in my reflection on what was happening within the relationship, helped to clarify my methodological approaches and theoretical frameworks of this and the other case studies. My own learning journey picks up Hughes' (2002) strong message that researchers have to develop a high level of skill in being critically reflexive. According to Hughes (2002) by putting the researcher, myself, into the research signals how the knowledge produced is located in the perspectives of the researcher. This was the case with Student B.

Student B

The request to change our original on-line tutor/student relationship came from her.

The request was buried inside a tutor/student e-mail about locating books for her assignment:

> – Second point Val – I am looking for a Mentor for myself, I wonder if you can help. I spoke to JW on Wednesday [she completed the Course some time ago and said you were a great support]. I am open to the idea of E-mentoring but would like some face-to-face as well –.

My response, on reflection, seemed guarded.

> Good to get a positive e-mail from you. Certainly I could offer some E-mentoring support [which would help my research]. Perhaps we could explore that and renegotiate our tutor/ student relationship

MENTORING GUIDE

MENTEE	MENTOR
1. Immobilisation	The need for reassurance and contact
2. Alliance	Negotiating the contract
3. Denial	Challenging
4. Assessment	Exploring the situation
5. Frustration	Tolerance and shared thinking
6. Analysis	Identifying patterns and trends
7. Acceptance	You decide!
8. Alternatives	Exploring the range of options
9. Development	Encouragement to seek training/coaching
10. Action planning	Choosing an option
11. Application	Support for the decision
12. Awareness	Supporting the here and now
13. Completion	Celebrate success
14. Appraisal	Reviewing the process of change

Figure 11.1   Mentoring Guide based on Hay's Stages of an Alliance (1995, p. 42)

We were exploring Stages 1 and 2 (Figure 11.1). We met at the second Workshop and set aside tutorial time so that we could negotiate our new mentoring relationship. She was keen to maintain the face-to-face meetings with e-mail contact in between, which somehow changed what I had envisaged. Reflecting on this I recognised that my 'anxiety' stemmed from a feeling of not being in control. In this I recognised the arguments put forward by Kelly, Burton and Regan (1994) about democratising the research process and that when embarking on feminist research it is crucial to think through what our power is as a researcher. Somehow I felt that we had reached Stages 4 and 5 (Figure 11.1) but it was me who was being challenged.

Student B set out in her follow up e-mail what we had agreed:

- To discuss career development.
- To analyse existing skills and experience.
- To explore time management skills.

However, she moved into issues we had not discussed:

– I would also like to explore the following: loss of status on many fronts; immigration; stress management; anxiety and sleep patterns. Also, I have decided that I would not like to set a time limit on the relationship.

Salmon (2000) points out that difficulties might come during an on-line relationship which 'slides' into an area of personal support where there has been no recognition that this has happened and where the ground rules and boundaries have not been defined at the beginning. In my relationship with Student B I had tried to set out a framework, had recognised that this was changing so my reply e-mail, which I delayed in order to think things through, attempted to bring us back on track – (my track?):

> Back in harness again! I think having set out your priorities to be addressed within our relationship will help us to focus clearly. However, is there is one issue that you feel impacts on all the others so that discussing that might clarify things. I am around this week –.
> Val

I found myself overwhelmed by her lengthy reply. She pointed out all her anxieties about immigration, her work abroad, her lack of interview success in Britain. She ended her e-mail:

> There is part of me that would really like to just hand over the controls to someone else for a while and give me a chance to breathe.

I was overwhelmed again. I delayed my reply but knew that I was experiencing a tension between my overall work load, my responsibilities as a tutor to her and to all my other students and a recognition that I was not qualified as a crisis Counsellor. I felt I could not offer Student B the kind of support I thought she needed.

I was conscious of interpreting the social existence she presented and the need for taking responsibility for its interpretation (Ramazanoglu with Holland, 2002). As the researcher I had the power to represent the life of the student I was researching, I was conscious about being a knowing self (Ramazanoglu with Holland 2002) and facing up to the interpretation that I would put on my findings.

I invited Student B to meet me so that I could explain my anxieties about those areas of her need I felt unable to support but offer her continued academic and professional on-line mentoring. She declined and I did not hear from her until I received some Course work. Our relationship tailed off and neither of us recognised the need for 'closure'. Somehow our relationship sat uncomfortably at Stage 8/9 (Figure 11.1). Our tutor/student relationship was not renegotiated and I am left with a feeling of guilt for the fact that she did not complete the Mentoring Course.

I am conscious that my reflection on this particular relationship has reiterated the place of the personal in feminist theory (Hughes, 2002. P.173). By reflecting I have not merely thought about something (my relationship with Student B) but that my portrayal of the social realities around the relationship simultaneously describe and constitute them. My position as a privileged feminist researcher is now even more obvious to me as I continue to reflect on my on-line tutor/student relationship.

Student C and Student D

My relationship with both students seems very clear. Student C used the momentum of the on-line tutor/student relationship to keep in contact mainly by e-mail but booking telephone tutorials and face-to-face meetings regularly. Her request for support, comments on her work and advice about 'direction' of her own career were always solidly within the kind of remit I would expect in a traditional tutor/student relationship:

> Hi Val -Just wanted to write a quick note to thank you for your support this morning – I found it to be very useful.
> Thought I would copy you in to this e-mail below – it would be good to be interviewed for a magazine on Mentoring wouldn't it?

Her method of using me as a 'sounding board', a recognisable element in traditional mentoring, continued but it became very intense as the months went by. We moved through Stages 1 to 11 and at Stage 11 (Figure 11.1) I recognised that though I was involved in much discussion/feedback about her own training and development as a Consultant our on-line relationship had not undergone any real 'shift'. What was obvious to me was that I was involved more within a 'coaching' relationship with Student C as she became more involved in her own career change. This is an acceptable component of a mentoring relationship but in our case we had not negotiated a mentoring relationship.

My relationship with Student D progressed in the same way but without the intense 'Coaching' element. It was a satisfying relationship on-line and developed in the traditional mentoring way. It seemed that in both cases my on-line relationship with these two students gave us a freedom in which there was no social distraction. My dilemma with Student B perhaps was that, according to Kiesler (2000, p. 2)

> On-line you don't have to deal with unpleasantness because if you don't like someone's behaviour, you can log off. In real life, relationships aren't always easy.

A mentoring relationship needs to be able to withstand challenge. As the key word in Hay's (1995) analysis is 'equal' then that challenge or confrontation will be a two way process. In my on-line relationship with Student B I reacted negatively to the challenge. Student C, Student D and I moved through Stage 13 (Figure 11.1) and celebrated the success of achieving the Award.

My relationship with StudentD has moved through Stage 14 (Figure 11.1) into a newly negotiated relationship in which I will be her mentor to support her in her role as mentor to the new professional mentors in schools in her Local Authority.

When I began to research the complexities of supporting mature women students on-line I realised that the students in my case studies so far could be described as white, middle class, Western women and as such, as Hughes (2002) points out, my contribution to feminist theory was over simplistic. However, my research is based on discovering what happens to the tutor/student relationship when it moves on-line. I am also exploring how the technology might be a barrier to the development of the relationships. Several of my relationships had developed in a way that I thought might contribute to new knowledge about women and mentoring on-line and women and technology and it was those relationships on which I focussed.

Interestingly I recently began to work with a group of Post-Graduate students who had elected to do the Mentoring Course. Nine of the students were from Mainland China. Two of these students are:

Student E and Student F

Both women were highly motivated, computer literate, new to Britain, the University and mentoring. They used e-mail frequently to contact me about their work and to arrange face-to-face tutorials. Student E began to use our on-line conversations to share information about cultural differences and how she felt about being in Leeds.

Hi Val!
Greetings! I have received your returned stuff including my diary and your comments. Thanks for your nice encouragement.

And again:

Dear Val
Nice to get your reply. I am in Shanghai for the Spring Festival. I am okay now. I did sustain a difficult period during my first month in Leeds since my life is so different from here. Your diary assignment helps me to track my changes as well as finding my own values while Mentoring.

Have a nice day

When we met face-to-face, which was frequent, always pre-booked and usually for an hour we discussed the Assignment, life in Britain and our relationship in which Student E spoke of me as a 'role model'. We had moved beyond the tutor/student relationship into one that could be tracked through the Mentoring Guide (Figure 11.1). At no time did either of us discuss this. As in a good mentoring relationship the learning takes place for both mentor and mentee and in this relationship I was in a privileged position to learn about Chinese culture.

Student F used an interesting method. She kept in touch about the Course with frequent e-mails. My insight into our relationship came through her reflective diary that I would often find had been put through my study door at night. In her diary she explored her observations about her working life in Britain (she was working as a University cleaner) and about mentoring in the workplace:

Of course this job is not only to gain work experience in Britain. The more important objective is to increase my knowledge and understanding of learning and Mentoring. I want to test the theories.

It seemed as though her diary replaced meeting me face-to-face.

Both Chinese students successfully completed the Mentoring Course and thanked me my support. Student E has asked me if I would be interested in doing some training for her Company when she returns to China. Our relationship has therefore moved into a phase similar to that which I have now with Student D. There has been 'closure' of the tutor/student relationship and a new relationship negotiated.

The literature, language and philosophy surrounding the concept of mentoring today are positively projected. Gulam and Zulfiqar (1998) highlighted the contemporary feel and flavour it appears to have. Again, this is where Hay's (1995) concept gains strength. By referring to it as a 'developmental alliance' she relates it the 'whole person'. This is an approach that covers long term, significant growth. By using the word 'alliance' the feeling of 'coming together' for a common purpose is re enforced. The word also implies some kind of negotiation and contract with the potential for rules and boundaries which can be re visited and reviewed by the two people involved.

In the tutor/student relationships I have explored I have recognised when the on-line relationship moved into something new and re-negotiated, new and not re-negotiated or when the relationship deepened but did not move out of that which might be determined as an acceptable tutor/student relationship.

Throughout I have been aware that my descriptions of events within these relationships also interpret them. According to Maynard (1994) the researcher is involved in interpretation and that no feminist study can be politically neutral but Cain (1986) argues that we need to take our own theory seriously and to use the theory to make sense of the experience. I have engaged in a synthesising process that connects experience to understanding.

This 'story' about on-line mentoring and the mature woman student has helped me to develop a higher level of skill in being critically reflexive:

> There is then a difference between claiming that experience does not give us the truth and concluding that experience cannot tell us anything except stories. (Ramazanoglu and Holland, 1999. p. 387)

By this I do not mean I have merely turned things over in my mind but by engaging with a reflective diary I have been able to portray the social realities of on-line tutoring and simultaneously describe and constitute the realities of the relationships with my on-line students.

This study shows how the six students responded to on-line tutor support and two students in particular, Student A and Student B negotiated an on-line mentoring relationship with me to focus on their needs. They also recognised that the relationship could help them achieve success. For me, the researcher/tutor, the experience demonstrated the importance of developing a tutor/student relationship of trust and open communication with students before expecting honest and open communication on-line. The breakdown of my relationship with Student B has helped me to understand that in order to create and maintain intensive relationships, mentors need to invest plenty of time and energy (Ragins and Scandura, 1999) and like other close relationships personality and other more dysfunctional outcomes can result (Eby et al, 2000).

All six relationships began face-to-face. An issue for further research for me will be to follow the progress of tutor/student relationships that begin, and continue, only on-line. Also, my exploration of my tutor/student on-line relationships with Student E and Student F gave me an opportunity to begin to compare group differences and experiences based on culture.

This is a small, select study that has produced a wealth of information I have not been fully able to use. I have not explored my on-line relationships with men students, for example. Some of my initial thoughts, as I began this study, centred on the possible barrier that the technology itself might present. All six students in the study were computer literate and had access to e-mail at work and at home in their own right. However, all six students, through choice, used a mix of e-mail and face-to-face contact to sustain a relationship with me. Perhaps, according to Spender (1995), we need to continue to work hard to convince women of the communication potential of the computer.

The most revealing aspect of this study for me has been recognising the power relations between the researcher and the researched. This might in itself affect the core relationship of tutor and student.

The strength of this research is the fact that it is new knowledge and it will contribute to the debate about being able to identify a shift from on-line tutoring to on-line mentoring, the implications of this shift if it happens and the impact of this shift on the original tutor/student relationship

References

Aburdene, P. and Naisbitt, J. (1993), *Megatrends for women*, Random House, London.

Appelbaum, S.H. and Shapiro, B.T. (1993), 'Why can't men lead like women'? *Leadership and Organizations Journal*, vol. 14(7), pp. 28–32.

Benjamin, A. (1994), 'Affordable, restructured education: a solution through information technology', *RSA Journal*, May, pp. 45–49.

Belenky, M.F. et al (1986), *Women's ways of knowing: the development of self voice and mind*, Basic Books, New York.

Bennet, D. et al (1998), *Critical issues in design and implementation of telementoring environments*, New York Education Development Centre's Centre for Children and Technology.

Besser, H. and Donahue, S. (1996), 'Introduction and overview: perspectives on distance independent education', *Journal of The American Society for Information Science*, vol. 47(11), pp. 801–804.

Blackburn, R.T., Chapman, D.W. and Cameron, S.M. (1981), 'Cloning in academe: mentorship and academic careers', *Research in Higher Education*, vol. 15, pp. 315–327.

Bleir, R. (1984), *Science and gender: a critique of biology and its theories of women*, Pergamon, Oxford.

Burkeman, O. (2001), 'Post modern', *The Guardian G2*, 20 June, p.

Cain, M. (1986), 'Realism, feminism, methodology and law', *International Journal of the Sociology of Law*, vol. 14, pp. 255–267.

Carli, D. (1994), 'A designers guide to the internet', *Step by Step Graphics*, Peoria, Illinios, November-December.

Clutterbuck, D. (1992), *Everyone needs a mentor*, 2nd ed. London, IPM.

Conefrey, T. (1993), *Internet communications gender the NET*, 22 April.

Cook, J.A. and Fonow, M.M. (1990), 'Knowledge and women's interests: issues of epistemology and methodology in feminist sociological research', in J.M. Neilsen, *Feminist research methods: exemplary readings in the social sciences*, Westview Press, Boulder, Col.

Davidhizer, R.W. (1998), 'Mentoring in doctoral education', *Journal of Advanced Nursing*, vol. 13(6), pp. 775–781.

Deem, R. (1995), *Do methodology and epistemology still matter to feminist educational researchers?*, ECER, University of Bath.

DeMarco, R. (1993), 'Mentorship: a feminist critique of current research', *Journal of Advanced Nursing*, vol. 18, pp. 1242–1250.

Devins, D. et al (2003), *Connecting communities to the internet*, PRI, Leeds Metropolitan University.

Earwalker, J. (1992), *Helping and supporting students*, SRHE and Open University Press, Buckingham.

Eby, L.T. et al (2000), 'The protege's perspective regarding negative mentoring experiencies: the development of a taxonomy', *Journal of Vocational Behaviour*, vol. 57, pp. 1–21.

Eisenman, G.T. and Thornton, H.J. (1999), 'Telementoring: helping new teachers through the first year', *Technological Horizons in Education Journal*, vol. 26(9), pp. 79–82.

Evans, J. (1995), *Feminist theory today: an introduction to second wave feminism*, Sage, London.

Fagenson, E.A. (1989), 'The mentor advantage: perceived cover job experience of protégé's versus non – protégé's', *Journal of Organizational Behaviour*, vol. 10, pp. 309–320.

Fennell, H.A. (1997), 'A passion for excellence: feminine faces of leadership', *Annual Meeting of the American Educational Research Association*, Illinios, Chicago.

Fonow, M.M. and Cook, J.A. (eds) (1991), *Beyond methodology: feminist scholarship as lived research*, Indiana University Press, Bloomington.

Friedan, B. (1963), *The feminine mystique*, Victor Gollancz, London.

Frierson, H.T. Jr. (1997), *Diversity in higher education mentoring and diversity in higher education*, vol. 1, J.A. Press, Greenwich, CT.

Future Foundation Study (2003), 'Tracking equality says report', *The Guardian 2*, July.

Garvey, B. (1999), 'Mentorship and the changing paradigm', *Mentoring and Tutoring*, vol. 7(1), pp. 41–54.

Gibbs, G. and Durbridge, N. (1976), 'Characteristics of Open University tutors (Part 1)', *Teaching at a Distance*, vol. 6, pp. 96–102.

Gibb, S. and Megginson, D. (1993), 'Inside corporate mentoring schemes: a new agenda of concerns', *Personnel Review*, vol. 22(1), pp. 40–54.

Glazer, N. (1997), *We are multiculturalists now*, Harvard University Press, Cambridge, M.A.

Golde, P. (1970), *Women in the field: anthropological experiences*, University of California Press, Berkeley.

Grant, J. (1988), 'Women as managers: what they can offer to organizations', *Organizational Dynamics*, vol. 16(3) Winter, p. 57.

Griffiths, M. (1995), *Feminisms and the self: the web of identity*, Routledge, London.

Gulam, W. and Zulfigar, M. (1998), 'Mentoring – Dr Plumbs elixer and the alchemists stone', *Mentoring and Tutoring*, vol. 5(3) Spring, pp. 39–45.

Hara, W. and Kling, R. (2001), *Students' distress with a web-based distance education course*, Research Report, Indiana University Press, Bloomington.

Harrington, A. (1999), *E-mentoring: the advantages and disadvantages of using e-mail to support distant mentoring*, Herts TEC.

Hawkridge, D. (1978), 'Seven years of tuition and counseling at the Open University', in *Feruniversitat Conference.1978 Hagen, West Germany*, Open University, Milton Keynes.

Hawks, J.H. (1991), 'Powers: a concept analysis', *Journal of Advanced Nursing*, vol. 16, pp. 754–762.

Hay, J. (1995), *Transformational mentoring*, McGraw – Hill, Maidenhead.

Herring, S., Johnson, D. and Di Benedetto, T. (1992), 'Participation in electronic discourse in a feminist field', in K. Hall, M. Bucholtz and B. Moonwomen (eds), *Proceeding of the Second Berkeley Women and Language Conference*, University of California, Berkeley.

Homer. (1946), *The Odyssey*, Penguin Classics, Harmondsworth.

hooks, B. (1984), *Feminist theory: from margin to center*, South End Press, Boston.

Hughes, C. (2002), *Key concepts in feminist theory and research*, Sage, London.

Jones, K. (1990), 'The gender difference hypothesis: a synthesis of research findings', *Educational Administration Quarterly*, vol. 26(1), pp. 5–37.

Kanter, R.M. (1979), 'Differential access to opportunity and power', in R. Alvarez and K.G. Lutterman (eds), *Discrimination in organizations*, Jossey-Bass, San Francisco.

Keisler, S. et al (1997), *Recent results from a field trial of residential internet use*, Research Report. Carnegie Mellon University, Pittsburgh.

Kelly, L. Burton, S. and Regan, L. (1994), 'Researching women's lives or studying women's oppression', in M. Maynard and J. Purvis (eds), *Researching women's lives from a feminine perspective*, Taylor and Francis, London.

Kling, R. (1994), 'Reading "all about" computerization', *The Information Society*, vol. 10(3), pp. 147–172.

Kram, K.E. (1983), 'Phases of the mentor relationship,' *Academy of Management Journal*, vol. 26(4), pp. 608–625.

Lee, W.Y. (1999), 'Striving towards effective retention: the effects of race on mentoring African American students', *Peabody Journal of Education*, vol. 74, pp. 27–43.

Lewis, C.W. (2002), *International telementor programme: executive summary – evaluation results from teacher surveys May 2000–March 2002*, Colorado State University, Fort Collins.

Lewis, M. (1990), 'Interpreting patriarchy politics resistance and transformation in the feminist classroom', *Harvard Educational Review*, vol. 60(4), pp. 467–488.

Limerick, B. (1995), *Women and mentoring for change*, beyond the status quo. Queensland University of Technology, Report. Mentorship.

Linn, M.C. and Kessal, C. (1996), 'Success in mathematics: increasing talent and gender diversity among college majors', *CBMC Issues in Mathematics Education*, vol. 6, pp. 101–144.

Loader, D. (1993), 'Reconstructing an Australian school', in I. Gasso and M. Fallshaw (eds), *Reflections of a learning community*, Methodist Ladies College, Melbourne.

Maynard, M. (1994), 'Methods practice and epistemology: the debate about feminist research', in M. Maynard and J. Purvis (eds), *Researching women's lives from a feminist perspective*, Taylor and Francis, London.

Mayhard, M. and Purvis, J. (eds) (1994), *Researching women's lives from a feminist perspective*, Taylor and Francis, London.

Maykut, M. and Moorhouse, R. (1994), *Beginning qualitative research: a philosophical and practical guide*, Falmer Press, London.

Megginson, D. and Garvey, B. (2001), *Odysseus, telemachus and the mentor*, Research Report, Sheffield Hallam University.

Mills, A.J. (1989), 'Gender sexuality and organization theory', in J. Hearn, et al (eds), *The sexuality of organizations*, Sage, London.

Murphy, K. (2001), 'High-tech reading is low on meaning, says report', *Times Higher Education Supplement*, 3 March, XX Feature.

Neilson, J. (1990), 'Introduction', in J. Neilson, (ed.), *Readings in feminist methodology*, Westview Press, San Francisco, pp. 1–37.

O'Neill, D.K. Wagner, R. and Gomez, L.M. (1996), 'on-line mentors: experimenting in science class', *Education Leadership*, vol. 54, pp. 39–42.

O'Shea, T. (2001), 'How to please all the people says report', *Guardian Education*, vol. 3 July, pp. 13.

Packard, B.W. and Hudgings, J.H. (2002), 'Expanding college women's perception of physicists lives and work', *Journal of College Science Teaching*, vol. 32, pp. 164–170.

Palloff, R.M. and Pratt, K. (2001), *Lessons from the cyberspace classroom: the realities of on line teaching*, Jossey-Bass, San Francisco.

Powell, B.J. (1999), 'Mentoring: one of the masters tools', *Initiatives*, vol. 59, pp. 19–31.

Preece, J. (1999), 'Empathetic communities: balancing emotional and factual communication', *Interacting with computers*, vol. 12, pp. 63–67.

Price, M.A. and Hui-Hui, C. (2003), 'Promises and challenges: exploring a collaborative telementing programme', *Mentoring and Tutoring*, vol. 11(1), pp. 105–117.

Ragins, B.R. (1989), 'Barriers to mentoring: the female manager's dilemma', *Human Relations*, vol. 42, pp. 1–22.

Ragins, B.R. and Cotton, J.C. (1991), 'Easier said than done: gender differences in perceived barriers to gaining a mentor', *Academy of Management Journal*, vol. 34(4), pp. 939–951.

Ragins, B.R. and Cotton, T.A. (1999), 'Burden or blessing? Expected costs and benefits of being a mentor', *Journal of Organizational behaviour*, vol. 20, pp. 493–509.

Rahm, D. and Reed, B.J. (1998), *Tangled webs in public administration: organization issues in distance learning* [Internet], Public Administration and Management an Interactive Journal, 3 (1). Available from: <http://www.pamig.com/rahm> [Accessed August 2001].

Ramazanoglu, C. and Holland, J. (2002), *Feminist methodology: challenges and choices*, Sage, London.

Rosener, J.B. (1990), 'Ways women lead', *Harvard Business Review*, vol. 28(6) November, pp. 199–125.

Rossman, P. (1992), *The emerging worldwide electric university: information age global higher education*, Conn. Greenwood Press, Westpoint.

Salmon, G. (2000), *E-moderating: the key to teaching and learning online*, Kogan Page, London.

Sanchez, B. and Harris, J. (1996), 'Online mentoring a success story', *Learning and Leading with Technology*, vol. 23 May, pp. 57–60.

Seymour, E. and Hewitt, N.M. (1997), *Talking about leaving: why undergraduates leave the sciences*, Westview Press, Boulder, C.O.

Shakeshaft, C. (1989), 'The gender gap in research in educational administration', *Education Administration Quarterly*, vol. 25(4), pp. 324–337.

Sharma, S. (1990), 'Psychology of women in management: a distinct feminine leadership', *Equal Opportunities International*, vol. 9(12), pp. 13–18.

Single, P.B. and Muller, C.B. (2001), 'When e-mail and mentoring unite', *Creating Mentoring and Coaching Programmes*, The American Society for Training and Development in Action Series.

Sosik, J.J. and Godshalk, V.M. (2000), 'The role of gender in mentoring', *Journal of Vocational Behaviour*, vol. 57, pp. 102–122.

Spender, D. (1995), *Nattering on the net: women, power and cyberspace*, Spin Fex Press, Melbourne.

Staley, A. and Mackenzie, N. (eds) (2001), *Computer supported experimental learning*, University of Central England, Research Report 1. Birmingham.

Straw Poll (2001), *Privacy and the new technology*. BBC Radio 4, 25 June (audio), London.

Stone, L. (1855), 'Quoted', in B. Friedan, (1963), *The feminine mystique*, Victor Gollancz, London, p. 80.

Taylor, S. (1993), 'Transforming the texts: towards a feminist classroom practice', in C.L. Smith (ed.), *Texts of desire: girls, popular fiction and education*, Falmer Press, London.

Taylor, S. and Bogdan, R. (1984), *Introduction to qualitative research methods*, Wiley and Sons, New York.

Valian, V. (1998), *Why so slow?: The advancement of women*, MIT Press, London.

Wai-Ling Packard, B. (2003), 'Web-based mentoring: challenging traditional models to increase women's access', *Mentoring and Tutoring*, vol. 11(1), pp. 53–65.

Warren, K.J. and Rada, R. (1998), 'Sustaining computer-mediated communication in university courses', *Journal of Computer Assisted Learning*, vol. 14, pp.71–80.

Weiner, G. (1989), 'Professional self-knowledge versus social justice: A critical analysis of the teacher-researcher movement', *British Educational Research Journal*, vol. 15(1), pp. 41–51.

Weiner, G. (1994), *Feminisms in Education: an introduction*, Open University, Buckingham.

Willard, N. (2001), *Social dimensions of the use of interactive technologies by young people*, Research Report. University of Oregon, U.S.A.

Wills, (2001), in Smithers (2001). Education Guardian, 20 March.

Chapter 12

Afterword

Cedric Cullingford

In Homer's carefully constructed Odyssey there is always an essential duality, an ambiguity of interpretation. The human beings are aware of the many Gods' interference, their whims, their immediacy and their power. They call to the gods, they rail against them, and they sometimes think that they are actually present, which is a difficult insight because the Gods are always in disguise as known people.

The gods, meanwhile, act like humans; they quarrel with each other, they interfere and cause genuine problems for humans to rail against, they play with people as wanton boys with flies. They are in disguise so no one can tell if they are there. They are not founts of all seeing wisdom, no simple mechanism of support.

The concept of mentor is not a simple one. In the eighteenth and nineteenth centuries, the term was used as a guide, an authority. On a personal level, it would mean a patron. Nowadays the term is used so ubiquitously that it has come to mean many different things. Like Homer's hero, it is difficult to interpret their role from moment to moment. They should be in authority, and able to guide and instruct. And yet, when they start to try to control, and limit the actions of the mentee rather than support and encourage, they can be both resented and rejected.

The term 'Mentor' has some contrary meanings. There are some essential interpretations that need to be understood.

- Is the role to do with guidance, freely given, or does it carry elements of judgement and assessment?
- Is the mentor a peer sharing information or an authority imparting it?
- Is mentoring an induction programme giving a welcome, a wider insight, or an initiation, a way of making the new member fit in?
- Are mentors volunteers, chosen by mutual consent, or imposed by virtue of their experience or standing?
- Are mentors themselves expected to learn or purely impart knowledge?
- Should mentoring be restricted to one person or should it involve a whole community?
- Should the mentor be a member of the organisation or have some role outside it?
- Is mentoring a constant process or an occasional, formal review?
- Do mentors give instruction, deal with knowledge, or do they only give advice,

dealing not with 'what 'but only 'how'?

- Are the mentees willing to be part of this process or is it forced on them? Some might be too young to feel they need it, some too old to want it.

- Does mentoring foster personal beliefs and independence or conformity to professional practice?

Mentoring is not a universal panacea, although the way it is ubiquitously employed might make one think it is supposed to be. It is a concept and a practice that ranges widely over the extremes of national systems of induction to the casual and subtle support mechanisms of professional friendship.

Above all, the success of mentoring systems depends on motivation; those who genuinely have the best interests or their colleagues at heart will make the systems work; those who use it as a short cut or for their own ends will find it does not succeed.

The modern manifestation of mentoring is a curious mixture. One aspect is the old notion of the tutorial system in ancient Universities, where the onus was on the independent learning of undergraduates, tested in a tutorial against the judgement of the supervisor. The emphasis was on learning rather than being taught, but the efficacy of the process was constantly being critically evaluated.

The other end of such judgement is the informal 'buddy' system, with peer assessment, sharing of practice, with help and cajoling that does not carry the weight of authority. The mentor is the one to whom one chooses to go for support.

This book demonstrates the complexities of the concept and gives many examples of how it can function best. It goes to the heart of the debate on all educational practice.

Name Index

Subject Index

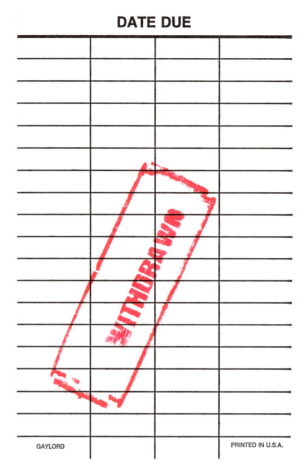